A WELCOMING NATION?

SERIES EDITORS' PREFACE

In a rapidly changing world, how we understand nations, their forma-
tions and contexts is being transformed. Across a range of disciplines,
the focus on race/ethnicity studies is growing. In recent decades, a
considerable body of writing and research has been produced that
details the place and reception of racial and ethnic minorities in
Welsh society, speaking more broadly to Wales's global encounters
past and present. These social, economic and cultural connections
shape Wales today. This research and cultural output has great significance to the general understanding of *stori Cymru*, the telling of how
Wales sees itself and how it relates to the wider world.

The series *Race, Ethnicity, Wales and the World* aims to consolidate
attention to this existing work, and to stimulate new and emerging
work in the field of study as part of more general trends in both the
globalising and *decolonising* of Welsh studies. The series is an exploration of the ways in which Wales has been and is being reshaped
and reimagined through its racial and ethnic diversity, showcasing
and stimulating multi-disciplinary research, and providing accessible
works to a broad public and available for cross national comparison
and scholarship.

Charlotte Williams OBE and Dr Neil Evans

A WELCOMING NATION?

Intersectional approaches to migration
and diversity in Wales

Edited by

Catrin Wyn Edwards, Laura Shobiye and
Rhys Dafydd Jones

University of Wales Press
2025

www.uwp.co.uk

British Library Cataloguing-in-Publication Data

A catalogue record for this book is available from the British Library.

ISBN   978-1-83772-231-0
e-ISBN   978-1-83772-232-7

The rights of authorship for this work have been asserted in accordance with sections 77 and 79 of the Copyright, Designs and Patents Act 1988.

For GPSR enquiries please contact:
Easy Access System Europe Oü, 16879218
Mustamäe tee 50, 10621, Tallinn, Estonia.
gpsr.requests@easproject.com

MIX
Paper | Supporting
responsible forestry
FSC
www.fsc.org   FSC® C013604

Typeset by Geethik Technologies

Printed by CPI Group (UK) Ltd, Croydon, CR0 4YY

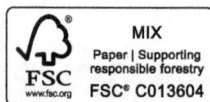

Contents

Series foreword   v

Acknowledgements   xi

List of illustrations, figures and tables   xiii

List of abbreviations   xv

List of contributors   xvii

1   Rethinking Migration and Diversity in Wales:
Towards an Intersectional Approach   1
Catrin Wyn Edwards, Laura Shobiye and Rhys Dafydd Jones

2   International Migration and the Welsh Language:
Exploring an Interdisciplinary Framework for
Linguistic Integration   31
Gwennan Higham

3   Speak to Me: A Creative and Participatory
Approach to Language Education for Inclusion   57
Barrie Llewelyn and Mike Chick

4   From City to Nation of Sanctuary?
Moving Scalar Imaginaries of Citizenship and
National Identity in Wales   77
*Franz Bernhardt, Catrin Wyn Edwards and
Rhys Dafydd Jones*

5   Creating a Welcoming Nation in a Hostile
     Environment: LGBTQ+ Precarious Experiences   103
     Ourania Vamvaka-Tatsi

6   Mothers' Narratives of Transitions and
     Resilience Through Social Learning   135
     Laura Shobiye

7   EU Migrants in Wales: Still Welcome?   165
     *Stephen Drinkwater, Taulant Guma,
     Bryonny Goodwin-Hawkins and Rhys Dafydd Jones*

8   Ageing and Migration into Rural Wales:
     A Counter-Narrative to the Rhetoric of
     Burden and Dependency   191
     Jesse Heley and Rachel Rahman

     Index   217

I bawb sydd wedi symud i, trwy, ac o Gymru.
To all those who've moved to, through, and from Wales.

Hedyn

Kate Bosse-Griffiths

(I ateb y cwestiwn, sut y gallwn berchen
gwreiddiau mewn dwy wlad.)

Hedyn wyf o wlad bell
wedi ei lyncu gan aderyn treigl
wedi ei gludo dros y môr gan wennol
Disgynnodd ar dir newydd ei aredig
a thaflu gwreiddiau

Glaswelltyn wyf ar borfa las
wedi fy mhlygu dan garn defaid
wedi fy nghnoi gan ddant bustach
Tyfais yn gnawd byw
Tyfais yn rhan o Gymru.

A Seed

Kate Bosse-Griffiths

*(To answer the question, how could I
possess roots in two countries.)*

*I am a seed from a distant land
swallowed by a wandering bird
taken over the sea by a swallow
It descended on newly ploughed land
and threw out roots*

*I am a blade of grass on green pasture
bent under sheep's hooves
chewed by a bullock's teeth
I grew into living flesh
I grew to be part of Wales.*

Acknowledgements

This volume began as a series of presentations at an online symposium for new and emerging migration researchers in Wales in January 2022. Organised by the Wales Institute of Social and Economic Research and Data's (WISERD) research network, Migration Research Wales, it provided an opportunity to showcase a range of issues related to migration research in and about Wales. The volume itself was conceived by the network in the autumn of 2020 as an opportunity to encourage collaboration among migration researchers, and to address important developments over the last twenty years. We are grateful to those who presented at and attended the symposium, and the network's other events and activities. James Atkinson, Liam Moylan, Kirsten Wain and Cara Rainbow provided invaluable assistance in promoting and supporting the network. We extend our thanks to Professor Sally Power and Professor Paul Chaney of WISERD for supporting the work of Migration Research Wales. We are grateful to our series editors, Professor Charlotte Williams and Dr Neil Evans, for their guidance and encouragement, and to Dr Llion Wigley of the University of Wales Press for his patience in dealing with our numerous queries. We would also like to thank the family of Kate Bosse-Griffiths for allowing us to include her poem, *Hedyn*, in the volume. We also wish to acknowledge the helpful discussions we had with Dr Hanin Abou Salem, Selina Lobina and Dr Adrian Marsh; our colleagues at the Departments of International Politics and Geography and Earth Sciences at Aberystwyth University and the School of Social Sciences, Cardiff University, for their collegiality, encouragement, and interest. Finally, we are grateful to our friends and families for their patience and support as we completed the volume.

List of illustrations, figures and tables

Images

6.1: 'Family Detention'   140
6.2: 'Open Prison'   143
6.3: 'Lone and Digital Motherhood'   144
6.4: 'One Day at a Time'   146
6.5: 'Continuing the Journey'   149
6.6: 'Growing Self-Care'   151
6.7: 'Surviving Alone'   152
6.8: 'Keep on Going'   155
6.9: 'Still Alone'   157

Figures

7.1: Estimated Population of Wales Born in
    EU Countries: 2000/1–2020/1   176

Tables

7.1: Population in Wales by Country of Birth: 2001–2021   171
7.2: Countries of Birth with Highest Number
    of Residents in Wales: 2021   172
7.3: Distribution of Residents Across Welsh Unitary
    Authorities by Countries of Birth: 2021   174
7.4: Labour Market Outcomes in Wales and
    Other Parts of UK by Countries of Birth:
    April 2022–March 2023   178

List of abbreviations

DPIA – Displaced People in Action
ELGCC – Welsh Parliament's Equality, Local Government and
            Communities Committee
ESOL – English for Speakers of Other Languages
EU – European Union
MP – Member of Parliament
MS – Member of the *Senedd* (the Welsh Parliament)
NGO – Non-Governmental Organisation
NoS – Nation of Sanctuary
SVPRP – Syrian Vulnerable Persons' Relocation Programme
TESOL – Teaching English to Speakers of Other Languages
USW – University of South Wales
WISERD – Wales Institute of Social and Economic Research and Data
WRC – Welsh Refugee Coalition
WSOL – Welsh for Speakers of Other Languages

List of contributors

Franz Bernhardt is a postdoctoral research fellow at Aalborg University in Denmark, and former ESRC Postdoctoral Research Fellow at Swansea University. He researches the intersections of migration and national identity.

Mike Chick has worked in language teaching for over twenty-five years. At the University of South Wales, he is a Teaching English to Speakers of Other Languages teacher education lecturer and is the University Refugee Champion. His research interests surround language education for migrants in Wales and he is currently researching social justice and language education.

Stephen Drinkwater is a professor of Economics at the University of Roehampton. He has researched several aspects of international migration, especially in relation to the labour market.

Catrin Wyn Edwards is a lecturer in the Department of International Politics at Aberystwyth University. She is an expert on migration, sanctuary, multi-level governance and nationalism. Catrin co-convenes Migration Research Wales, a WISERD research network.

Bryonny Goodwin-Hawkins is a senior research fellow at the Countryside and Community Research Institute at the University of Gloucestershire.

Taulant Guma is a lecturer in Human Geography at Edinburgh Napier University and was recently PI on an ESRC project examining the everyday experiences of asylum seekers living in temporary accommodation during the Covid-19 pandemic.

Jesse Heley is a reader in Human Geography at Aberystwyth University. His research is situated in the broad fields of rural studies, ageing and the sociology of elites. Jesse is a Co-Director of the Wales Institute of Social and Economic Research and Data (WISERD).

Gwennan Higham is a senior lecturer in Welsh at Swansea University. She researches the field of migration, the Welsh language and issues of citizenship, multiculturalism and belonging.

Barrie Llewelyn is a senior lecturer in Creative Writing at the University of South Wales whose research interests centre on creativity and well-being. She is also a qualified Coach and Mentor.

Rachel Rahman is a senior lecturer in Psychology and Director of the Centre for Excellence in Rural Health Research at Aberystwyth University. Her research focuses on the factors contributing to the health and well-being of rural communities, through understanding their lived experience of accessing health and social care services.

Laura Shobiye is currently a lecturer in the School of Education and Social Policy at Cardiff Metropolitan University. Her research specialises in anti-racism and gender equality, particularly refugee education. She completed her PhD at Cardiff University in 2023. Laura is an active member of the Welsh Refugee Coalition and the Migration Research Wales Network and is a co-founder and co-organiser of the UK's National Centre for Research Method's collaborative and participatory special interest group.

Ourania Vamvaka-Tatsi (she/her) gained her PhD from the School of Social Sciences at Cardiff University. She is a multi-award-winning Human Rights activist, who has undertaken significant work with and on behalf of LGBTQ+ people seeking asylum in Wales. Ourania has a comprehensive knowledge and understanding of UK Queer Policy and the asylum system and has volunteered in the Calais Refugee Camp. Ourania co-chairs Wales's leading People of Colour

LGBTQ+ grassroots organisation, Glitter Cymru, contributed to the LGBTQ+ Action Plan Expert Panel and is the Policy & Research Lead for Llamau.

CHAPTER 1

Rethinking Migration and Diversity in Wales: Towards an Intersectional Approach

Catrin Wyn Edwards, Laura Shobiye and Rhys Dafydd Jones

Introduction

As we prepared this manuscript for its initial submission, the UK parliament had just passed the Safety of Rwanda (Asylum and Immigration) Act 2024. This Act, which received Royal Assent on 25 April 2024, removed further judicial obstacles for the UK's Conservative government to enact parts of the UK and Rwanda Migration and Economic Development Partnership (commonly known as the 'Rwanda asylum plan'); the intention to remove people seeking asylum and crossing the border informally. The legislation was a response by the UK government to rulings by the Supreme Court in November 2023 that held that its plan to deport people crossing the English Channel was unlawful, as Rwanda is not a safe country. The Act effectively created a law stating that Rwanda is a 'safe destination', thus removing the safety argument in attempts to oppose the rendition of informal migrants and people seeking sanctuary to Rwanda. The Act and the plan's proponents claimed that this is the only way to stop 'the small boats' crossing the English Channel, leading to many deaths (in the week of writing twenty-seven people had died trying to cross), yet this costly approach is preferred over establishing safe and formal routes to sanctuary.[1] While many people – including ourselves – were appalled with a plan considered inhumane, irresponsible, ineffective and inefficient, we note that this Act is not an exception. The Illegal Migration Act 2023 prohibits those who arrive in an irregular manner from claiming asylum (although the Geneva Convention of 1951 does not specify that people need documentation or to arrive in a regular manner), while the Nationality and Borders Act 2022, effectively criminalises people seeking sanctuary coming through irregular routes, as well as facilitating the removal of British citizenship from those with two or more nationalities. In sum, these Acts make claiming asylum nearly impossible, potentially criminalising and deporting vulnerable people. International organisations such as Amnesty International (2022) condemned these Acts for racism. Both build on a long genealogy of legislation by the UK government demonising and marginalising migrants and people seeking sanctuary.

Alongside legislation in the early 2020s that aimed to reduce irregular migration (including musings at various stages of undermining the Laws of the Seas by criminalising the maritime rescue of irregular migrants), the Immigration Acts of 2014 and 2016 were the legislative cornerstones of Theresa May's 'hostile environment', which enforced a 'border within' (Yuval-Davis et al., 2018) requiring enforcement by untrained, unsupported lay people such as small employers and landlords, and created the new criminal offences of 'renting to disqualified tenants' and 'illegal working', and 'employing an illegal worker'. Other policies, such as restricting access to the NHS by introducing a surcharge for immigrants and increasing the threshold for spousal visas (resulting in 'Skype families' whereby partners or parents are unable to join loved ones within the UK), also play a role in marginalising and othering immigrants in the UK. As Yuval-Davis and her colleagues note, the effects of these hostile environment policies in the early 2010s (and, indeed, beyond) were 'to sensitise people to who carries a British passport and who does not' (2018: 238).

Yet, these policies and laws are not restricted to the Conservative party. The Liberal Democrats, their coalition partners between 2010 and 2015, facilitated the hostile environment, while the New Labour governments of Blair and Brown also played their role in differentiating immigrants, most notably through the Immigration and Asylum Act 1999, which exemplified the shift towards the legislative fixation on people seeking sanctuary and marked a turning point in restriction of fundamental rights. This Act restricted the rights of asylum seekers to work, and also brought in a policy of dispersal, which led to the 'dispersal' of asylum seekers outside London and southeastern England to locations elsewhere in England, Scotland, Wales and Northern Ireland.

Beyond highlighting issues with access and provision of services (Hynes, 2003: 46), in Wales, the effects were profound in bringing a shift from immigration associated with established diasporic communities in specific locations, to a more diverse and varied experience, including of forced migration.

Earlier in the twentieth century, however, was not some beacon of progressive policies. Several pieces of legislation from the 1960s to the 1980s define citizenship in racialised terms (Tyler, 2010). These include the Commonwealth Immigrants Act 1962, which made immigration from the Commonwealth of Nations and British colonies dependent on having a job to come to, possessing specific skills in short supply or being part of an 'undifferentiated group', the numbers of which were determined by labour requirements. Here, we see the Act construct migration as an economic phenomenon, and a reduction of a migrant as a worker. This was not a new phenomenon, with schemes such as the 'Balt Cygnet' being developed to encourage 'desirable' migrants – younger women without dependants – to move to the UK in the aftermath of the Second World War (McDowell, 2003, 2009). However, this scheme, named after a young swan and evoking the adult swan's symbolic whiteness, was part of a broader response which prioritised women from Baltic states above Ireland or Poland, which were preferred to the Caribbean in a racial hierarchy, infused with anti-Catholic sentiment (McDowell, 2003, 2009). Fifteen years later, the Commonwealth Immigrants Act would also construct citizenship in terms of race, with a distinction made for different kinds of British subjects: those born in the UK, or with a UK or Irish government-issued passport being immune from the above restrictions, and were far likelier to be White people.[2] Subsequent legislation continued with this racist construction of citizenship. The Immigration Act 1971 removed the British subject/aliens distinction, but introduced a further distinction among British citizens: 'patrial' and 'non-patrial'. 'Patrial' citizens were born or naturalised in the UK, had a parent (or grandparent, in the case of British citizens) born in the UK or were British or Commonwealth citizens who had been resident in the UK for five years and applied to register as a citizen; this category was free from controls. 'Non-patrial' citizens required a work permit to enter, had no right of permanent residence and had no right of entry for dependants. Again, the former, with immediate ancestors born in the UK or who had lived there for the required period, were again likelier to be white people, and the legislation remains considered racist (Solomos, 1989). The 1981 Nationality Act removed *jus soli* ('the right of the soil'), in that babies born in the UK were no longer automatically born into British citizenship; it also created further distinctions, with the categories of 'British Dependent Territory Citizen' and 'British Overseas Citizen' with inferior residency rights, removing residency rights from British citizens in the Commonwealth and in Hong Kong, and requiring an 'ancestral link' to be proved. As Tyler (2010: 63) notes:

> Whilst race and ethnicity were never directly named, the 1981 Act effectively designed citizenship so as to exclude black and Asian populations in the Commonwealth while leaving 'routes home' for white nationals born within the boundaries of the empire.

One of the most profound effects of these shifting constructions of British citizenship was the scandalous denial of citizenship and residency rights for the Windrush generation, which emerged in 2018. While not the only individuals who came to the UK for work or study from other parts of the Commonwealth at the time, hundreds of thousands of people responded to the call for people to come to work in the UK in the aftermath of the Second World War, with the *Empire Windrush* the best-known (but not the first) vessel to bring people to the UK from the Caribbean. As the British Nationality Act 1948 gave Citizenship of the UK and Colonies and rights of residency in the UK to British subjects in the British colonies and Commonwealth, there was no need to produce further papers on entry. However, as the legislation changed in the period between the 1960s and 1980s, around people who had been resident for several decades, and without the required proof of showing that they had been in the UK every year since their arrival (not least as the original landing cards had been destroyed by the Home Office), many people faced the threat of deportation (and some 164 were; see Goring et al., 2020: 276), as they could not meet the new legislative requirements introduced as part of the 'hostile environment' to prove their right to residency.

These pieces of legislation were in the backdrop of racial tensions in the UK, such as Enoch Powell's infamous 'rivers of blood' speech in 1968, which was itself made in opposition to the Race Relations Act as it was being debated in the UK parliament. The discriminatory barriers to immigration and constructions of citizenship noted above are based on a social construction of race that is rooted in colonialism and the ideology of white supremacy, and that creates hierarchies of human groups initially based on so-called phenological differences, such as skin colour. During the British Empire, this social construction and its relationship with migration was, for example, evident in power hierarchies in eastern Africa, with migrants from India deliberately brought into the region to support the white British ruling classes' efforts to maintain order over the Black local peoples. As the concept of race developed over time it become more nuanced and incorporated, on British shores, cultural and linguistic distinctions, leading to more detailed relevant academic discussions and definitions of race, notably by Hall (2021; Hall and Morley, 2018a; 2018b).

Race, as an evolving concept, cannot now be separated from the shifting concepts of racism and ethnicity. The evolving connection with racism has seen a change in scope from systemic discrimination based on phenotypes to include systemic discrimination based on factors such as culture, heritage, identity, religion and language. Hall (and Morley, 2018a; 2018b) called this broader concept 'cultural racism'. The concept of ethnicity relates to both race and racism. A person's ethnicity is typically defined by their ancestry in terms of culture and national origin, yet it also often includes a person's race based on skin colour (e.g., Black British). Race and ethnicity are both contextual social constructions that have evolved over time and that also differ across geographical locations. In the UK, for example Black used to be a political term referring to anyone who was not racialised as White. Now, more typically, it refers to those with 'black' skin and (/or) heritage from Africa or the Caribbean. Yet, in Australia, the term Black can include indigenous populations.[3] In this volume, these concepts are important in providing the context and language for us to define and explore the 'othering' of migrants and people seeking sanctuary as racism (Bulmer and Solomos, 2018; Cole, 2017).

The policies and laws discussed here focus on the response of the UK state, rather than the Welsh polity. This is unsurprising, given that much of the legislation pre-dates devolution, and that immigration itself is not a devolved field. However, there is a need to consider two interrelated aspects. First, the differential experiences of Wales as a distinct part of the UK, with its own national consciousness and culture, population dynamics, socio-economic conditions, and different experiences of migration, which are different to and distinct from other parts of the UK. Secondly, the emergence of a field of Welsh policy and practice related to migration that has emerged in the last quarter-century, as part of the broader devolution process. Although immigration is not a devolved field, there have been important policy developments related to migration, and immigration in particular, in Wales. Most apparent here is the commitment to become the world's first nation of sanctuary (NoS), but there are many other related dimensions, too. This includes distinct Welsh policies related to the rights of 'unsuccessful asylum seekers', such as receiving secondary medical treatment and to obtain medical training, and the provision of free bus travel for Ukrainian refugees. This 'clear water' between the Welsh and UK administrations can also be seen in criticism of the then Illegal Migration and Borders and Nationality Bills by Jane Hutt, then minister for Equality and Social Justice and then Counsel General, Mick Antoniw (Hutt, 2023; Hutt and Antoniw, 2021). The Welsh Parliament also refused legislative consent for these bills by voting against the Bill (under the Sewell convention of UK parliament legislation impacting on devolved fields), although this opposition did not prohibit the Bill becoming law.

Devolution has also fostered a distinct Welsh civil society that has developed to address specific issues in Wales (Chaney and Williams, 2003). Among these are organisations that constitute part of what Theodore and Martin (2007) call 'migrant civil society', namely the organisations and groups supporting migrants, such as the Welsh Refugee Coalition, the Wales Strategic Migration Partnership, cities of sanctuary groups, and Oasis in Splott, Cardiff. As Williams and Chaney (2003) noted, these groups find relative proximity and ease of access to Welsh ministers, even if the effects of austerity and the hostile environment mean that not enough is done to address their concerns (Guma et al., 2023).

Spurred by concerns regarding the disproportionate impact of Covid-19 on individuals from Black, Asian and Minority Ethnic backgrounds in Wales, the then First Minister, Mark Drakeford, launched a three-month investigation into the factors contributing to these uneven outcomes, and identified institutional racism as a key contributing factor (Welsh Government, 2020; Ogbonna, 2024). The inquiry findings, which coincided with the murder of George Floyd and the subsequent international response along with results of the wider British racial attitudes survey, highlighted the need for a race equality strategy (Ogbonna, 2024: 80). Following extensive collaboration with a variety of stakeholders, the Welsh Government published its vision for making Wales an anti-racist nation in its 'Anti-racist Wales Action Plan' (2022).

However, in drawing attention to these issues, we do not wish to reproduce the discourse of 'a tolerant nation' that Charlotte Williams and her colleagues critiqued twenty years ago. Similarly to the accounts in *A Tolerant Nation?* (2003), we are not seeking to make the case for Welsh exceptionalism in this volume; rather, we argue that we need to explore the different and distinct (and, indeed, similar) experiences of migration in Wales, including distinct Welsh problems and challenges. These challenges include a defensive mobilisation or retreat to the 'tolerant nation' discourse, a denial of racism, xenoracism and other prejudices, the mainstreaming and casualisation of anti-English racism, the fetishisation of Welsh-speaking migrants of colour as a symbol of inclusion, and the mischaracterisation of a history of conquest as that of being colonised and a reluctance, if not a refusal, to acknowledge Wales and Welsh people's entwining with colonialism and enslavement.

Colonial Entanglements

The summer of 2020 saw increased and overdue reflection on racism and white supremacy in everyday life in the Anglosphere. The murder of George Floyd by Minneapolis police officers in May 2020 emphasised the way race features prominently in quotidian

power-relations. While it should be questioned why it took the hor-
rific events in Minnesota to prompt action across the Atlantic, there
was, nonetheless, a significant response. In Bristol, enslaver Edward
Colston's statue was thrown into the harbour, while renewed attention was given to Welsh figures involved in chattel slavery, such as
Thomas Picton and the Pennants of Penrhyn Castle. Picton, who was
impeached in the 1800s for his torture of Luisa Calderón during his
tenure as Governor of Trinidad, had his portrait removed from the
'Faces from Wales' gallery and redisplayed in a travel frame as part of
the Reframing Picton exhibition at the National Museum in Cardiff,
2022–5, while his statue among the eleven 'Heroes of Wales' in the
neighbouring Cardiff City Hall was boxed off, pending its removal.
His monument and commemoration in the streetscape of Carmarthen remains, despite some consultation by Carmarthenshire
County Council (Hoskins and James, 2024). The National Trust
had also begun to engage with the enslaver legacy of its properties.
Penrhyn Castle, home to the notorious quarry-owners, the Pennant
family, had its interpretation revised to acknowledge that its splen-
dour was financed by enslaved people in plantations in Jamaica.
This development is not without its contestation, either: the pressure group Restore Trust was formed in opposition to the National
Trust's acknowledgement of the role of slavery in the establishment
and maintenance of country estates.

    While these cases are quite well-known (and have presented a
challenge to the previous dominant narratives of Picton as a high-pro-
file casualty at Waterloo and the Pennants as harsh employers during
Streic Fawr 1900–3), these were not the only Welsh people[4] involved
in chattel slavery and the colonial enterprises that accompanied it,
drawing on the same narratives of white supremacy. Folk heroes such
as the pirates Harri Morgan and Barti Ddu were involved in colonialism and enslavement, and the settler-colonisation of Patagonia
has, until very recently, been approached uncritically (Taylor, 2025).
However, this is not a volume focusing on the history of chattel slavery and colonialism, although their legacies persist, and themes such
as race, 'othering' and exclusion are entwined with this volume. Nor
is it one that is solely concerned with the emigration of people from
Wales to elsewhere. This is a volume concerned with migration, to,
through and from Wales.

A Welcoming Nation?

Twenty years ago, Charlotte Williams, Neil Evans and Paul O'Leary (2003) edited the ground-breaking volume, *A Tolerant Nation?*, which took a much-needed critical study of race and diversity in Wales. Set against the backdrop of devolution and the first term of the National Assembly for Wales, the volume was concerned with both historical accounts of race and diversity, immigration and emigration (Evans, 2003), and empire and colonialism (Jones, 2003), as well as new policy developments in the fledgling Welsh polity, and the existing and potential effects of UK (i.e., non-devolved) policy in Wales, such as the dispersal of asylum seekers under the 1999 Immigration and Asylum Act (Robinson, 2003a). In the intervening two decades much has changed around migration and migration policy in Wales. In 2015, the book was updated to address and respond to developments in devolution, such as the Government of Wales Act 2006, and clear support for further devolution in 2011, against the backdrop of anti-multicultural narratives and a backlash against multiculturalism as a public policy alongside global events, migration, and the European Union (EU)'s enlargement and its approach to racism, xenophobia, religious diversity and institutional racism (Evans et al., 2015).

First, there have been many new and different experiences of migration to, from and through Wales in the first quarter of the twenty-first century. One notable dimension is the migration enabled by the expansions of the EU since 2004. The accession of former Communist states (the 'A8' or 'EU8' group of countries) in 2004 meant that millions more people could benefit from the free movement of labour for EU citizens. Against the backdrop of a growing economy and labour shortages (particularly in areas such as plumbing), the UK was one of three member states (along with Ireland and Sweden) not to place restrictions on these member states' citizens treaty rights. While it is methodologically difficult to calculate exact migration patterns, as well as the fact that EU migration may be shorter-term and 'liquid' (Lulle et al., 2018) in nature, staying for shorter periods of time, it was estimated that there were around 80,000 EU citizens living in Wales shortly after the 2016 EU membership referendum (Welsh Government, 2017). The largest national group were Polish citizens, and concentration of Polish nationals in areas like Llanybydder and

Wrexham existed alongside earlier, post-1945 waves of Polish migration to Lampeter and Rhosllanerchrugog, as well as areas which had experienced relatively little migration in the past, such as Llanelli (Thompson et al., 2010). The 2021 Census shows a decline in EU citizens resident in Wales, attributable to the 'double whammy' of the UK's eventual withdrawal from the EU in January 2020 and the Covid-19 pandemic, with fewer work opportunities and uncertainty around recourse to state funds. The same Census also recorded a small increase in Wales's population, showing how Wales's current population of 3.1 million is sustained by net migration (approximately 55,000 usual residents) (Office for National Statistics, 2022).

Another important example that has unfolded in the last two decades are the experiences of people seeking sanctuary in Wales. The new dispersal system ushered in with the Immigration and Asylum Act 1999 led to the arrival of new asylum seekers in Wales and changed the landscape of migration and sanctuary. Robinson (2003a) discusses how unprepared Wales was for the dispersal of asylum seekers, and there have been several important developments since. These include more people seeking sanctuary coming to Wales. Some include community sponsorship programmes, such as people who fled Syria and Iraq (including during the turbulent summer of 2015) becoming resident in smaller towns such as Aberystwyth (Guma et al., 2020). These are not the first people seeking sanctuary to live in such settlements: there were Belgian refugees resident in Wales during the First World War, Basque refugees from the Spanish Civil War, evacuees from larger cities in the UK, refugees from Nazism (Hammel, 2022) and Communism (including some of the Polish communities mentioned above). It is notable that much discourse, policy and academic analysis, has focused on metropolitan experiences. Paying attention to the experiences of migrants, including people seeking sanctuary, in these smaller cities and towns, as well as the countryside, are particularly important. While there may be an emphasis on a 'community spirit' and accounts of being welcomed, there are also challenges, which can include the Whiteness of rural areas and the hostility towards people of colour in the Welsh countryside (Robinson, 2003b; Robinson and Gardiner, 2004), a lack of religious services and challenges for maintaining faith-based networks (Dafydd Jones, 2010, 2012), and travel difficulties in accessing cultural services and diasporic networks also found in metropolitan areas.

More broadly, the story of Wales is the story of migration. The initial settlers came to Wales several thousand years ago, followed by the Celts and the Romans, who left, among their legacies, the Roman road of Sarn Helen, an ancient precursor to the A470, connecting Neath with Caernarfon (Bullough, 2023). The next few centuries defined Wales, or, rather, Welsh territoriality. The establishment of Angle, Saxon and Jute kingdoms in what is now England demarcated the 'foreign' ('Welsh') lands, eventually reinforced by the construction of Offa's Dyke as a more permanent boundary-marker. There was also extensive exchange between Ireland and Wales: St Patrick was, reportedly, born in Banwen, at the head of the Dulais valley, before being captured by pirates and taken to the island he now patronises, while parts of southern Wales were settled by Irish groups, most notably Brychan, who gives his name to Brycheiniog (Brecknock). The exchange of saints' sacred scholarship is also attested to by the formation of Brittany. In the following centuries, sacred mobilities were also marked by pilgrimages, education, service, and religio-political conflict: Gerald of Wales's journey in 1188 to raise armies for the 'Second Crusade' is an example of mobility within Wales before the soldiers were shipped to the Middle East. The role of Welsh clergy in medieval geopolitics is also noted (Emlyn, 2012, 2018), with many receiving an education in Oxford before taking posts throughout Europe.

The so-called 'early modern period' also highlights significant mobility. Harri Tudur's armies were raised from Brittany before landing in Pembrokeshire and proceeding to Bosworth Field through Wales, while many aspirational Welsh people moved to London hoping to find new opportunities with an enthroned Welsh dynasty. Seafaring also accounted for trade as well as colonial expansion. Parts of North America were settled by Welsh people, including Quakers fleeing religious persecution in the 1670s: the most noted is Rowland Elis, the real-life protagonist of Marion Eames's historical novels *Y Stafell Ddirgel* ('The Secret Room') and *Y Rhandir Mwyn* ('The Mild Tract'). Areas of West Virginia and Ohio were also associated with emigrants from Wales seeking employment in mining in those coalfields. As Chris Evans (2010, 2017) has shown, Welsh people and industry – whether based in cities or rural Wales – were also close-ly entwined and 'structurally embedded' (2010: 25) in enslavement; Welsh woollens, known as 'Welsh plains', were produced in rural mid-Wales to clothe the enslaved, while copper made in Swansea was used to make commodities to purchase enslaved individuals.

We also know of some instances of people of colour 'moving' to Wales in this period. Nathaniel Wells, a magistrate, landowner and plantation owner, moved to Wales from St Kitts for education as a child, and is believed to be Britain's first Black sheriff after becoming Sheriff of Monmouthshire. John Ystumllyn, however, was forcibly re-moved and abducted from Africa in the first half of the eighteenth century (Evans-Jones, 2024). Yet, his story is often told with a focus on his life as a gardener in Cricieth in northern Wales with an emphasis on his fluency in English and Welsh and his marriage to a white Welsh woman from Trawsfynydd. Enslavement, loss, childhood trauma, rac-ism and violence are seldom discussed in relation to his experiences of 'moving' to and living in Wales. His story reminds us that we must not sensationalise a few cases as evidence of a tolerant nation. Indeed, the Race Riots in Cardiff and elsewhere in 1919 showed much hostility to people of colour (Caballero and Aspinall, 2018), taking place some eight years after communal violence against the Jewish and Chinese community in southern Wales (Evans, 2015: 134–5). Prisoners of war and other combatant detainees were also held in Wales. In 1916, near-ly two thousand prisoners who fought in the Easter Rising, including Michael Collins, were held in a camp in Frongoch, near Bala, that had been converted from a distillery (Ebenezer, 2005), while Italian and German prisoners of war were held in Llandysul, Bridgend and else-where. There are accounts of some of these prisoners subsequently remaining or returning to Wales, either on a long-term basis or in frequent visits. A small but celebrated contingent of around 300 peo-ple also travelled to Spain to fight in the International Brigade against the Nationalist forces in the Spanish Civil War. People also sought sanctuary in Wales during conflict. In the 1930s, people fled Nazism and came to Wales, while evacuees from major English urban centres – mainly younger children – came to Wales during the heaviest peri-od of the Blitz. Post-war migration from central and eastern Europe also featured, as people fled the Soviet occupation or took advantage of work programmes recruiting labour from abroad. From the 1940s onwards, migrants from the Caribbean, Africa and southern Asia came to live and work in Wales. As the Race Council Cymru film, *Windrush Cymru @ 75*, commissioned to celebrate seventy-five years since the Windrush generation came to the UK, shows, many people's experiences were of hostility and racism.

Following the eastward expansion of the EU in 2004, thousands of people moved to Wales from central Europe (particularly Poland, but also Romania from 2014) to take advantage of the opportunities afforded by the free movement of people. This post-2004 wave of EU migrants is notable, as there were far more experiences of settling in rural and non-metropolitan areas, compared to other waves and cohorts. The industrial niche occupied by workers from central and eastern Europe included hospitality, food processing and construction, and, consequently, areas like Llanybydder (with its abattoir) registered a high number of non-UK born residents.

One aspect that receives scant attention is the emigration of people from Wales during the Great Depression. Some 430,000 people – nearly a quarter of its population – left Wales during the 1920s and 1930s (Morgan, 1980: 231), with the population only returning to the level of the 1921 Census in 1961. The disruption is likely to have come from the effects of the First World War ('the lost generation'), as well as the Great Depression, with better opportunities and quality of life offered elsewhere. Much of the migration at this period was to the English metropolises, highlighting the significance of internal migration.[5] More recently, around 29,000 people usually resident in Wales study at a university outside Wales, most of whom are younger people studying in England. Opportunities related to courses (until recently, veterinary science could not be studied at a Welsh institution, while medicine could only be studied in Cardiff) or institutions, as well as Welsh Government funding schemes and the promotion of the Russell Group by the Seren Network contribute to this educational mobility. Conversely, Wales attracts substantial numbers of undergraduates from England, and international student migration has also been an important aspect for many institutions for decades. Historically, Malaysia had much connection with Aberystwyth, and, in response to a volcanic eruption on the island in 2021, Lampeter now offers scholarships for students from St Vincent;[6] its theological legacy also attracted many Islamic studies students from Malaysia and the Persian Gulf to the Teifi valley. However, very little is known on the onward mobility of these students: some may return, while others remain nearby, and others, still, move elsewhere. Another little-researched phenomenon that emerged in the early twenty-first century is the movement of younger people to Cardiff, generally characterised by young graduates moving south and eastwards to search for professional opportunities in the capital, which have been bolstered by devolution. Attributed as a major contribution to gentrification in Canton, Riverside and Grangetown, such developments are seen as allowing people to remain in Wales. Yet, at the end of the nineteenth century, Grangetown was a home to many dock workers, of which many were migrants from rural parts of Wales and England and Irish towns and cities (Inam, 2022; Grangetown Community Action, 2019).

This 'Cardiff experience' – akin, perhaps, to the 'overseas experience' associated with middle-class Australian and New Zealander youth crossing the threshold into adulthood – appears as a form of lifecourse mobility; there are recent accounts of some of these in-migrants returning or moving to more rural areas (Owen, 2018). Quality of life factors, such as cheaper or more spacious housing, proximity to parents (and the associated childcare opportunities) and living in areas with higher percentages of Welsh-speakers are all factors associated with this return migration of 'older younger people' (Goodwin-Hawkins and Dafydd Jones, 2022).

While some émigré(e)s returned to Wales (or the parts thereof that they are from), this exodus has received less attention than traffic going the other way on east–west travel corridors, and the vilification of English migrants to Wales. Again, much of this movement is associated with quality of life associated with living in Wales, and in rural Wales in particular (Goodwin-Hawkins and Dafydd Jones, 2022; Stockdale, 2014). As many studies over the last thirty years or so have noted, some migration has been driven by spiritual and counter-cultural motivations, such as the 'back-to-the-land' movement associated with John Seymour as well as neo-Pagan and New Age movements (Jones, 1993). Consequently, 'English migrants to Wales' are as diverse a group as any other. However, this group has also faced much casualised and mainstreamed vilification, including being portrayed as extractive either as a group that has been 'moved on' from local authorities in England and foisted on Wales or as a wealthy, second-home owning group responsible for the decline in the Welsh language in northern and western Wales. Such sentiments were also apparent during the Covid-19 pandemic, where visitors crossing into Wales and breaking Welsh restrictions (possibly unaware of the differences at work) were seen as some glee-inducing folk devil, along with those visitors (with 'English' number plates) who had parked in irresponsible places when permitted to visit popular Welsh beauty spots during the summers of 2020 and 2021.

Against this backdrop of migration experiences, there is another, second aspect: the development of distinct Welsh policy responses. The 2010s have seen much development in this field. A major aspect is the development of the NoS. This flagship approach is grounded in the grassroots responses to 'refugee crises', which saw the consolidation of city (and other communities) of sanctuaries and community sponsorship programmes emerge as local responses to global issues. In 2019, the Welsh Government's declaration to become a 'true Nation of Sanctuary' placed 'clear water' between the Welsh approach to asylum and the UK state's hostile environment approach (Closs Stephens and Bernhardt, 2022; Bernhardt, 2022), highlighting the way in which the national scale provides an alternative locus for progressive sanctuary measures (Edwards and Dafydd Jones, 2024). Policies and programmes in devolved fields such as housing, education and healthcare are examples of divergent policy approaches for people seeking sanctuary (Bernhardt, 2022; Edwards and Wisthaler, 2023). While the NoS approach enables Wales to position itself as more progressive and open than the UK's draconian policies, portraying Wales as a uniformly welcoming, tolerant nation has been the focus of many critical discussions, along with scholarly work on the limitations and drawbacks of a range of policies in devolved fields such as mental health, language and translation, along with lack of infrastructure, challenges of connectivity and potential for greater isolation in non-urban spaces (Schmid-Scott et al., 2020: 147).

An Intersectional Approach

Intersectionality developed in Black feminism in the late 1980s. While Kimberlé Crenshaw (1989, 1991) is credited with its definition, associated with the 'third wave' of feminism, its genealogy can be traced to women's role in emancipation in the USA and colonial resistance in India, such as Maria Stewart and Sojourner Truth in the former and Savitribai Phule in the latter. Intersectionality engages with the multiple subjectivities that are co-produced from multiple forms of marginalisation. It is important to emphasise that intersectionality is not about intersecting identities but about specific and nuanced multiple layers and forms of systemic and structural discrimination. For Black women in the USA, issues relating to racism and segregation were marginalised within the feminist movements, while women's rights affairs were considered peripheral to the Civil Rights movements. As the UK is not the USA, and has its own distinct dimensions of racialisation through legislation and societal culture, it is important not to rely too closely on US approaches and overlook those of Black British scholars, as Warmington (2012) notes (see also Shobiye, 2023: 23), established British scholars, such as Heidi Mirza (1992, 2014) and Yasmin Gunaratnam (2014), Gargi Bhattacharyya (2018), Nira Yuval-Davis (2011) and Kalwant Bhopal (2020) who are, arguably, at the forefront of work in the UK. While race and gender were the central aspects of intersectionality, as it developed from Black feminism, class, sexuality and disability have always been focuses of intersecting systems of oppression. The last thirty years have seen the extension of intersectional analysis to incorporate intersecting categories of social analysis, without always including the emphasis on race or gender, bringing some critique that the concept has been colonised from its origins in Black feminism (Puar, 2012; Hopkins, 2019). Indeed, there is very real concern that it has 'often been misused, thrown out as a buzzword by managers with no understanding of intersectionality's theoretical ground or intellectual framework' (Crenshaw et al., 2024: 1).

There is a need to locate intersectional analysis within the broader British context, which has distinct histories to the USA. These include the UK's position as 'colonizer-in-chief' of a 'large and diverse' empire (Crenshaw et al., 2024: 13), distinct immigration histories and patterns, specific policy and legislative responses, and its own long and distinct histories of anti-racist activism. Yet, the UK is also territorially diverse. London, Manchester and Glasgow are large and 'hyper-diverse' cities, but these are not uniform; outside such settlements, people of colour may be at once invisibilised and hyper-visibilised (Sobande, 2024; Robinson and Gardiner, 2004; Scourfield and Davies, 2005). The UK as a 'union state' – or, as James Mitchell (2010) once called it, a 'state of unions' – reflecting its constitutional status as a union of three states (and the annexation of a conquered territory) over some 150 years (and the subsequent secession of most of one of the 'junior partners') means that there is a need to ground studies in specific localities within the UK. The emergence of devolved governance over the last quarter-century means increasingly different policies and practices. So, too, are there impacts of distinct national stereotypes, such as the construction of absence of Black people in Scotland and Wales (Sobande, 2024; Robinson, 2003b; Robinson and Gardiner, 2004). As Sobande (2024: 53) notes:

> as long as discussions of the lives of Black women in Britain are predicated on the interchangeability of 'Britain' and 'England', both the nuances of their lives, and those of British regional relations, will be overlooked.

While Scotland has received considerable attention in intersectional studies (Hopkins, 2006; Bassel and Emejulu, 2018; Sobande 2024), there has been limited engagement with Welsh case studies. This neglect risks overlooking the distinct experiences at work in Wales, from governance, demographics, socio-economic conditions and identity, and creating an assumption that the lived experiences are the same as those in England.

This volume draws on these approaches to understand the contemporary varied lived experiences of migrants to Wales. It builds on two landmark volumes. First, the groundbreaking *A Tolerant Nation?*, first published in 2003 and updated in 2015. This volume was critical in establishing Wales as a diverse country. Drawing on both historical accounts from the beginning of the industrial revolution onwards, as well as the new developments emerging from early years of devolution at the dawn of the twenty-first century, the volume cemented the research on diversity in Wales firmly on the research agenda. We note that the first edition was published as the effects of dispersal under the Immigration and Asylum Act 1999, began; the second emerged before the effects of Brexit and the so-called 'refugee crisis' of 2015 could be recorded. This volume appears after the enactment of the Nationality and Borders Act 2022 and the Illegal Migration Act 2023, but before we can study their impact.

Secondly, the recent collection *Welsh (Plural)* (2022) edited by Darren Chetty, Hanan Issa, Grug Muse and Iestyn Tyne. While *A Tolerant Nation?* is fairly limited in its intersectional approach, *Welsh (Plural)* engages extensively with intersectional accounts. Drawing primarily on the lived experiences of younger creative people (writers, poets and musicians), the volume provides a valuable insight on race, gender, sexuality, class, rurality and language against a backdrop of a maturing Welsh polity getting to grips with expressing its identity more confidently on the world stage and considering its constitutional future. This volume emerges from the same socio-temporal context and similarly approaches its commitment to intersectionality in its engagement with empirical studies.

About This Book

This book brings together a range of scholars studying migration and diversity in Wales. We have deliberately sought a diversity of topics that address contemporary issues at work in Wales with the intention of centring the experiences of individuals with lived experience and reflecting on the notion of Wales as a welcoming nation against the backdrop of the Welsh Government's NoS vision (2019). We consider the way in which migration is an appropriate lens through which to consider important contemporary concepts and narratives such as: hospitality, sanctuary, and responsibility towards (not-so-distant) others; the relationship between devolved and reserved powers; belonging, non-belonging, and recognition; citizenship, denizenship and statelessness; racism, exclusion, cohesion, inclusion and isolation.

Our volume begins with a focus on questions around language acquisition for migrants to Wales, encompassing both Welsh and English languages. In Chapter Two, Gwennan Higham focuses on international migration and the role and potential of the Welsh language to contribute to a multilingual and inclusive approach to integration in Wales. Largely influenced by UK government policies and ideologies, there has been a long-standing perception of English as the sole language of linguistic integration in Wales. Given the ingrained assumption that the UK is a monolingual state, the ability of the Welsh language to contribute to efforts to create an inclusive and civic Wales, and function as a language of migrant integration within a multicultural nation-building project has been overlooked (Higham, 2020). Yet, the Welsh Government's increasingly distinct approach to migrant integration has opened up new opportunities and discussion regarding the role of the Welsh language in belonging and participation in a multicultural (Welsh) nation. This chapter focuses on two Welsh language initiatives, Welsh for Speakers of Other Languages (otherwise known as the WSOL provision), and the bilingual welcome of the youth movement, Urdd Gobaith Cymru ('The Welsh League of Hope'), to advance an interdisciplinary framework where linguistic hospitality and an intercultural language provision play a central role. Beyond challenging the entrenched assumption that the Welsh language, as a minority language, is inherently exclusive, the chapter's innovative framework allows for a new thinking on integration as a two-way process and addresses the ongoing linguistic inequalities of society with the aim of transforming notions of belonging and participation in a multicultural nation.

Language and its role in the lives and experiences of people seeking sanctuary is also the focus of Chapter Three. In their chapter, Barrie Llewelyn and Mike Chick reflect on the findings of an initiative, 'Speak to Me', that began as a way of using creative thinking and storytelling to improve the language acquisition experiences of sanctuary seekers taking English for speakers of other languages (ESOL) classes in southern Wales. Without the pressure of tests and attending formal classes that add to already stressful lives, informal learning experiences and opportunities such as 'Speak to Me' provide the room and space for integrative experiences where students have the agency to decide on the focus and direction of each class. This participatory, student-led model allows for topics to emerge organically, leading to meaningful and honest discussions on finding worthwhile employment and suitable accommodation, experiences of trauma, culture shock, and family separation along with money worries. More than just language acquisition, the 'Speak to Me' project shows the way in which language education initiatives can respond to the psychological, practical and emotional needs of people seeking sanctuary as an ecological approach to education that 'intentionally connects classroom learning with the real-world' (Cox and Phipps, 2022: 3). Chick and Llewelyn highlight the role that language and language education classes play in bringing people together to foster friendships, support and mutual understanding. This chapter situates language initiatives and learning within the Welsh approach to sanctuary and the Nation of Sanctuary Plan (2019) as the only nation in the UK to have a language education policy for migrants (Welsh Government, 2019).

Chapter Four builds on key themes introduced in Chapters Two and Three, notably belonging, citizenship and nation-building in Wales, by examining the emerging political geographies of sanctuary discourses in Wales. By drawing on data collected during two research projects on the NoS vision, Franz Bernhardt and colleagues trace the emergence of the NoS discourse and explore scalar imaginaries of hospitality and citizenship. Following from these examinations, the chapter advances two findings that contribute to the critical literature on citizenship and migration. The first finding concerns the emergence of the NoS vision and highlights the influence of both third-sector organisations and the urban grassroots movement on the Welsh Parliament and subsequently the Welsh Government's decision to establish Wales as the world's first NoS. The second finding relates to the shift from urban discourses around a 'culture' of welcome and hospitality on a city scale to a national scale and the implications of this move for understandings of citizenship. While the literature on regional citizenship has engaged so far with the re-scaling of citizenship rights from the state to the city scale in a 'downwards' manner, this chapter shows that, in the Welsh context, the sanctuary discourses which emerged on a city scale were rather 'levelled-up' to impact on national discourses too. This allows us to problematise the existing over-simplified scalar thought on sanctuary and show the important relation between understandings of citizenship as a set of legal rights and as a practice and culture of claiming such rights.

Chapter Five examines the intersectional identities experienced by LGBTQ+ forced migrants living in Wales within the framework of the UK government's asylum policies. Through a focused exploration of their lived experiences upon arrival and settlement in Wales, Ourania Vamvaka-Tatsi's chapter delves into themes of otherness, belonging, community and the expression of sexual orientation and gender identities. By analysing the narratives of participants, this chapter contributes to a broader dialogue on the necessity for sustainable and inclusive asylum policies along with existing research on queer asylum policy. Their testimonies shed light on how UK asylum policies both construct and shape the experiences of a marginalised group, while simultaneously perpetuating social barriers for vulnerable populations. The precarious journey of LGBTQ+ forced migrants highlights the complex interplay of identity and policy within the asylum system. Their arrival and settlement experiences in Wales serve as a lens through which to examine the challenges they face in navigating societal norms and legal frameworks. By centring the voices of these individuals, we gain invaluable insights into the ways in which UK asylum policies impact their sense of self, community and belonging. Furthermore, this research underscores the urgent need for policies that recognise and address the unique vulnerabilities faced by LGBTQ+ individuals within the asylum process. Through a comprehensive analysis of these experiences, the chapter contributes to ongoing efforts to advocate for more equitable and inclusive asylum policies that uphold the rights and dignity of all forced migrants, regardless of their sexual orientation or gender identity. Similarly to previous chapters, we see a tension between the UK government's asylum policies and the NoS vision, with Ourania Vamvaka-Tatsi calling on the Welsh Government to address the needs of asylum seekers and refugees within its jurisdiction and for a Welsh approach that can respond to the specific needs of vulnerable groups such as LGBTQ+ individuals, women and non-binary people.

Chapter Six explores the role that learning plays in transitions and social resilience experienced by mothers seeking sanctuary in Wales. Laura Shobiye analyses the UK government's racialised asylum system, the intersectional harms and abuses imposed by it along with the gendering of immigration through hierarchies of immigration and citizenship status. By drawing upon social learning as a social process or phenomenon of active participation through which individuals and communities develop individual identities and a shared sense of belonging, Shobiye explores the experiences of three mothers through ethnographic, creative and collaborative multi-modal methods. Shobiye reveals the importance of education in

journeys of survival, well-being and resilience within Welsh communities and the significance of adopting a social learning perspective in
understanding how Wales might achieve its aim of becoming a NoS.
Together, Chapters Six and Three provide valuable insights into the
significance of informal education strategies for the lives and experiences of migrants living in Wales.

Chapter Seven turns our focus to the nature and experiences of EU citizens' migration to Wales, notably those who arrived
in Wales from the eight central and eastern European states that
joined the EU in May 2004. Stephen Drinkwater and colleagues'
chapter, which echoes some of the themes already encountered
in the volume, that of 'othering', racism and exclusion, begins by
providing an analysis of how the number and origin of international migrants living in Wales has evolved over recent decades.
Unlike most other existing EU member states, the UK placed few
restrictions on migration from the EU8 to the UK immediately
following the accession, which led to more than 1 million EU8 migrant workers moving to the UK between May 2004 and June 2010
(McCollum and Findlay, 2011). It also uncovers the various experiences of EU citizens in Wales during the 2016 Brexit referendum
campaign, its aftermath, and the run-up to the UK's withdrawal
from the EU in January 2020 by focusing on everyday hostilities.
Testimonies of EU citizens in Wales reveal how the hostility, stigmatisation and racialisation promoted by British media and political discourses (Burrell, 2010; Fox et al., 2012; Rzepnikowska,
2019) that were directed mainly to 'East Europeans' and pre-dated
Brexit are now affecting a wider range of EU citizens, including
groups such as those from northern and western Europe. Accounts
of a sense of 'othering' and non-belonging, uncertainty and xenoracism are but a few of the sentiments expressed that highlight the
impact of the hostile environment policies on individuals living in
Wales and the limitations of Wales as a tolerant and welcoming nation. Drinkwater and colleagues adopt an intersectional approach
to explore the way in which individuals living in Wales encounter
everyday hostilities and 'othering', based on national origin informed by geopolitical imaginations ('EU14' v 'EU8' and 'EU2' or
'western'/'northern' v 'eastern'/'southern'), race and ethnicity, and
gender. Significantly, it also highlights the need to incorporate EU

citizens living in Wales into the NoS vision and ensure that they are not overlooked.

Chapter Eight explores the nexus between migration, ageing and health, notably migration to rural mid-Wales, and focuses on the lived experiences of an often disregarded and misrepresented group, that of older in-migrants in Wales. By drawing on a qualitative study in one community in mid-Wales, as well as within a wider suite of research in this field nationally and internationally, Jesse Heley and Rachel Rahman's chapter unpacks the complexities of individual migrant rationales for moving to mid-Wales and present a heterogeneity of experiences between communities and individuals. While mid-Wales's attractiveness as a destination for retirement in-migration has precipitated concerns regarding the social, cultural and economic vitality of its constituent communities in the mid-to-long term, with older people being perceived as service users and a relative 'burden' to wider society, this contribution provides a much-needed alternative, fresh account of older in-migration into rural Wales that challenges and discredits broad-brush stereotypes from both an economic, cultural and social standpoint. By underscoring some of the more encouraging aspects of older age in-migration, the authors present a more positive picture of rural in-migration including the significant voluntary contributions of older adults to the Welsh health and social care sector, along with the technological interventions that are supporting healthy and independent living.

We have sought to include authors from a range of institutions in Wales (and beyond), and to include people at a range of career stages: from current PhD students to a professor. We have also deliberately engaged with early career researchers, who are often producing work on these cutting-edge themes. Many chapters included were originally contributions to a symposium for early career researchers organised by the editors in their capacities as co-convenors of the Wales Institute of Social and Economic Research and Data (WISERD)'s Migration Research Wales network.

However, any volume on migration will be incomplete, and this one is no exception. There are only so many studies that can be fitted within a 72,000-word volume. We also had some colleagues who, unfortunately, had to withdraw during the process, and we were unable to find alternative contributions in the timeframe. We recognise that there are omissions in this volume. There are no chapters, for example, on Roma and Travellers' experiences of mobility in Wales. Nor are there discussions on younger people's migrations, including international student mobility and unaccompanied children who are seeking sanctuary. A chapter on the experiences of disabled migrants in Wales is also missing. Return migration is not an explicit focus, although one which seems increasingly pertinent with some evidence of younger in-migrants beginning to leave Cardiff and return to western parts of Wales. More significantly, there is no discussion of emigration in this volume. Some of these omissions reflect a lack of Welsh case studies in these themes at the moment, and there is a need for these, and many other aspects, to receive scholarly attention. While, undoubtedly, it would have been richer through including these and other accounts, we should concentrate on what this volume *does* include, and the potential for beginning a discussion on people's experiences of moving to, from and through a 'welcoming' Wales.

Notes

1   The scheme was scrapped by the new Labour government in July 2024.
2   Despite this privileged status, the discrimination and othering experienced by Irish people in Britain is well-documented.
3   For further discussions on race, racism and ethnicity, see Hall (2021) and Hall and Morley (2018a; 2018b).
4   We use 'Welsh' in a broad sense, including both demonym as an inhabitant of Wales as well as those who identify as Welsh.
5   While migration of this type is within the UK state borders, its also crosses national boundaries.
6   Lampeter is entwined with enslavement on St Vincent through Thomas Phillips, who was a benefactor to St David's College in the 1830s. His bust was subsequently removed from the university in 2021. The scholarships, effective from 2021–2, were in response to the eruption of La Soufière, rather than as part of engaging with its institutional legacy of enslavement. However, it is unknown whether these scholarships, brokered by the then Prince Charles, were targeted for Lampeter specifically because of these connections. See Bevan (2023) and Scott (2024).

Bibliography

Amnesty International. n.d. 'UK: Priti Patel's racist Nationality and Borders Bill "drags the UK's reputation through the mud."' *https://www.amnesty.org.uk/*

press-releases/uk-priti-patels-racist-nationality-and borders-bill-drags-uks-reputation-through-mud

Bassel, Leah and Emejulu, Akwugu. 2018. *Minority Women and Austerity: Survival and Resistance in France and Britain*. Bristol: Policy Press.

Bevan, A. n.d. *https://www.iwa.wales/agenda/2023/03/wales-oldest-university-and-its-slavery-links-with-st-vincent-in-the-caribbean/?lang=cy*

Bhattacharyya, Gargi. 2018. *Rethinking Racial Capitalism: Questions of Reproduction and Survival*. London: Rowman & Littlefield International.

Bhopal, K. 2020. 'Gender, ethnicity and career progression in UK higher education: a case study analysis'. *Research Papers in Education*, 35/6, 706–21.

Bullough, Tom. 2023. *Sarn Helen: A Journey Through Wales, Past, Present and Future*. London: Granta.

Bulmer, M. and Solomos, J. 2018. 'Migration and race in Europe'. *Ethnic and Racial Studies*, 41/5, 779–84.

Caballero, C. and Aspinall, P. J. 2018. *Mixed Race Britain in The Twentieth Century*. London: Palgrave Macmillan.

Chaney P. and Williams, C. 2003. 'Getting involved: Civic and political life in Wales'. In C. Williams, N. Evans and P. O'Leary (eds), *A Tolerant Nation? Exploring Ethnic Diversity in Wales*. Cardiff: University of Wales Press, pp. 201–19.

Chetty, D., Issa, H., Muse, G. and Tyne, I. (eds). 2022. *Welsh (Plural): Essays on the Future of Wales*. London: Repeater Books.

Cole, M. 2017. 'Racism in the UK'. In M. Cole (ed.), *Education, Equality and Human Rights: Issues of Gender, 'Race', Sexuality, Disability and Social Class*. London: Routledge, pp. 52–98.

Cox, S. and Phipps, A. 2022. 'An ecological, multilingual approach to language learning with newly reunited refugee families in Scotland'. *International Journal of Educational Research*, 115, 101967.

Crenshaw, K. 1989. 'Demarginalizing the Intersection of Race and Sex: A Black Feminist Critique of Antidiscrimination Doctrine, Feminist Theory and Antiracist Politics'. *University of Chicago Legal Forum*, 1/8, 139–67.

Crenshaw, K. 1991. 'Mapping the Margins: Intersectionality, Identity Politics, and Violence against Women of Color'. *Stanford Law Review*, 43/6, 1241–99.

Crenshaw. K., Andrews, K. and Wilson, A. 2024. 'Introduction: Reframing Intersectionality'. In K. Crenshaw, K. Andrews and A. Wilson (eds), *Blackness at the Intersection*. London: Bloomsbury, pp. 1–20.

Dafydd Jones, Rh. 2010. 'Islam and the rural landscape: discourses of absence in west Wales'. *Social and Cultural Geography*, 11/8, 751–68.

Dafydd Jones, Rh. 2012. 'Negotiating Absence and Presence: Rural Muslims and "Subterranean" Sacred Spaces'. *Space and Polity*, 16/3 (2012), 335–50.

Ebenezer, Lyn. 2005. *Y Pair Dadeni: hanes gwersyll y Fron-goch*. Llanrwst: Carreg Gwalch.

Emlyn, Rh. 2012. 'Serving Church and State: the Careers of Medieval Welsh Students'. In Linda Clark (ed.), *The Fifteenth Century XI: Concerns and Preoccupations*. Woodbridge: Boydell, pp. 25–40.

Emlyn, Rh. 2018. 'Migration and Integration: Welsh Secular Clergy in England in the Fifteenth Century'. In Patricia Skinner (ed.), *The Welsh and the Medieval World: Travel, Migration and Exile*. Cardiff: University of Wales Press, pp. 75–130.

Engbersen, G. and Snel, E. 2013. 'Liquid migration: Dynamic and fluid patterns of post-accession migration'. In B. Glorius, I. Grabowska-Lusinska and A. Rindoks (eds), *Mobility in Transition: Migration patterns after EU enlargement*. Amsterdam: Amsterdam University Press, pp. 21–40.

Evans, Chris. 2003. *Slave Wales: the Welsh and Atlantic slavery 1660–1850*. Cardiff: University of Wales Press.

Evans, N., O'Leary, P. and Williams, C. 2015. 'Race, Nation and Globalization in a Devolved Wales'. In C. Williams, N. Evans and P. O'Leary (eds), *A Tolerant Nation? Revisiting Ethnic Diversity in a Devolved Wales*. Cardiff: University of Wales Press, pp. 1–23.

Evans, N. 2003. 'Immigrants and Minorities in Wales, 1840–1990: A Comparative Perspective'. In C. Williams, N. Evans and P. O'Leary (eds), *A Tolerant Nation? exploring ethnic diversity in Wales*. Cardiff: University of Wales Press, pp. 14–34.

Evans, N. 2015. 'Through the Prism of Ethnic Violence: Riots and Racial Attacks in Wales, 1826–2014'. In C. Williams, N. Evans and P. O'Leary (eds), *A Tolerant Nation? Revisiting Ethnic Diversity in a Devolved Wales*. Cardiff: University of Wales Press, pp. 128–52.

Evans-Jones, G. 2024. 'The "Descendant of Ham": A Critical Analysis of the Biography of John Ystumllyn by Alltud Eifion'. In N. Evans, and C. Williams (eds), *Globalising Welsh Studies: Decolonising History, Heritage, Society and Culture*. Cardiff: University of Wales Press, pp. 41–69.

Goodwin-Hawkins, B. and Dafydd Jones, Rh. 2022. 'Rethinking lifestyle and middle-class migration in "left behind" regions'. *Population, Space and Place*, 28/8, e2495.

Goring, N., Beckford, B. and Bowman, S. 2020. 'The Windrush Scandal: A Review of Citizenship, Belonging and Justice in the United Kingdom'. *European Journal of Law Reform*, 22/3, 266–302.

Grangetown Community Action. 2019. *http://grangetowncardiff.co.uk/Twenties2.htm*

Guma, T., Drinkwater, S. and Dafydd Jones, Rh. 2023. '"They were chasing me down the streets": Austerity, resourcefulness, and the tenacity of migrant women's care-full labour'. *Geoforum* 144, 103822.

Guma, T., Woods, M., Yarker, S. and Anderson, J. 2020. '"It's That Kind of Place Here": Solidarity, Place-Making and Civil Society Response to the 2015 Refugee Crisis in Wales, UK', *Social Inclusion*, 7/2, 96–105.

Hall, Stuart. 2021. *The hard road to renewal: Thatcherism and the crisis of the left*. London: Verso.

Hall, Stuart and Morley, David, 2018a. *Essential Essays, Volume 1: Foundations of Cultural Studies*. New York: Duke University Press.

Hall, Stuart and Morley, David. 2018b. *Essential Essays, Volume 2: Identity and Diaspora*. New York, USA: Duke University Press.

Hammel, Andrea. 2022. *Finding Refuge: stories of the men, women and children who fled to Wales to escape the Nazis*. Aberystwyth: Honno.

Hopkins, P. 20026. 'Youthful Muslim masculinities: gender and generational relations'. *Transactions of the Institution of British Geographers*, 31/3, 337–52.

Hopkins, P. 2019. 'Social Geography I: Intersectionality'. *Progress in Human Geography*, 43/5, 937–47.

Hoskins, G. and James, L. 2024. 'Commemorating Picton in Wales and Trinidad: Colonial legacies and the production of memorial publics'. *Journal of Historical Geography*, 83, 68–79.

Hutt, J. 2023. 'Written statement: safe and legal routes for asylum seekers'. Cardiff: Welsh Government. Available at: *https://www.gov.wales/written-statement-safe-and-legal-routes-asylum-seekers*

Hutt, J. and Antoniw, M. 2021. 'Written statement: UK Nationality and Borders Bill'. Cardiff: Welsh Government. Available at *https://www.gov.wales/written-statement-uk-nationality-and-borders-bill*

Hynes, Patricia. 2003. *The Dispersal and Social Exclusion of Asylum Seekers. Between liminality and belonging*. Bristol: Policy Press.

Inam, A. 2022. 'Designing an equitable city: confronting gentrification in studio pedagogy'. *Journal of Urbanism: International Research on Placemaking and Urban Sustainability*, 1–24.

Jones, A. 2003. 'The other internationalism? Missionary activity and Welsh Nonconformist perceptions of the world in the nineteenth and twentieth centuries'. In C. Williams, N. Evans and P. O'Leary (eds), *A Tolerant Nation? Exploring ethnic diversity in Wales*. Cardiff: University of Wales Press, pp. 49–60.

Jones, Noragh. 1993. *Living in Rural Wales*. Llandysul: Gomer.

Lulle, A. 2018. 'And then came Brexit: experiences and future plans of young EU migrants in the London region'. *Population, Space and Place*, 24/1, e2122.

McCollum, D. and Findlay, A. 2011. 'Trends in A8 migration to the UK during the recession'. *Population Trends*, 145, 77–89.

McDowell, L. 2003. 'Workers, migrants, aliens or citizens? State constructions and discourses of identity among post-war European labour migrants in Britain'. *Political Geography*, 22/8, 863–86.

McDowell, L. 2009. 'Old and New European economic migrants: Whiteness and managed migration policies'. *Journal of Ethnic and Migration Studies*, 35/1, 19–36.

Mitchell, J. 2010. 'The Westminster Model and the State of Unions'. *Parliamentary Affairs*, 63/1, 85–8.

Mirza, Heidi Safia. 1992. *Young, Female and Black*. London: Routledge.

Mirza, H. S. 2014. '"The Branch on Which I Sit": reflections on Black British Feminism'. *Feminist Review*, 108/1, 125–33.

Morgan, Kenneth O. 1980. *Rebirth of a Nation: Wales, 1880–1980*. Oxford: Oxford University Press.

Office for National Statistics. 2022. 'Population and household estimates, Wales: Census 2021'. Available at: *https://www.ons.gov.uk/peoplepopulationandcommunity/populationandmigration/populationestimates/bulletins/popula-tio nandhouseholdestimateswales/census2021*

Ogbonna, E. 2024. 'Making Wales an Anti-racist Nation: A "Public Value Mission" in Action'. *Business Focus Annual Research*, 2, 78–83.

Puar, J. 2012. '"I would rather be a cyborg than a goddess": Becoming intersectional in assemblage theory', *Philo-SOPHIA*, 2/1, 49–66.

Robinson, V. 2003a. 'Croeso i Gymru – Welcome to Wales? Refugees and Asylum Seekers in Wales'. In C. Williams, N. Evans and P. O'Leary (eds), *A Tolerant Nation? Exploring ethnic diversity in Wales*. Cardiff: University of Wales Press, pp. 179–200.

Robinson, V. 2003b. 'Exploring Myths about Rural Racism: A Welsh Case Study'. In C. Williams, N. Evans and P. O'Leary (eds), *A Tolerant Nation? Exploring ethnic diversity in Wales*. Cardiff: University of Wales Press, pp. 160–78.

Robinson, V. and Gardiner, H. 2004. 'Unravelling a stereotype: the lived experience of black and minority ethnic people in rural Wales'. In N. Charkraborti and J. Garland (eds), *Rural Racism*. Cullompton: Willan, pp. 85–107.

Rzepnikowska, A. 2019. 'Racism and xenophobia experienced by Polish migrants in the UK before and after Brexit vote'. *Journal of Ethnic and Migration Studies*, 45/1, 61–77.

Schmid-Scott, A., Marshall, E., Gill, N. and Bagelman, J. 2020. 'Rural Geographies of Refugee Activism: The Expanding Spaces of Sanctuary in the UK'. *Revue européenne des migrations internationales*, 36/2, 137–60. https://doi.org/10.4000/remi.15482.

Scott, A. 2024. 'Phillips Must Fall: Histories and Legacies of Slavery and Colonialism at St David's College, Lampeter'. In N. Evans, and C. Williams (eds), *Globalising Welsh Studies: Decolonising History, Heritage, Society and Culture*. Cardiff: University of Wales Press, pp. 171–203.

Scourfield, J. and Davies, A. 2005. 'Children's accounts of Wales as racialized and inclusive'. *Ethnicities*, 5/1, 83–107.

Shobiye, L. 2023. '"I survive on people": (Mis)recognising the value of social learning for mothers seeking sanctuary in Wales'. Unpublished PhD thesis, Cardiff University.

Sobande, F. 2024. '(In)visible Black women (be)longing in Scotland'. In K. Crenshaw, K. Andrews and A. Wilson (eds), *Blackness at the Intersection*. London: Bloomsbury, pp. 53–66.

Solomos, John. 1989. *Race and Racism in Contemporary Britain*. London: Palgrave.

Taylor, Lucy. 2025. *Global Politics of Welsh Patagonia: Settler Colonialism from the Margins*. Cardiff: University of Wales Press.

Theodore, N. and Martin, N. 2007. 'Migrant civil society: new voices in struggle over community development'. *Journal of Urban Affairs*, 29/3, 269–87.

Thompson, A. 2010. '"Welcome to Llaneski": Polish Migration in South West Wales'. *Contemporary Wales*, 23/1, 1–16.

Tyler, I. 2010. 'Designed to fail: A biopolitics of British citizenship'. *Citizenship Studies*, 14/1, 61–74.

Warmington, P. 2012. '"A tradition in ceaseless motion": Critical race theory and black British intellectual spaces'. *Race Ethnicity and Education*, 15/1, 5–21.

Welsh Government. 2019. 'Nation of Sanctuary: Refugee and Asylum Seeker Plan'. Available at: *https://www.gov.wales/sites/default/files/publications/2019-03/ nation-of-sanctuary-refugee-and-asylum-seeker-plan_0.pdf*

Welsh Government. 2020. 'First Minister of Wales Black, Asian and minority ethnic COVID-19 socio-economic subgroup report'. Available at: *https:// www.gov.wales/sites/default/files/pdf-versions/2021/12/1/1638805480/cov- id-19-bame-socio-economic-subgroup-report-welsh-government-response.pdf*

Welsh Government. 2022. 'Anti-Racist Wales Action Plan'. Available at: *https:// www.gov.wales/sites/default/files/publications/2022-06/anti-racist-wales-ac- tion-plan_0.pdf*

Williams, C., Evans, N. and O'Leary, P. (eds). 2003. *A Tolerant Nation? Exploring ethnic diversity in Wales*. Cardiff: University of Wales Press.

Yuval-Davis, Nira. 2011. *The Politics of Belonging: Intersectional Contestations*. London: SAGE Publications.

Yuval-Davis, N., Wemyss, G. and Cassidy, K. 2018. 'Everyday Bordering, Belong- ing, and the Reorientation of British Immigration Legislation'. *Sociology*, 52/2, 228–44.

CHAPTER 2

International Migration and the Welsh Language: Exploring an Interdisciplinary Framework for Linguistic Integration

Gwennan Higham

Introduction

This chapter investigates linguistic integration in Wales and the potential for the Welsh language to contribute to a multilingual and inclusive approach to integration. It opens with the transformation in the twenty-first century from viewing minority languages as belonging to a particular homogeneous group to perceiving them as valuable resources to speakers from multiple backgrounds. In addition, the chapter contextualises the role of language(s) in integration policies in Wales which, until recently, have been significantly influenced by the UK's centralised immigration policy and the emphasis on the hegemony of the English language. The chapter also underscores the recent change in Wales, embodied in its Nation of Sanctuary plan, towards an alternative approach to linguistic integration which includes elements of learning Welsh as well as English.

The study therefore advances an interdisciplinary framework which combines sociolinguistic research with political theory to provide empirical ground and legitimacy to a context-sensitive notion of linguistic integration in Wales. By using sociolinguistic research methods, the chapter analyses the case of two Welsh language initiatives: Welsh for Speakers of Other Languages (otherwise known as the WSOL provision) and the bilingual welcome of the youth movement, *Urdd Gobaith Cymru* ('the Welsh League of Hope', 'the Urdd' hereafter). It further draws out findings from language teachers and community activists concerning the potential of Welsh to play a part in an intercultural language provision as well as to provide linguistic hospitality (Kearney, 2019). The chapter concludes by emphasising the need for a holistic, context-sensitive and two-way approach to linguistic integration in Wales.

New Speakers of Minority Languages

The traditional view of minority languages belonging to a homogeneous group of speakers has been widely challenged by researchers over the last decades (O'Rourke and Pujolar, 2015). The latter half of the twentieth century saw a rise in claims over minority rights within a wider movement of liberal democracy in the West. National language groups, including in Wales, Catalonia, Québec and Scotland, were mobilised in the effort to affirm and have recognised their minoritised languages. In Wales, this movement initiated *Cymdeithas yr Iaith Gymraeg* (the Welsh Language Society) in 1962, bilingual road signage from the late 1960s, the Welsh language television channel S4C in 1982, as well as the 1993 Welsh Language Act, which gave a legal basis for the Welsh language alongside English in public services and justice. Educational opportunities for children, as well as adults, thus became a key factor in language revitalisation efforts (Williams, 2023). For example, in Wales, Welsh became a compulsory subject for all schools from 1990 and Welsh-medium education thereafter increased in popularity, particularly amongst non-Welsh speakers (Jones and Jones, 2014). Likewise, Welsh language courses for adults were introduced in the 1970s and led to the establishment of Welsh for Adults teaching centres across Wales, now coordinated by the National Centre for Learning Welsh (NCLW).

Many minority nations also gained political powers during this period, which led to the formation of sub-state governments. This has enabled minority nations to legislate and create strategies to further promote the use and prestige of their national minority languages. Devolution for Wales in 1999, for example, which decentralised certain powers from the UK government to Welsh Government, included powers and oversight over the Welsh language. This subsequently led to significant language strategies and measures by the Welsh Government, such as *Iaith Pawb*: A National Action Plan for a Bilingual Wales (Welsh Government, 2003), the Welsh Language (Wales) Measure in 2011, in which the position of Welsh as an official language was strengthened and given an equal status with English, and *Cymraeg 2050*, the current Welsh language strategy to reach a million Welsh speakers by 2050 (Welsh Government, 2017).

National minority languages like Welsh, although previously associated with cultural heritage and identity, are increasingly connected with added value and economic advantage (Duchêne and Heller, 2012). Governmental efforts in sub-state contexts aim to portray these languages as equally accessible to everyone, moving away from an ethnolinguistic focus to promoting the plurality of language, nationhood and belonging. In sub-state contexts such as Québec, there are noticeable efforts to strike a balance between preserving existing linguistic heritage and upholding the ethnolinguistic rights of newcomers, as further elaborated upon in this study. In Wales, there has been more ambiguity in public policy and scholarly debate regarding its role in the future of an inclusive and civic Wales (Higham, 2020). Despite language revitalisation efforts, public discussions related to migration and the Welsh language have tended to focus more on the threat of migration to the vitality of the national minority language. Questions have also arisen in scholarly debate concerning the inclusivity of the Welsh language and its ability to function as civic, open and inclusive language within a multicultural nation-building project (e.g., Turnbull, 2004; Scourfield and Davies, 2005). This is also connected to wider discussions that have tended to categorise minority languages as ethnic languages related to exclusion and ethnocentrism (Barry, 2001).

The legitimation of new speakers of Welsh, particularly from immigrant and minority ethnic communities, is therefore an increasingly forefront matter for Welsh language policies. The *Cymraeg 2050* strategy, for example, emphasises the role of Welsh in welcoming newcomers and notes that that Welsh 'can also be an opportunity to demonstrate how the language can be used to embrace multicultur-alism and diversity' (Welsh Government, 2017: 69). The Welsh Gov-ernment's Anti-racist Wales Action Plan stresses that attention will be directed towards Black, Asian and Minority Ethnic Welsh speakers and ensuring access for ethnic minority communities to education and language learning (Welsh Government, 2022). Nevertheless, these efforts are met with increasing challenges for the future of the Welsh language. International migration has trebled in Wales over the last decade and the decline in Welsh language speakers, accord-ing to the two last Censuses, has been partly attributed to increased internal and external migration (Jones, 2015). Concerns have also been raised regarding internal migration and second home owners, often from outside Wales, and the effect of this on the vitality of the Welsh language in rural Welsh speaking communities (Edwards, 2017). For international migration, the focus of this study, there are added complexities arising from Wales's political status as part of the United Kingdom and its adherence to the regulations of the UK gov-ernment's Home Office. The next section will elaborate further on this relationship.

Policy Developments in Linguistic Integration in Wales

The highly centralised nature of immigration policy in the UK means that the issue of linguistic integration of migrants in Wales has been largely influenced by UK government policies and ideol-ogies. The idea that the UK is a monolingual state, and that English is the only suitable language for integration, has been propagated by policy moves by the Home Office (Simpson, 2015). The Nation-ality, Immigration and Asylum Act, introduced by the Labour gov-ernment in 2002, emphasised the importance of English language proficiency and initiated national discussions on the relationship between English, British identity and belonging in the UK. In 2013, British citizenship requirements were updated to include manda-tory English language competency. While English for Speakers of Other Languages (ESOL) serves as the primary English language provision for adult migrants in the UK, it operates under a mono-lingual ideology, despite being devolved and separate from British citizenship requirements. Recent anti-immigrant discourse and the rise of far-right populism in the UK, especially around the Brexit referendum, have further reinforced the idea of linguistic hegemony and linked state monolingualism to the securitisation of nation-states (Khan, 2022). Moreover, the UK government's hostile environment policies, measures introduced in 2012 to prohibit the rights and freedoms of refugees, asylum seekers and other migrant groups in the UK, are also accompanied by discourses on the acquisition of English as a prerequisite for integration and social cohesion (Simpson and Hunter, 2023). Thus, as Fournier points out, 'the way that language and integration are linked in government policy consistently locates the "problem" of integration in "English-free homes"' (Fortier, 2017: 1258.

Discussions on diversity management in Wales have (until recently) been dominated by UK government's policy direction, particularly the focus on the necessity of the English language. Nevertheless, important changes are underway as a result of the Welsh Government's increasingly divergent approach to migrant integration. This is most clearly seen in the Welsh Government Refugee and Asylum Seeker Plan with the ambition for Wales to become the world's first Nation of Sanctuary and help migrants, particularly refugees and asylum seekers, integrate well in the communities of Wales (Welsh Government, 2019). While the role of the Welsh language has not featured prominently in the strategy, key developments regarding migrant integration has led to Welsh featuring in the official welcome given to certain cohorts of migrants. The most prominent example is the resettlement of over 100 Afghan refugees in 2021 by the Urdd, a Welsh language voluntary youth organisation. This came as a result of what is named a 'Team Wales' approach, a concentrated cross-sector partnership, led by the then First Minister of Wales, Mark Drakeford, that negotiated with the Home Office regarding the conditions for Afghan refugee resettlement in Wales. Although there was no official remit to introduce the Welsh language to these cohorts of refugees, the Welsh language became a natural part of their settlement and daily activities. The Head of Inclusion and Cohesion for the Welsh Government, for example, noted that the 'Team Wales' partnership with the Urdd developed 'a ground-breaking approach to refugee re-settlement and seeing refugee children singing in the Welsh language before learning English is something we haven't been able to achieve before' (Urdd Gobaith Cymru, 2022).

In addition, a WSOL provision for adult migrants has been established since 2018. Delivered by the NCLW, the *Croeso i Bawb* (Welcome to All) course is directed at a diverse and international audience. This provision entails a ten-hour taster course and ensures follow-on Welsh courses are offered free of charge for migrant students. While funding for NCLW is provided by the Welsh Government, the WSOL developments are driven by language practitioners (directors and teachers), community activists and migrants themselves (Senedd Cymru, 2016). In 2014, the Welsh Government introduced its first ESOL policy for Wales, initially viewing the Welsh language as a challenge for migrants already learning English (Welsh Government, 2014). However, the WSOL developments have led to a shift in perspective, recognising the Welsh language in subsequent policy reviews as an asset for social integration and belonging in Wales (Welsh Government, 2023). It nevertheless calls into question the role of a minority language in the wider linguistic integration process and the extent to which including both host English and Welsh languages is fair and inclusive of immigrants' own linguistic backgrounds.

Framing an Interdisciplinary Approach to Linguistic Integration

The present study identifies with a growing body of literature on linguistic justice in the field of political theory. This emerging new field engages with normative theory on the just treatment of speakers of different languages, such as in minority language and multicultural settings. Although academic literature has largely focused on the linguistic integration of migrants through the majority language of nation-states, debates on linguistic justice consider contexts with more than one potential host community language for integration (Kymlicka, 1995; Patten, 2014; Van Parijs, 2011). Much of this literature is based on liberal democratic theory, particularly liberal multiculturalism, as defined by Will Kymlicka. In his theory of multiculturalism, he distinguishes rights of both national minority/substate groups, indigenous and immigrant groups and argues that a fair and multicultural society must acknowledge and protect the cultural and collective rights of its minority groups (Kymlicka, 1995). Granting special cultural or linguistic rights to non-dominant groups is believed to put these groups on a more equal footing with dominant majority groups. The practical implications of linguistic integration in a national minority/sub-state context are nevertheless complex. While multiculturalism defines distinct rights accorded to minority/sub-state and immigrant groups, literature in linguistic justice considers how the linguistic rights of both these groups intertwine within one given (sub-state) context. As Riera-Gil points out, minority/sub-state contexts which experience increased immigration and where the sub-state language plays a significant role (e.g., Québec, Catalonia, Wales), must address the additional challenge of balancing two types of minority language rights, those of long-settled populations and those of immigrants (Higham, 2020). While there is a general consensus on newcomers learning the sub-state language for instrumental purposes, discussions on the rights and duties of host communities and newcomers often neglect the identity-based values of minority languages (see, for example, May, 2022; Riera-Gil, 2022). There is also less clarity concerning how linguistic integration in these contexts can truly claim to be plural and inclusive without considering the contribution of immigrants' own language and identities within the new host society.

While linguistic justice debates contribute to normative discussions, this study recognises the importance of addressing the nuanced needs of the specific context in question. Oakes and Peled (2017) call for a holistic and more context-specific study of linguistic integration which incorporates both normative and sociolinguistic research methods. They use the case of Québec, and its distinct sub-state form of interculturalism, to highlight how identity interests related to promoting French are based on an open and plural notion of inclusion and participation. Québec's interculturalism, as defined by Bouchard (2012), balances preserving the French language with promoting ethnocultural diversity, including the minority anglophone community and immigrant groups. It emphasises a shared public space where both host and immigrant communities contribute to Québec's identity and social cohesion. While critics have labelled it as assimilationist,

Bouchard argues that the survival of the language requires language promotion and newcomers learning it. Québec's intercultural model promotes an additive approach to developing linguistic repertoires, resulting in more multilingual competencies for immigrants compared to other parts of Canada (Corbeil and Houle, 2013).

This context-sensitive and language-focused approach to interculturalism is also related to the notion of linguistic hospitality, as discussed in the field of sociolinguistics (Phipps, 2012). Linguistic hospitality, as originally conceived by Paul Ricoeur (2007) in hermeneutics, involves mediating between languages without compromising their integrity. For Kearney (2019), it is a two-way integration model that promotes equitable relations between people, honouring both host and guest languages while preventing one from dominating the other. Rather than framing linguistic integration in terms of linguistic competency and/or deficiency, it focuses on the kind of meaningful interaction that can happen and which can transform both parties in their understanding and belongings. Sociolinguistic research by Cox and Phipps (2022) on language education for new refugees in Scotland shows how linguistic hospitality promotes a multilingual, ecological approach to linguistic integration. This research highlights how putting the dominant language (in their case English) last in the language classroom can have a powerful decolonising effect on language pedagogy and promote feelings of empowerment and self-worth amongst refugees and asylum seekers. Both linguistic hospitality and a context-sensitive approach to interculturalism imply that both parties are considered as agents that strive together through dialogue and mutual learning to rethink the possibilities of integration.

The following sections of this chapter will focus on the Welsh context, where both English and Welsh languages may serve as a language of integration. Based on the Welsh Government's pro-migration stance, embodied in its Nation of Sanctuary strategy, this study will consider the potential role of the Welsh language in facilitating an intercultural and hospitable approach to linguistic integration. Focusing particularly on data from language teachers and community activists, it will further consider whether there is scope, despite the minoritised position of the Welsh language, to develop an interdisciplinary approach to linguistic integration, drawn from both sociolinguistic and normative research approaches that support both the inclusion of minority and immigrants' languages.

Methodology

Context

The following paragraphs are based on sociolinguistic research that records the new developments regarding the new WSOL provision for adult migrants and recent efforts to accommodate Afghan refugees at the Urdd. The data used forms part of a critical participatory action research on a project entitled 'Pathways to the Welsh Language for International Migrants' which has two main impact research strands. It is part of a continuous research involvement in the field which is aimed at improving access of international migration to Welsh language learning opportunities.[1] For this chapter, the data will focus primarily on extracts from interviews taken with host community representatives (community activists and language teachers) between 2021 and 2022. Although the findings from the language teachers and community activists do not necessarily represent the views of the general public in Wales, the research intends to highlight the potentially significant and mediatory role of the host community in a pluralist approach to linguistic integration (see also Higham, 2024).

CPAR and Researcher Positionality

The critical participatory action research (CPAR) was adopted as a research approach based on its emphasis on collaborative inquiry. While CPAR and participatory action research (PAR) both share a commitment to collaborative research, CPAR focuses on the notion of researching with others with the aim of transforming dominant thinking and practices that can better individuals' lives and consequently the community practices in which these individuals interact (Kemmis et al., 2014). CPAR is also shaped by an emancipatory impulse to create space for alternative and underrepresented narratives (Kemmis et al., 2014). In this respect, the writer's role as researcher was also as collaborator amongst other language teachers and community activists. The work was carried out with an ongoing reflexivity with collaborators about the research process and how their understandings of language and integration can inform new ways of thinking and collective action. As writer, personal engagement was designed to give a platform to the views of the different actors as well as to co-develop and implement new practices and policy processes.

Participants
The two WSOL teachers were experienced ESOL teachers and were selected because of their instrumental position in leading the WSOL developments. Language Teacher 1 is a first language Welsh speaker while Language Teacher 2 is a new speaker of Welsh. Despite ESOL remaining their main brief, both are committed to giving their time to raise awareness of, coordinate, as well as teach the WSOL courses. As a result, these teachers are involved in training other WSOL teachers and demonstrating good practice for WSOL courses elsewhere in Wales.

The community activists are part of the 'Team Wales' partnership and were involved in the Urdd's Afghan resettlement scheme. Both community activists are first language Welsh speakers and experienced in the field of community work. Community Activist 1 specialises in interethnic relations in Wales and was influential in facilitating the Welsh Government's 'Nation of Sanctuary' vision. Community Activist 2 is experienced in promoting youth relations in Wales and was instrumental in housing Afghan refugees within the Welsh language youth organisation and in highlighting the role of the Welsh language for successful integration in Wales.

Analysis
The data (interview transcripts with elements of field notes and informal conversations) were analysed using Braun and Clarke's (2006) six-step thematic analysis as follows:

1) becoming familiar with the data by transcribing the interview recordings, then reading and engaging with it whilst searching for meanings and patterns;
2) identifying and labelling preliminary codes for the data;
3) beginning the interpretative analysis by compiling relevant extracts via common and recurring themes;

4) reviewing these themes against the coded extracts and the general data set;
5) refining the themes; before
6) writing up the findings – interviews were transcribed fully and, in the case of all but one, the interviews were translated from Welsh to English.

Welsh as a Language of Hospitality

Language teachers and community activists acknowledge that the general position towards language policy in institutions and government bodies in Wales (as with the rest of the UK) has traditionally privileged English language learning. As WSOL Teacher 1 puts it:

> I think there's a utilitarian attitude around the support for refugees coming here. It's very practical. Accommodation, basic integration. Welsh is seen as a luxury, fun, but not important on a practical level.

The English language retains a hegemonic position in Wales, in relation to Welsh, regarding language learning for adult migrants. The host community note this disparity in language education policy and in practice, yet also point to initiatives that embrace support for both community languages: the Welsh Government's Nation of Sanctuary ambition and activities undertaken by the Urdd to resettle Afghan and Ukrainian refugees. According to Community Activist 1:

> *Mae byd croesawu mewnfudwyr yn heriol a chymhleth ac mae'n naturiol i bobl feddwl bod 'na flaenoriaethau eraill ond yn achos yr Urdd roedd yn allweddol bod hynny'n realiti. Mae [integreiddio] yn digwydd trwy bethau fel 'pen, ysgwyddau, coesau, traed' a chysylltu'r Gymraeg â chwarae a hwyl. Beth wnaethon nhw o'r cychwyn un oedd dweud bod gan y teuluoedd fraint o gael mynediad at y Gymraeg. Y peth mwyaf grymus oedd fe ddysgodd i bobl eraill nad oedd [dysgu Cymraeg] yn broblem rhyfeddol fel oedd pobl yn ei feddwl.*

[The world of welcoming migrants is challenging and complex and it's natural for people to think there are other priorities but in the case of the Urdd they made it a reality. It [integration] happens through things like 'head, shoulders, knees, and toes' and connecting Welsh to play and fun. What they did from the very start was to say that the families would have the privilege of having access to Welsh. The most powerful thing was that it taught others that it [learning Welsh] wasn't a massive issue like they had thought.]

In response to this, the outcomes of being hosted in a Welsh language organisation have encouraged this cohort of migrants to identify with the Welsh language, as Community Activist 2 points out:

Y flaenoriaeth oedd eu helpu ond yn fuan iawn datblygon nhw identity *fel Cymry. Roedd y Gymraeg yn gyson yn y cefndir, yn gyfochrog â'r Saesneg ac roedd hyn yn grymus. Maen nhw uniaethu profiadau da gyda phethau Cymreig, tra bod y cysylltiadau â'r Swyddfa Gartref ddim cystal. Mae ambell Sir wedi cael sioc bod teuluoedd y plant yn gofyn i roi eu plant mewn ysgolion Cymraeg. Mae'n ymwybyddiaeth* identity *newydd i sawl un.*

[Although the priority was helping them, very soon they developed an identity as Welsh. The Welsh language was in the background, alongside English and this was powerful. They identify good experiences with things that were Welsh, while their links with the Home Office were not as good. Some Counties have been shocked that the families of the children have been asking to put their children in Welsh schools. It's a new identity awareness for many.]

This identification with Welsh contrasts with these migrants' experiences in England, namely those that relate to policy at national government level. Indeed, this community activist further explained the negotiation between Welsh Government and Home Office officials regarding the appropriateness of sending refugees and asylum seekers to rural Welsh-speaking communities. The discussion referred to the Home Office sending a cohort of Syrian refugees to Ceredigion, a rural region in mid-Wales with many Welsh speakers, in 2016. This led to some refugees learning Welsh and being recognised by the community for their efforts – see the example of Mohamad Karkoubi (Learn Welsh, 2019). In addition, the extract notes that local authorities in Wales did not anticipate that introducing the Welsh language to Afghan families could influence their decisions to send their children to Welsh-medium educational settings in Wales.

Despite claims that Welsh is ethnocentric (Turnbull, 2004), the findings suggest that a distinct sub-state version of integration is also tied to a desire to show Welsh speakers and Welsh culture as embracive of multi-/interculturalism, and which contrasts with the UK's hostile environment. Community Activist 1 refers to an ambition to be hospitable to migrants in Wales, particularly amongst Welsh speakers:

> *Mae yna syniad gyda rhai ein bod ni'n geidwadol, yn ymylol, ac nid yn progressive. Mae'r naratif mor wrthyn i'r rhan fwyaf o siaradwyr Cymraeg. Mae'n anodd iawn i ddeall. Dyn ni wedi manteisio ar ddatganoli i greu 'Cenedl Noddfa'. Yn y cyfamser, mae diwylliannau Seisnig yn anfon mewnfudwyr yn ôl ac yn erbyn eu hewyllys i Rwanda. I ni, fel Cymry Cymraeg, dyn ni'n sylweddoli nad dyna yw ein traddodiad ni.*
>
> [There's an idea with some that we are conservative, marginal, and not progressive. The narrative is ridiculous to most Welsh speakers. It's hard to understand. We have taken advantage of devolution to create a 'Nation of Sanctuary'. In the meantime, English cultures are sending migrants back and against their wills to Rwanda. We, as Welsh language speakers, we realise that we have a different tradition.]

Rather than aligning with the dominant ideologies about migration and integration in UK policy and in public discourse, there is confidence concerning possible alternative pathways for integration in Wales. Here, the idea of sanctuary and Welsh hospitality is contrasted with 'English cultures', referring to the UK's Conversative government's attempts (elected primary by inhabitants in England) to deport asylum seekers to Rwanda as a third country.[2] As well as the clear contrast in integration approaches, these comments evoke the notion of linguistic hospitality, as defined by Kearney, which challenges the idea of integration as primarily undertaken by the migrant and shifts equal, or even more, responsibility to the host, as those in positions of power. Further to this, Community Activist 1 comments:

> *Tua diwedd y prosiect ... dw 'di treulio blynyddoedd yn credu mai ein gwaith ni yw eu croesawu [newydd-ddyfodiaid] a gwneud ein gorau i leddfu anawsterau. Beth ddysgodd yr Urdd oedd dych chi'n gwneud yn dda pan dych chi'n gadael iddyn nhw ein croesawu ni.*
>
> [Towards the end of the project ... I've spent years believing that our work is welcoming them [newcomers] and doing our best to alleviate difficulties. What the Urdd did was show that you're doing well if you let them welcome us.]

The comment illustrates a desire to provide a view of integration which allows newcomers to occupy a space in which they can communicate their own cultural and linguistic values. As suggested, the most powerful tool for integration is when guests become hosts, given freedom, opportunity to regain dignity, self-worth to participate in a new life. While the Nation of Sanctuary Plan is in its early stages of development, the findings from this research suggest that there is an opportunity to define integration in Wales as two-way process, where languages can play a forefront role in facilitating this.

An Intercultural Language Provision for Migrants

Monolingual ideologies regarding language learning have traditionally dominated state language policies as well as influenced sub-state language policies (Blackledge, 2000). Indeed, previous research in the field of ESOL suggests that little knowledge of and consequently limited demand for the Welsh language amongst migrants is based on the assumption that students prefer to focus on learning English (Higham, 2014). What is notable about the new WSOL provision is that language teachers in general observed that the classes facilitated multilingual exchange as well as enhancing English language skills. Language classes did not replace one monolingualism with another: that is, Welsh instead of English. Language classes were a means to supporting a multilingual approach to language provision in Wales.

The reason for this, according to WSOL Teacher 2, is that participants did not feel the same pressure learning Welsh as they did with English, which in their view is associated with assessment, examinations and the gaining of qualifications:

> There is a different tone in the WSOL classes. People are turning up of their own volition. There is a levity, a conviviality in the class that you don't always see in the ESOL class. There's a multilingual element, the idea that ... it's like multiple languages rather than just English and learners use their own languages and make comparisons. Not an intimidating monolingual atmosphere.

In this respect, language teachers comment on how the new WSOL provision can enrich the teaching of languages to migrants in Wales by making it more inclusive, multilingual and emancipatory for migrants in contrast to the mandatory English classes and requirements imposed upon migrants to reach a certain level of English. WSOL Teacher 2 noted the following:

> I think that it [WSOL] will sort of radically change the way ESOL is framed, taught and presented in different ways. I think one big one is that it's part of a new movement towards seeing ESOL classes as social justice rather than trying to fit learners in with the state and try to meet the requirements of the state. So, it's about language learning, community, culture without that massive crushing pressure that you absolutely have to learn English, or the job centre is mandating it, to just turn yourself into a citizen which fits in with the state.

Thus WSOL, according to the language teachers, provides a new perspective on adult language provision for migrants in Wales. By aligning with the multiplicity of migrants' backgrounds and languages, it also provides a learning environment based on human connections which reflects the way that students use languages outside the classroom (Duff and Van Lier, 1997). Rather than the obligation to 'fit in' with state requirements by learning English, WSOL classes offer a meaningful way for students to express notions of belonging. The language teachers' vision is to challenge a monolingual provision of ESOL by bringing the new WSOL provision – which is multilingual and inclusive – to the forefront of adult education for migrants in Wales. This would also necessitate that access to Welsh language opportunities for adult migrants become equal to opportunities available to learn English.

However, language teachers acknowledge that they are often lone agents in pursuing WSOL for migrants, and that the work of promoting the classes is done in their spare time. Despite expressing a desire to transform teaching systems, some language teachers admitted that there are limitations (in terms of time and feasibility) to their ability to incorporate Welsh or other languages in their teaching. In an earlier sociolinguistic study on the experiences of adult migrant learners of Welsh, the present writer indicated that ESOL teachers in Wales were often monolingual English speakers and that they assumed that learning an additional language would be confusing for ESOL students (Higham, 2020). While not many ESOL teachers have embraced the WSOL provision so far, WSOL Teacher 2 expressed an understanding of the reason for not doing so:

> I think a lot of tutors … there's an attempt to challenge the system, bottom-up learning instead of authoritative and learner-led instead of textbook based. I think there's limitations in the system as it's so dominated by assessment bodies. So, the tutors have very little wiggle room and the funding that colleges get are dependent on these exams being put in place and students passing them. Even creative approaches in ESOL classes, people are desperately trying to shoehorn them in … they are really hamstrung.

While there is much scope for developing WSOL, WSOL Teacher 2 explains that any additional creativity relating to language teaching is challenging, given ESOL teachers' increasing workloads and frequent assessment requirements. From informal conversations with WSOL teachers, it was noted that the current WSOL course material is at times tokenistic in its attempt to include multicultural elements, such as focus on stereotypical elements within middle eastern culture. Observations in the field indicate that cooperation between both ESOL and WSOL language teachers to improve course material would be beneficial, as would training for Welsh language teachers to deal with multicultural classes and the linguistic and cultural differences between migrant students. Despite the development of a Welsh approach to migrant integration, which includes elements of learning Welsh, only a small number can take advantage of it at present, according to Community Activist 2:

Mae lot o bolisïau ar waith a diolch ein bod yn gallu gwahaniaethu fel uned ddatganoledig, ond eto nid ydym yn ddigon cryf, ddim â'r pwerau datganoledig a all wneud mwy o wahaniaeth. Y realiti yw nad ydyn nhw [mewnfudwyr] yn canfod y dyhead hwn [i fod yn Genedl Noddfa] yn eu profiadau bob dydd. Yr hyn sy'n fy nharo yw bod yna elfen o hap a damwain. Mae yna fylchau ac mae Covid yn enwedig wedi datgelu hyn mewn bob math o feysydd. Mae angen mwy o drefniant arnom.

[There are a lot of policies in place and it's good that we can differentiate as a devolved unit, but we are still not strong enough without the devolved powers that can make a difference. The reality is that they [migrants] don't find this desire [to be a Nation of Sanctuary] in their everyday experiences. What strikes me is that there is an element of hit and miss. There are gaps and Covid has revealed this in many ways. We need more structure.]

Even though language teachers and community activists note a shift towards a sub-state position on migrant integration, immigration and integration are still tied to UK hegemonic integration models. Although there are creative cross-agency partnerships to support migrant integration and refugee resettlement in Wales, the Nation of Sanctuary ambition is far from fully realised. Likewise, the Welsh and English adult migrant language learning sectors still work separately: ESOL provides monolingual language instruction for most adult migrants in Wales while NCLW provides Welsh language instruction for UK-born citizens. Regardless of plans to revamp the Welsh Curriculum in statutory education, there is no nation-wide discussion about how Welsh or multilingualism can or should be integrated into the adult language learning sector for migrants.

Discussion

The sociolinguistic research in this study has considered the perceptions of language teachers and community activists regarding Welsh language learning for migrants and the possible implications on linguistic integration approaches in Wales. For both language teachers and community activists, the desire to provide a hospitable welcome to newcomers through the Welsh language is evident. The inclusion of the Welsh language in their initiatives is portrayed as both positive and distinct integration practices which contrast with UK norms of monolingual integration. First, the Urdd's work is contrasted with traditional resettlement practices by the Home Office which often house asylum seekers in dilapidated accommodation with little financial support.[3] Asylum seekers and refugees, in these cases, are distanced or cut off from integration support in the wider community, which hinders rather than empowers language learning (Peled, 2003). Secondly, the WSOL provision is framed as a way of revolutionising the monolingual ESOL provision which is traditionally concerned with meeting state requirements for the English language and 'fitting in' to a new host society, as described by Language Teacher 2.

Thus, the findings suggest that integration approaches in Wales are increasingly divergent and in line with the Welsh Government's vision to become a Nation of Sanctuary. The difference between the UK's official stance on migration is noteworthy, especially in the context of its hostile environment policies and its emphasis on the dominance of the English language. Thus, evidence from this study challenges a simplistic, one-way approach to language integration in Wales which views the need to acquire the host language without considering the role of the minority national language as well as the difficulties and trauma placed on newcomers in a new host society. Although prior evidence has highlighted the challenges of integrating the Welsh language into linguistic integration in Wales (as seen in the Welsh Government's 2014 ESOL policy), the current study indicates that it can serve as a means to promote social participation and a feeling of belonging in Wales.

In this respect, the Welsh language has distinctive function and utility in linguistic integration. The examples taken from the language teachers indicate that the learning of Welsh, a minoritised language, opens up opportunities for discussion relating to power structures and thus makes a suitable platform to negotiate and transform perspectives around identity and belonging as well as to pave the way towards linguistic hospitality (Phipps, 2012). They observed that WSOL classes were a means of foregrounding multilingualism as well as facilitating English language acquisition.

By intertwining Welsh and Welsh culture with migrants' linguistic backgrounds (many of which include knowledge of lesser-used languages), the WSOL class is a space for sharing experiences, translanguaging and mediation (García and Wei, 2015). The ease and freedom of the WSOL classes, according to the language teachers, is contrasted with the obligation and burden that is often connected with ESOL and learning English.

Likewise, the examples taken from the Urdd's bilingual welcome highlights the role of the minority Welsh language in facilitating and promoting connectivity between host community members and newcomers. Rather than emphasising the ability to converse through Welsh or the need to affiliate with the identity of the language, emphasis was placed on the language as a platform to provide hospitality and promote the ethics of care and co-learning. Although studies reveal that the Welsh language and its speakers are not exempt from racism and colonial logic (Williams, 2007), findings in this study suggest that introducing the Welsh language can facilitate the inclusion of migrants' own backgrounds and linguistic repertoires in community integration practices. The views of these four individuals certainly do not claim to represent the general host society in Wales, including both English and Welsh speaking communities. Nevertheless, the findings highlight how the host community, through a minority language, can help challenge hegemonic notions of integration and monolingualism and facilitate a two-way relational approach to integration with a view to transforming and empowering individual lives.

The question remains regarding the role of the Welsh language in integration and social cohesion policies. Language teachers comment on how WSOL is not yet widely promoted by ESOL providers in Wales, and resources and capacity are limited for developing bilingual and multilingual provision for adult migrants in Wales. Despite gestures from the Welsh Government towards supporting the Welsh language in their ESOL policy, it is questionable the extent to which WSOL can be supported without a thorough revision of adult language education for migrants in Wales. Likewise, the bilingual approach to refugee resettlement, as shown in the example of the Urdd, has so far only been offered to specific groups of refugees who have escaped war and conflict situations. Wales's Nation of Sanctuary ambition and its 'Team Wales' approach have not explicitly included Welsh as part of resettlement projects. While the aspiration to become a Nation of Sanctuary might inspire individuals and institutions to offer a welcoming environment, language teachers and community activists are often lone agents, and require wider support from local actors and national institutions to transform language practices for migrants in light of the prevailing monolingual practices in the UK. Carlsson points out that policy formation in linguistic integration frequently overlooks the narratives of minority language communities and thus notes that 'integration policy ends up serving majority identities and nationhood rather than those of minorities' (Carlsson, 2021: 68). With the limitations of sociolinguistic research, this study acknowledges the importance of interaction with top-down policies and frameworks.

Conclusion: Working Towards an Interdisciplinary Framework for Linguistic Integration

This chapter has drawn from political philosophy as well as sociolinguistics to discuss the possibility of an interdisciplinary language policy and theoretical reference point to guide thinking on linguistic integration in Wales. Oakes and Peled (2017) refer to this as a 'normative language policy' which seeks to capture the strength of language policy research in political philosophy and sociolinguistics. They argue in favour of a holistic, ethical and up-to-date understanding of linguistic integration practices in minority contexts which re-evaluate changing political structures and education practices. In view of the debates on linguistic justice, the principles of maintaining a minority language and promoting immigrants' languages can be ethically justified (Riera-Gil, 2022). Moreover, there is justification to support the duty of migrants to learn the national minority language to better integrate into the sub-state culture. Nevertheless, there are limitations in normative thinking to be specific concerning the context in question and delve into the nuances of the culture in question. Québec is an example in which academics have noted the strengths of its linguistic integration framework, which is both context-specific and based on liberal democratic principles. Its notion of interculturalism explicitly defines the role of the French language and its relationship with immigrant languages. Catalonia, too, is an example of a sub-state nation that adopts a tailored approach to interculturalism in its integration policies (Conversi and Jeram, 2017: 54). It advocates the Catalan language as a key capability for migrants to develop within a framework of multilingual education (Zapata-Barrero, 2015).

While linguistic integration in Wales has traditionally adhered to the UK government's monolingual ideology, this research highlights the emergence of innovative multilingual approaches. This study has attempted to show that combining sociolinguistic research with political theory on liberal democracy and minority rights may deepen insights, provide empirical grounding and increase the legitimacy of these practices for linguistic integration in Wales. The new WSOL provision and the bilingual welcome of the Urdd are examples of how sociolinguistic research can stimulate theoretical and policy discussions about the possibilities of integration in the Welsh context. Although the Welsh language is demographically weaker than English in Wales, the research suggests that the minority language can assume an important role in integration endeavours by facilitating a two-way relational equality between host communities and newcomers. Integration, after all, according to Klarenbeek (2021), is essentially about promoting moral worth between people.

Calls for a diversity management model in the Welsh context highlight the need for defining the role of the Welsh language as well as considering the place of migrant and heritage language rights (Williams, 2015). This would mean rejecting former integration models based on an anglophone version of multiculturalism, as seen in the rest of the UK. According to Brooks (2021), anglophone multiculturalism in the UK excludes the role of the Welsh language and other migrant languages and cultures by placing English as the sole bearer of democratic participation. Brooks proposes that a model of Welsh multiculturalism, defined as a non-hegemonic cultural diversity model, should interconnect Welsh, English and other migrant languages, and promotes minority hybridity.

Should Welsh become more prominent in future integration policies, this research suggests that the interconnection of the minority language with other languages is necessary to promote a holistic and principled approach to linguistic integration. Rather than focusing on an outcome, such as the revitalisation of the Welsh language or the acquisition of English, an interdisciplinary framework ensures that the fair treatment of all speakers is met. A future interdisciplinary model for linguistic integration in Wales could, nevertheless, change the discourse from viewing migration as a threat to minority languages cultures towards seeing migrant new speakers as an opportunity for supporting language revitalisation efforts (Augustyniak, 2021). Research indicates that adult migrant learners of Welsh show affinity with the Welsh language's struggle for survival and consider this a motivation to endeavour with language learning and promote it amongst non-Welsh speakers in Wales (Higham, 2015).

The UK government's emphasis on hostility towards international migrants and the increasing burden placed on migrants to learn the English language is likely to continue for the foreseeable future. Indeed, solely placing the burden on newcomers to learn the host society language and regarding them as objects rather than agents of integration may only hinder personal integration experiences (Peled, 2003). In Wales, there is an opportunity to 'do things differently' (Bernhardt, 2023). As Peled (2003: 591) points out:

> a host society that is conscious of its own diverse linguistic constitution is likely to fare better in establishing the kind of relational basis that can better facilitate the process of linguistic integration.

In terms of linguistic integration, the examples of the WSOL provision and the Urdd's bilingual welcome demonstrate the potential to establish an interdisciplinary framework where linguistic hospitality and an intercultural language provision play a central role. The aim of such a framework could rethink integration as a two-way process and address the ongoing linguistic inequalities of society with the aim of transforming notions of belonging and participation in a multicultural nation.

Notes

This chapter has benefited from the financial support of the Leverhulme Trust Research Project Grant (RPG-2024-032), awarded as part of the project 'The Ethics of Linguistic Integration: Realities, Expectations, Prospects'.

1   'Pathways to the Welsh Language for International Migrants' is funded by Arts and Humanities Research Council Impact Acceleration Account from 2022–4, awarded by Swansea University, and is in partnership with IAITH: the Welsh Centre for Language Planning.

2   At the time of writing, no asylum seekers had been sent to Rwanda by the UK Home Office. The UK government's five-year trial to send asylum seekers to Rwanda, launched in April 2022, was rejected by the Supreme Court in 2023. The UK's Conservative government was seeking measures to pursue with their Rwanda plan, before it was scrapped by the incoming Labour government in July 2024.

3   A notable example was the housing of asylum seekers by the Home Office in disused military barracks in Penally, in western Wales. Penally closed six months later due to complaints about the poor living conditions and its contradiction to the Welsh Government's Nation of Sanctuary ambition.

Bibliography

Augustyniak, A. 2021. 'Migrant learners of Basque as new speakers: Language authenticity and belonging'. *Languages*, 6/3 (116), 1–19.

Barry, Brian. 2001. *Culture and Equality: An Egalitarian Critique of Multiculturalism*. Cambridge: Harvard University Press.

Bernhardt, F. 2023. '"In Wales … we do things differently". The politics of asylum dispersal in the UK and emerging national (self-) imaginaries of hospitality in Wales'. *Political Geography*, 103, 102886.

Blackledge, A. 2000. 'Monolingual ideologies in multilingual states: Language, hegemony and social justice in Western liberal democracies'. *Estudios de sociolingüística*, 1/2, 25–45.

Bonotti, M., Carlsson, N. and Rowe, C. W. 2022. 'Introduction: Linguistic justice, migration and the nation-state'. *Nations and Nationalism*, 28/2, 379–86.

Bouchard, Gérard. 2012. *Interculturalisme: d'un point de vue québécois*. Montréal: Éditions Boréalt.

Braun, V. and Clarke, V. 2006. 'Using thematic analysis in psychology'. *Qualitative research in psychology*, 3/2, 77–101.

Brooks, Simon. 2021. *Hanes Cymru: Lleiafrifoedd Ethnig a'r Gwareiddiad Cymraeg*. Cardiff: University of Wales Press.

Carlsson, Nina. 2021. *One Nation, One Language?: National minority and Indigenous recognition in the politics of immigrant integration*. Doctoral dissertation, Södertörns högskola.

Conversi, D. and Jeram, S. 2017. 'Despite the crisis: The resilience of intercultural nationalism in Catalonia'. *International Migration*, 55/2, 53–67.

Corbeil, Jean-Pierre and René Houle. 2013. 'Trajectoires linguistiques et langue d'usage public chez les allophones de la région métropolitaine de Montréal'. Montréal: Office québécois de la langue française.

Cox, S. and Phipps, A. 2022. 'An ecological, multilingual approach to language learning with newly reunited refugee families in Scotland'. *International Journal of Educational Research*, 115, 101967.

Duchêne, A. and Heller, M. 2012. 'Pride and profit: changing discourses of language, capital and nation-state'. In Monica Heller and Alexandre Duchêne (eds), *Language in Late Capitalism: Pride and Profit*. New York: Routledge.

Duff, P. and Van Lier, L. 1997. 'Approaches to observation in classroom research: Observation from an ecological perspective'. *Tesol Quarterly*, 31/4, 783–7.

Edwards, C. W. 2017. 'Language policy, in-migration and discursive debates in Wales'. *Language Policy*, 16, 165–88.

Fortier, A.-M. 2017. 'On (Not) Speaking English: Colonial Legacies in Language Requirements for British Citizenship'. *Sociology*, 52/6, 1254–69.

García, O. and Wei, L. 2015. 'Translanguaging, bilingualism, and bilingual education'. In Wayne E. Wright, Sovicheth Boun and Ofelia García (eds), *The handbook of bilingual and multilingual education*. Malden, MA: Wiley-Blackwell, pp. 223–40.

Higham, G. 2014. 'Teaching Welsh to ESOL Students: issues of intercultural citizenship'. In David Mallows (ed.), *British Council Innovation Series: Language and Integration*. London: British Council, pp. 111–22.

Higham, Gwennan. 2020. *Creu Dinasyddiaeth i Gymru: Mewnfudo Rhyngwladol a'r Gymraeg*. Cardiff: University of Wales Press.

Higham, G. 2024. 'Developing personal integration projects through a Welsh language provision for adult migrants in Wales'. In James Simpson and Sari Pöyhönen (eds), *Minority Language Learning for Adult Migrants in Europe*. London: Routledge.

Jones, Hywel. 2015. 'Poblgaeth Cymru'n Newid' [online]. Available at: *http://www.bbc.co.uk/cymrufyw/34260651*

Jones, Meirion Prys and Ceinwen Jones. 2014. 'Welsh: The Welsh Language in Education in the UK'. Regional Dossiers Series, 2nd edn. Mercator European Research Centre on Multilingualism and Language Learning.

Kearney, R. 2019. 'Linguistic hospitality – The risk of translation'. *Research in Phenomenology*, 49/1, 1–8.

Kemmis, Stephen, Robin McTaggart and Rhonda Nixon. 2014. *The action research planner: Doing critical participatory action research*. Springer.

Khan, K. 2022. 'The Securitisation of Language Borders and the (Re) production of inequalities'. *TESOL Quarterly*, 56/4, 1458–70.

Klarenbeek, L. M. 2021. 'Reconceptualising "Integration as a Two-Way Process"'. *Migration Studies*, 9/3, 902–21.

Kymlicka, Will. 1995. *Multicultural Citizenship*. Oxford: Oxford University Press.

Learn Welsh. 2019. 'Welsh Learner Award for Mohamad from Ceredigion' (July) *https://learnwelsh.cymru/news/welsh-learner-award-for-mohamad-from-ceredigion/*

May, S. 2022. 'Sociolinguistic and political theory perspectives on language rights'. In Tove Skutnabb-Kangas and Robert Phillipson (eds), *The Handbook of Linguistic Human Rights*. Oxford: Wiley, pp. 39–54.

O'Rourke, B. and Pujolar, J. 2015. 'New speakers and processes of new speakerness across time and space'. *Applied Linguistics Review*, 6/2, 145–50.

Oakes, Leigh and Yael Peled. 2017. *Normative language policy: Ethics, politics, principles*. Cambridge: Cambridge University Press.

Patten, Alan. 2014. *Equal recognition: The moral foundations of minority rights*. Princeton University Press.

Peled, Yael. 2023. 'The practical ethics of linguistic integration: Three challenges'. *Metaphilosophy*, 54/5, 583–97.

Phipps, A. 2012. 'Voicing solidarity: Linguistic hospitality and poststructuralism in the real world'. *Applied linguistics*, 33/5, 582–602.

Riera-Gil, E. 2022. 'Linguistic rights and duties of immigrants and national identity in Catalonia: between accommodation and transformation'. *Nations and Nationalism*, 28/2, 483–500.

Scourfield, J. and Davies, A. 2005. 'Children's account of Wales as racialized and inclusive'. *Ethnicities*, 5/1, 83–107.

Senedd Cymru. 2016. 'Equal Access to Welsh Language'. Available at: *https://business.senedd.wales/mgIssueHistoryHome.aspx?IId=14556*

Simpson, J. 2015. 'English language learning for adult migrants in superdiverse Britain'. In James Simpson and Anne Whiteside (eds), *Adult language education and migration: Challenging agendas in policy and practice*. London: Routledge, pp. 200–13.

Simpson, J. and Hunter, A. M. 2023. 'Policy formation for adult migrant language education in England: national neglect and its implications'. *Language Policy*, 22, 155–78.

Turnbull, J. 2004. 'Educating for Citizenship in Wales: Challenges and Opportunities'. *Welsh Journal of Education*, 12/2, 65–82.

Urdd Gobaith Cymru. 2022. 'Urdd Gobaith Cymru's ground-breaking provision to support the Afghan Refugees'. Cardiff: Urdd Gobaith Cymru.

Van Parijs, Philippe. 2011. *Linguistic Justice for Europe and for the World*. Oxford: Oxford University Press.

Welsh Government. 2023. 'A review of English for Speakers of Other Languages (ESOL) policy for Wales'. Cardiff: Welsh Government.

Welsh Government. 2022. 'An Anti-Racist Wales Action Plan'. Cardiff: Welsh Government.

Welsh Government. 2019. 'Nation of Sanctuary – Refugee and Asylum Seeker Action Plan'. Cardiff: Welsh Government.

Welsh Government. 2017. 'Cymraeg 2050: A million Welsh Speakers'. Cardiff: Welsh Government.

Welsh Government. 2014. 'ESOL policy for Wales'. Cardiff: Welsh Government.

Welsh Government. 2003. 'Iaith Pawb: A National Action Plan for a Bilingual Wales'. Cardiff: Welsh Government.

Williams, C. 2007. 'Revisiting the rural/race debates: A view from the Welsh countryside'. *Ethnic and Racial Studies*, 30/5, 741–65.

Williams, Colin H. 2023. *Language Policy and the New Speaker Challenge*. Cambridge: Cambridge University Press.

Williams, Daniel, G. 2015. *Wales unchained: Literature, politics and identity in the American Century*. Cardiff: University of Wales Press.

Zapata-Barrero, Ricard. 2015. 'Interculturalism: main hypothesis, theories and strands'. In R. Zapat-Barrero (ed.), *Interculturalism in Cities: Concept, Policy and Implementation*. Cheltenham: Edward Elgar Publishing, pp. 3–19.

CHAPTER 3

Speak to Me: A Creative and Participatory Approach to Language Education for Inclusion

Barrie Llewelyn and Mike Chick

Introduction

In 2021, nearly 5,000 people enrolled on English for Speakers of Other Languages (ESOL) courses across Wales (Welsh Government ESOL review, 2023). At the same time as coping with the demands of resettlement in an unfamiliar country and through a foreign language, many of those registering on ESOL courses are also seeking sanctuary in Wales. These language learners are often people dealing with the trauma associated with forced displacement, as well as the stress involved in navigating a hostile and complex asylum process. Becoming competent in English is critical for people looking to rebuild their lives and to develop a sense of belonging. What is more, being able to communicate in English, or Welsh, is crucial in finding a way through the health, employment, social security, housing and education systems involved in building a new life. Zaina Aljumma is one such person who has lived experience of all the above. A single mum of two, Zaina arrived in Wales in 2019 and has since completed a Master's degree, won prizes for charity work and gained full-time employment with a refugee charity. Zaina worked hard on a number of the Speak to Me activities and we would like to acknowledge here her important contribution to the success of the project.

This chapter will detail a project designed to complement and enhance the language learning journey of such sanctuary seekers in Wales through an attempt to provide creative language learning opportunities that bring people together to foster friendships, support and mutual understanding. The project, Speak to Me, began as an intervention to add creative thinking and storytelling to the experience of acquiring language in a new and welcoming country and this chapter will outline the various forms the project has taken, and attempt to explain how these fit both with the Welsh Government's Nation of Sanctuary aspiration and with contemporary approaches to migrant language education. Throughout the chapter, the term people seeking sanctuary is used to cover all categories of forced migrants in the UK which includes, for example, people with refugee status and people still in the asylum process. To begin this chapter, the reader is invited to take a creative, imaginative approach in an attempt to understand how a sanctuary seeker might feel upon arriving in Wales:

> Imagine that you find yourself in a strange new world in which you do not speak the language or even understand the alphabet from which it is formed. Imagine that you want to do something quite simple like bake your child a cake for their birthday, but when you go to the store for the ingredients, you cannot tell which is sugar, which is salt, and which is flour. And you do not know how to ask and would be too embarrassed to try.
>
> Now imagine that your child becomes sick and, when you take the child to the doctor, you cannot communicate the symptoms and do not understand the instructions to help them get better.

You are here, reading this book, *A Welcoming Nation?*, because, more than likely you are interested in the challenges and opportunities societies face in offering a place of sanctuary to those escaping war, persecution, terror or climate change. Think about it this way for a moment or two: if you could not communicate effectively in a new place and you could never go home, how would you feel?

Speak to Me

The ideas behind the Speak to Me project, which began at the University of South Wales (USW) in January 2020, were inspired by the research and practice of participatory methods in the delivery of ESOL classes to a group of people who had been resettled in southern Wales. Additionally, Teaching English to Speakers of Other Languages (TESOL) students at the university were learning about these methods and incorporating them into their live teaching practices in a variety of contexts including at the Welsh Refugee Council in Cardiff. In response, Speak to Me was designed by Barrie Llewelyn, a creative writing lecturer and researcher who, in her teaching practice, uses a variety of strategies to encourage writing students towards creativity to improve both their creative writing and their well-being. Barrie was curious to explore the extent to which those strategies could be useful for those seeking sanctuary in Wales. Funding became available from Literature Wales's Writing for Well-being Fund and the university supported the project with a meeting space and other resources. The initial project lasted seven weeks and partnered the people seeking sanctuary mostly, but not exclusively, from Syria, who had been resettled in Pontypridd for approximately four years, with local English-speaking residents in the area. Some of the English speakers were TESOL students; others were academics and administrators from all parts of the university and several of them were local people who had heard about the project and wanted to be included. The English language learners were also attending traditional language classes at local colleges, so Speak to Me activities were an addition to the language provision they were already engaged in and was not intended to replace it.

The people who have participated in the Speak to Me project since January of 2020 have almost universally had some working knowledge of the English language. Yet when they became comfortable enough to share stories about their experiences, they have sometimes talked about a time when they could not read well enough to understand which was the flour or the sugar in the supermarket; when they were presented with official forms that they could not understand; when they could not move around a new area easily by public transport; when they could not fathom the currency or how to buy a stamp – and then they also told the stories about those people and those institutions who helped them. One simple comment summed the complex experience of learning a new language in a new place. A young woman said:

> When I was in my country, I had banter and flirted and had something amusing to say to new friends, but when I came here to Wales and I lost my language and because I could not make people laugh anymore, I lost some of my personality.

Understanding the role that language and education can play in addressing the anxiety and trauma associated with forced migration is a growing field and recent research exploring a trauma-informed pedagogy has illuminated practice (e.g., Palanac, 2019). Expressing oneself through language, with the confidence to be ironic, self-deprecating, funny, and when necessary, serious, to the point, deadpan and non-negotiable is fundamental to who we are and who we will become within a new context or a familiar one. It is essential to our successes, too, in terms of life and work, family dynamics and friendships. So, when the previously uncomplicated act of communicating suddenly becomes less easy and automatic, and instead becomes an act fraught with difficulty and embarrassment, the need to learn a new language in a new place, particularly for adult forced migrants, is of paramount importance (Ćatibušić et al., 2021).

A Welcoming Nation

It follows, then, that a welcoming nation must create language learning environments which recognise the importance of viewing language as far more than the acquisition of knowledge of grammar and vocabulary, and the evidencing of this learning through the constant taking of exams and assessments. Although immigration to Wales is not a devolved power and the Welsh Government does not control how and how many people seeking sanctuary are dispersed across Wales, it does control matters of health, education, housing and employment and, in those areas, can enact policies that directly affect the well-being of people seeking sanctuary and attempting to build new lives. Indeed, the very act of designing and implementing a Nation of Sanctuary plan (2019) sends a 'powerful message of inclusivity to political and social actors' (Edwards and Wisthaler, 2023: 3620). In the Nation of Sanctuary Plan, the Welsh Government has acknowledged that much needs to be done to support inclusion, welfare and integration and it aims to utilise its devolved powers to improve the welfare of people seeking sanctuary. It is significant for this chapter that the provision of appropriate language education is one of the central components of the plan and is complemented by the fact that Wales is the only country in the UK to have a language education policy for migrants (Welsh Government, 2019).

For people already dealing with the stress, trauma and worry of having to start life from scratch in a new country, learning the dominant language is essential. However, conventional, formal ESOL classes for migrants are required to evidence learning through constant tests and assessments – leaving little or no time for learners to practise talking about their real life needs or concerns or to use language for authentic purposes such as making friends and sharing experiences (Cooke, 2019). In other words, for many people seeking sanctuary, their experience of language learning can be demotivating (Sidaway, 2021), with the pressure of tests and attending formal classed adding to already stressful lives. For this reason, initiatives such as Speak to Me provide the room and space to offer the type of integrative experiences that are often missed by conventional language classes (Chick and Hannagan-Lewis, 2019; Court, 2017).

Finally, it is important to note how the Nation of Sanctuary ambitions differ from the UK government's approach towards people seeking sanctuary. For instance, the suite of policies that have come to be known as the hostile environment, introduced in 2012 by then Home Secretary, Theresa May, are aimed at making life in the UK difficult for people seeking sanctuary. For example, people claiming asylum in the UK are prevented from working, taking voluntary jobs or accessing university while their claim for asylum is assessed by the Home Office – a process which can take years. The result is that thousands of individuals are left in limbo each year, forced to subsist on under £6 a day and unable to develop their talents fully or begin integrating in their local community. Edwards and Wisthaler (2023: 6) describe how the Welsh Government's Nation of Sanctuary ambition 'stands in clear contradistinction' to this hostile approach and is 'antithetical to the UK's immigration policy'.

A Participatory Approach

Since the turn of the twenty-first century, there has been a growing appreciation amongst those involved in teaching people seeking sanctuary of the relevancy of a participatory approach to language education. Although there are different understandings and interpretations of participatory pedagogy, all have a primary focus on dialogue and discussion and on the real-life experiences and needs of the learners. To those involved with supporting forced migrants in developing their language competency and their sense of belonging in their new communities, viewing education from a participatory pedagogy perspective can be particularly helpful. From this pedagogical perspective, it is the students who decide on the focus and direction of each class, meaning that the content comes 'from the students to the curriculum rather than from the curriculum to the students' (Auerbach, 1993: 19; see also Cooke and Simpson, 2008). When people are given the space to speak from within and to talk about what they wish, topics emerge such as finding meaningful employment, the effects of trauma, culture shock, family separation, money worries and finding accommodation.[1]

In the planning stages, Speak to Me was thought of as a writing class that would encourage the topics to emerge from the participants themselves – possibly with a book of poetry as an output. After much research and plenty of conversations with ESOL colleagues, Barrie understood that writing poetry might not come easy to those learning English as adults. To mitigate some of the issues the language learners would encounter when writing creatively, participants would work together in partnerships for the duration of the project. Throughout the project, participants were provided with notebooks and writing implements. They were also provided with a variety of paper: lined, coloured, A3, etc., and whiteboards were also available for use. The concept was that partners were to be given a topic at each session and the English speaker and the English learner would talk about it and write about it. 'Even just a few words' was the instruction. After each session, the facilitator would collect the notebooks, papers and photograph the white boards in order to capture the words. By the end of a very noisy and lively first session, however, the focus changed. After that first meeting, while writing materials were still provided, the activity became conversational; participants were encouraged – it hardly took any encouragement at all – towards story sharing. The output changed. Now, the goal was that participants spoke out loud in English to the whole group every week. This output emerged organically.

The activities were purposely focused on what participants had in common. It was envisioned that this approach would facilitate the bonding experience for partners and encourage them to speak freely about life experiences. The purpose of Speak to Me was never to harvest stories of forced migration. If such stories emerged within other conversations, that was fine, but pointed questioning about traumatic events was never on the agenda. During the planning stage it emerged that four of the original sixteen participants were celebrating their birthdays on the first day of the programme. It was an easy decision to turn the first meeting into a birthday party with cake, candles, balloons and banners. As they entered the large room, which was accidentally, but also serendipitously, not a traditional classroom, people were introduced to their partners for the first time. General chatter and brief introductions were carried out. More formally, partners were asked to find out each other's names, where they were from and something unusual or quirky to share with the entire group; and after a few minutes, the couples introduced each other to the entire group. This introductory activity was followed by the birthday party in which participants sang happy birthday in English, Welsh and Arabic. Everyone was then asked to find out more about their partner's personal experience of other celebrations and how they had been marked. The stories that emerged were then shared with the entire group. When English learners told the stories that they had heard out loud, they were encouraged and helped, but not corrected. The focus was completely on oral communication, not on the grammatical accuracy of the language used.

The theme of celebration almost naturally morphed into conversations about food. For the second meeting, participants were asked to bring with them a food from their culture which they could talk about. Passion for food and the desire to share it seems to be universal and this session cemented the group dynamic of friendly conversation. There was evidence of the warm friendships growing between partners as they shared food and recipes as well as stories about social and family gatherings and, again, celebrations. One of the highlights of that meeting was when one adult woman, a housewife and mother from Syria, who had found formal English classes difficult even after attending for several years, stood in front of the entire group and proudly spoke about the chicken and salad that she had prepared and presented. Also, in that second session and in all subsequent sessions of the first Speak to Me project, more people came. They had heard about the group from the original participants and asked if they could come along, and no one was turned away.

The following week, the theme was 'my uniform' and Barrie adapted creative writing exercises in relation to the clothes and shoes people were wearing to prompt the discussions. In creative writing classes, these same prompts had guided students towards writing stories of memory and identity. The same occurred within Speak to Me, except instead of writing the stories they were shared in conversations. In all the Speak to Me sessions, a good proportion of time was allocated to allowing partners to find space for speaking to each other exclusively or within small groups. Conversations were never moderated, but the level of hubbub in the room and the sound of laughter attested to the success of the idea of partnering people. It was also evident that although people used a variety of methods to communicate, including *Google Translate*, the main language people were speaking was English. Towards the end of the 'my uniform' session, a guessing game was played in which everyone in a large circle had to guess who was being described by one person in terms of their clothing. This game produced some of the most creative language, with English learners naturally using similes to describe another person's clothing.

On week four, the topic focused on the way in which people greet each other in various cultures. By this time, there were people involved in the project from Syria, Sudan, Iran, Iraq, Wales, Poland, Czechia, Hungary, England, China, Thailand, India, Italy and Romania. Many of the participants from various countries outside Europe were students of the university who had joined for the purpose of capturing the impact of the project to produce an exhibition of sound and photographs. The students were visual artists, photojournalists and sound technicians, who recorded the conversations between partners.[2]

Speaking and demonstrating greetings was just one example of a topic that went beyond language acquisition and encouraged people to share cultural modes and practices. Much of the feedback from participants in the first Speak to Me project commended the opportunity for understanding each other's cultures. In this way, the Speak to Me project added to its original goal of adding creativity to language education by also promoting understanding, acceptance and well-being for all the participants.

For the friendship-themed week, small items of bric-a-brac were sourced from participants' homes and charity shops. One table in the room was filled with an array of items including cookbooks, dainty dessert forks, makeup, gloves, a toy Eiffel Tower and many other curios. During the session, participants were invited to choose one item from the table and, in front of the entire group, present their gift to their partner saying why they had chosen it. Again, this activity served to cement partnerships which almost universally had turned into friendships. This was to become even more important because, within a few weeks, the project came to an end just as lockdowns to combat the Covid-19 pandemic began. Throughout those uncertain months, which began in March 2020, people who had met, become partners and then friends continued to check in with each other and in that way the Speak to Me project began to extend beyond its original fixed time plan.

Café Chit Chat

A group of women, some of whom had been participants in Speak to Me and others who were recommended to the group by their ESOL tutors, met online weekly from the Spring of 2020 as a response to the Covid-19 lockdowns. Inevitably, forced isolation was, at least at first, detrimental to language education for those seeking sanctuary in Wales, but it was possibly more devastating in terms of integration, work experiences and the progression towards feeling more at home within a new culture. It is true, too, that many people seeking sanctuary are homed in places which are small and do not have gardens, and they often live alone – far from family and friends. Although online language classes were soon organised, these other issues of social isolation could only be partially met by online English classes. The Speak to Me online group for women was envisioned as something that would add to the experience of formal online English lessons by employing the same strategies as Speak to Me, only via Zoom. The group members, who eventually named themselves Café Chit Chat, met weekly. Each week there were between eight and twenty participants, but attendance was much more fluid, so partnerships also had to be less fixed. Participants came and went and came back again according to their other duties and pressures. There was still a mixture of women who were learning English and native English speakers, and each week they were put into small groups and sent into breakout rooms to discuss specific topics, or to work with creative exercises and prompts. They then came back into the main room and shared the stories they had told each other with the entire group. As in Speak to Me, the initial planning was around topics and activities were focused on the things the participants had in common. And as the group matured, topics were suggested and facilitated by the members themselves. The unique situation of pandemic lockdowns meant that the women, no matter where they came from or how well they spoke English, were living through an unfamiliar situation and negotiating a new way of being. Though this was not expressed overtly, it certainly was understood and helped the group toward very quick cohesion and understanding. In this way, Café Chit Chat became focused on well-being and less on language acquisition.

Although adopting to the online format was at times a challenge for everyone involved, some of the creative activities that emerged were surprising and energising. For example, regular participants quickly and organically created their unique gesture to tell a member, 'You're on mute'. As it was said, participants put their fingers to their foreheads as if they were saluting and moved their heads from left to right as if searching. This gesture was used so often that, besides becoming a running joke, some participants reported they had habitually continued to use the gesture when anyone was muted in any online meeting anywhere, even after the lockdowns were eased. Weekly sessions began with a check-in. Questions like: Tell us the best thing about your week? Any news? What amused you today? were asked to warm the participants into speaking. With some people spending many hours each day alone, gentle warm-up conversations were essential. Some weeks participants were asked in advance to wear a certain colour, a hat or sunglasses, or to bring a favourite item of jewellery, and the opening questions were about describing those things. As in Speak to Me, each session was themed, but, unlike Speak to Me, participants were involved in choosing themes and issues and topics to discuss so they had an idea of what the content was to be in advance and were able to prepare if they wished to. Some of the themes were: your heroes, people who inspire you and why; the story behind our names; a great friendship and what makes a friend? In one poignant session, the questions were about where people would like to go when they were free to go anywhere. Who would they choose to go with? It was a topic that resonated widely.

Sometimes, women came into the room and were not in the mood for light-hearted conversation or to be directed into themes. They wanted to and did share some of the problems they were facing to do with housing, health issues and worries about family, whether they were local or overseas. Sometimes a woman wanted to share something personal or ask for advice from the other women in the room. At such times, the weekly theme could be dropped and, instead, the sessions became reactive to the needs of the group. Nothing was ever wrong or taboo. At such times the value of a group for women only was evident, proving the power and possibilities of a participatory approach. Possibly because the group were working online, the conversations, as compared to the original Speak to Me project, were both more intimate and seemed somehow more private. The women became very caring for each other's welfare and very close friends, very quickly.

A moment of significance for Café Chit Chat was that members volunteered to be recorded for a Refugee Week presentation in late spring of 2021 in which they freely spoke,, with the camera turned on, about the kinds of food they enjoy. Using the camera to record for the presentation was an exception. Although notes were kept about the sessions, weekly meetings were not recorded, to give the participants more freedom to speak as they wished without fear of being judged for using the wrong word or not speaking grammatically. Taking part in the presentation illustrated growing confidence and ease with the use of English.

After the project was over, one participant wrote:

> I want to especially say thank you for the amazing group, Café Chit Chat, where we could communicate despite the Covid-19 pandemic. This gave us the opportunity to keep up to date with our English skills, always learning more. It was a great way to get out of being lonely, we had a lot of laughter and interesting conversations that included everyone. Overall, it was the one thing that I looked forward to every day in lockdown.

Another said:

> Café Chit Chat was invaluable for me as an asylum seeker. Not only did it offer a platform for improving language skills, but, later, our trips to London, Tenby and other places provided the opportunities to socialise, gain confidence, and form meaningful friendships with other people seeking sanctuary as well as with people local to the area. These projects directly led to my successful application for a University of South Wales sanctuary scholarship to study for a MA in Animation, which I completed last year.

Walking and Talking

As lockdown restrictions were eased, the value of meeting was evident and, by the time groups were allowed to gather in outside settings, the Café Chit Chat group was keen to meet in person. The first meetings were in local parks and public areas, lasting just a couple of hours and involving some birthday celebrations and the sharing of food, but no organised transportation. As rules about space and meeting changed, trips were organised, which required buses or carpooling and often there was financial support from university funds and grants. The group naturally expanded to include men, women and children; whoever wanted to join in was welcomed. Whether walking in Bannau Brycheiniog National Park or Bath or Tenby or London or over the Cardiff Bay Barrage, it became evident that when people walk together, they speak to each other in a less formal and scripted or self-conscious way. Even on buses or in cars when travelling together to various destinations, people continued to share their stories, but it happened naturally without any prompts or expectations. And it was on a walk up Skirrid Fawr in Abergavenny, when the young woman said:

> In my own language I had a lot of banter, and it was fun flirting with boys and chatting with my friends. Now I am in Wales, I have to communicate in English, as a learner. I don't sound like myself anymore. I've lost my personality and people do not know me.

It is worth repeating because it gives context to what Speak to Me is about, especially now that it was so far from the original intention to write creatively and perhaps produce a book of poetry.

While walking and talking, some of the stories that were shared were more personal too. Some participants spoke about the journeys they had undertaken, frustrations with the 'hostile environment' (Travis, 2013) of the asylum system and their worry for family members who have been left behind.

There might be something liberating about moving forward (walking) and not looking directly at each other that allows people to say things about themselves that they otherwise would not do. Also, for a language learner, the lack of direct eye contact might mean less worry about using the 'correct' grammar and word choices – and ease the anxiety around the possibility of seeing judgment in the facial expressions of those being spoken to. Talking while not looking directly at each other seems to be a very good way to share problems and find understanding.

After a trip to Tenby one participant wrote:

> Embarking on a day trip to Tenby wasn't just a journey of exploration; it is a profound step towards nurturing well-being and healing. For people seeking sanctuary, these moments

of escape and connection hold the power to mend the spirit, reminding us that amidst challenges, the embrace of nature and community can mend the heart.

Speak to Me Some More ...

In some of the most recent Speak to Me sessions, guest practitioners have been invited to run specialist sessions. Laughter Yoga was used to break barriers with a new group of participants in a new location. Trinity Centre, a Methodist church project in central Cardiff, hosts many projects which support people seeking sanctuary, and was the venue for the Speak to Me group in Spring 2022. The people in this group had very mixed levels of English competency. Laughter Yoga uses very little language and focuses on something we all share and enjoy sharing – laughter. It was a very good icebreaker, and participants were immediately aware that Speak to Me was not an English language class, but a place to meet new people and have fun doing a range of activities to complement their more formal English classes. A good percentage of the people involved had not yet gained their refugee status, and were thus not allowed to work, were living within a very tight budget and often dealing with a range of settlement and well-being issues. Laughter Yoga was a very good way in which to start – a fact even more evident when the power of word of mouth, in any language, enticed even more people to come along to the sessions which followed. Over seven weeks, approximately forty participants took part in language games like charades (except words were, of course, encouraged!) and a music therapy session delivered by a specialist practitioner, in which instruments from around the world were passed around and experimented with – by the end of the session a new song and dance was created.

This version of Speak to Me was co-facilitated by Zaina Aljumma, a sanctuary seeker with newly granted refugee status. Zaina is a special educational needs teacher from Syria, and, at the time of the project, a postgraduate student at USW. She had been a member of Café Chit Chat and found the connection with a group of women especially beneficial in view of her unique circumstances – unique, but unfortunately, not unheard of. She was moved by the Home Office, with only a few days' warning, from Newport, southern Wales to Wrexham, in northeastern Wales, during the early days of the pandemic. Zaina knew no one in Wrexham or even where the city was located until she arrived after a long taxi ride. Eventually, the exacerbated feelings associated with social isolation led her to reach out to contacts she had made at USW and to a recommendation to join the online women's group. When Zaina achieved refugee status she almost immediately resettled (again) in southern Wales where she felt supported by USW and began to involve herself in university life: 'Being given a position to co-organise the Speak to Me Too project has empowered me on so many levels', Zaina said.

The advantages someone with lived experience brought to the Speak to Me group were immensely important. There was a seamless shift of focus to some of the matters that most impact the actual lives of those seeking sanctuary in Wales, thereby embracing more of the principles of a participatory pedagogy. For example, during Ramadan, Zaina brought a map to the group and she dressed some of the women in traditional Ramadan clothing from several countries. People then explained how Ramadan is observed in their various countries, while others talked about other family traditions around Easter and Passover. The map was also used to plot the journey people had taken. Whether from the US, Canada, India or from countries in the Middle East or Africa, knowing and understanding what had brought this group of people to a room in the centre of Cardiff in early spring to share their experiences was powerful.

One of the successful things about the first Speak to Me sessions was that there was an almost magical consistency to the partnerships, which remained constant from week to week. In subsequent Speak to Me groups there had to be more flexibility, possibly because these sessions were often scheduled in the daytime, rather than the evening, and people sometimes came a few times, disappeared to other responsibilities, and then came back again when they could. In the most recent Speak to Me session, in July 2023, there were people from Syria, Iraq, Ukraine, Russia and Wales and the participants were prompted over two hours to create fictional stories. Again, the stories they created were not written down or recorded in any way, but they were told out loud to the entire group and everyone spoke without fear of correction. The group did not know each other before they came together for this one-off session, but by the time they left, they had spoken creatively with someone, whom they had never spoken to before, for two hours, formed a story based on a photograph, first, and then another about an empty box. What's in it? What might happen if you opened it?

It is wonderful when there is money to spend on Walk and Talk trips and guest practitioners, but there is something satisfying about going back to the original ideas of using creative prompts to encourage people to speak to each other. One participant wrote afterwards:

I'm happy to share my impressions of that lovely session. It was fun and unexpected for me. It is an interesting idea to make couples with Welsh and Ukrainian people to do the joint task. I was really enjoying the creation of stories and listening to them.

Another said: 'Everyone enjoyed the creative workshop, had a lot of fun, practised English, met new people and exercised their imagination.' And someone else wrote:

I loved taking part in the Speak to Me session at USW. Everyone was so optimistic, enthusiastic, and creative in their story-making endeavours. I had expected people to be sad or negative about what had happened to them in their home countries, but it was quite the opposite. A demonstration of human spirit at its best.

What's Next?

Speak to Me is not a wholly unique idea; there are groups all over the UK dedicated to helping people who are seeking sanctuary in a new country to feel welcome and supported. They are responding to events in all parts of the world in which people absolutely have had to leave their homes and restart their lives in a new place – often a place in which learning a new language and the local customs is key to integration, acceptance and leading a meaningful, dignified life. Conversation Clubs are commonplace within organisations such as STAR

(Student Action for Refugees), a UK-wide student-led network committed to 'building a more just society where refugees are welcomed and can thrive'. English for Action, an educational charity which seeks to provide 'accessible, participatory, and empowering' English language classes for migrants has a long partnership with academics from King's College London. Hearts and Parcels is based in Manchester and brings 'people together through cooking, making, sharing, eating, celebrating food and using English language skills'. Hearts and Parcels is supported by various organisations in and around Manchester including Big Lottery funding and Manchester Wellbeing. It would be easy to dismiss conversations about food and cooking as a soft domestic skill, but Hearts and Parcel are also able to support women to complete Health and Safety certificates, therefore opening a door to future employment or entrepreneurial possibilities. Their website is impressive, with links to some inspiring blog posts written by participants, all English language learners.

Like Speak to Me, these projects were imagined and initiated by people who were moved by world events and the UK government's hostile response to displaced people who came to seek sanctuary. They wanted to do something to welcome those people arriving from troubled parts of the world who really needed to be welcomed and nurtured. For every one of those individuals seeking sanctuary who have benefited from a group like Speak to Me, Hearts and Parcel or STAR, there are thousands of others who have not yet had access to organisations and people who want to offer them a welcome and help in their resettlement. These projects are often supported by community organisations like the Trinity Centre and Oasis in Cardiff. Cardiff University, Swansea University and USW have all been awarded University of Sanctuary status by the City of Sanctuary charity. They were assessed on their commitment to creating a welcoming supportive environment. Some examples of supporting actions are: providing sanctuary scholarships for people awaiting their asylum claim to be processed and thus not yet having refugee status; supporting displaced academics with resources; and providing accessible language education, and supporting projects like Speak to Me.

Speak to Me has received a lot of attention. Not only has USW enthusiastically supported the initiative in terms of resources and funding, Barrie has also been invited to talk or write about the project for organisations such as: the Wales Institute of Social and Economic Research and Data (WISERD), City of Sanctuary, Social Care Wales, Lapidus International and for USW research events and publications. The project was a finalist for an Impact Award at USW in 2022 and an Inspire award at the Adult Learning Celebration in 2023. This attention and the accolades are very welcome and it is hoped that they will inspire other practitioners to design similar projects to benefit those seeking sanctuary in Wales and learning to speak English. There are, of course, the usual challenges in relation to resources. Although a project like Speak to Me does not require large amounts of funding, it does require suitable spaces, time and effort to reach a community of participants. Innovative projects require creative people who may or may not be ESOL teachers to step out of their comfort zones and suggest activities which may or may not be successful – although, most of the time, just providing safe, positive spaces for people to meet and speak to each other without judgement can be tremendously gratifying to all involved.

In sum, this chapter has detailed a language education project that is more closely linked to the real-life psychological, practical and emotional needs of people seeking sanctuary and its attempt to provide what Cox and Phipps (2022: 3) describe as an ecological approach to education that 'intentionally connects classroom learning with the real-world'. That real world is a superdiverse, multilingual community in which many of the learners face an uphill struggle to build new lives. Projects such as 'Speak to Me' demonstrate how language education can indeed be viewed from a humanistic rather than a purely 'skills' perspective and thus be an effective vehicle for migrant well-being, belonging and inclusion. The hope is that, in reading this account, more individuals will be inspired to become involved in projects that help play a part in making Wales a Nation of Sanctuary.

Notes

1   For a discussion of some of the ethical issues in these kinds of initiatives, see Simpson and Chick (2024).
2   A link to the online iteration of the exhibition, held in September 2021, can be found here: *https://gallery.southwales.ac.uk/past-exhibitions/speak-me/*.

Bibliography

Auerbach, E. R. 1993. 'Reexamining English only in the ESL classroom'. *TESOL Quarterly*, 27/1, 9–32.

Ćatibušić, B., Gallagher, F. and Karazi, S. 2021. 'Syrian voices: An exploration of the language learning needs and integration supports for adult Syrian refugees in Ireland'. *International Journal of Inclusive Education*, 25/1, 22–39.

Chick, M. and Hannagan-Lewis, I. 2019. 'Language education for forced migrants: governance and approach'. *Languages*, 4/3, 74.

Cooke, M. 2019. 'ESOL Teachers as Mediators of the Citizenship Testing Regime'. In M. Cooke and R. Peutrell (eds), *Brokering Britain, Educating Citizens: Exploring ESOL and Citizenship*. Bristol: Multilingual Matters, pp. 63–82.

Cooke, M., Bryers, D. and Winstanley, B. 2019. 'Our Languages: Sociolinguistics in multilingual participatory ESOL'. In M. Cooke and R. Peutrell (eds), *Brokering Britain, Educating Citizens: Exploring ESOL and Citizenship*. Bristol: Multilingual Matters, pp. 137–54.

Cooke, Melanie and Simpson, James. 2008. *ESOL: A Critical Guide*. Oxford: Oxford University Press.

Court, J. 2017. '"I feel integrated when I help myself": ESOL learners' views and experiences of language learning and integration'. *Language and Intercultural Communication*, 17/4, 396–421.

Cox, S. and Phipps, A. 2022. 'An ecological, multilingual approach to language learning with newly reunited refugee families in Scotland'. *International Journal of Educational Research*, 115, 101967.

Edwards, C. W. and Wisthaler, V. 2023. 'The power of symbolic sanctuary: insights from Wales on the limitations and potential of a regional approach to sanctuary'. *Journal of Ethnic and Migration Studies*, 49/14, 3602–28.

Goodey, C. 2021. 'Collaboration and learning in the community: Shifting the focus'. *New York State TESOL Journal*, 8/2, 29–38.

Palanac, A. 2019. 'Towards a trauma-informed ELT pedagogy for refugees'. *Language Issues*, 30/2, 3–14.

Simpson, J. and Chick, M. 2024. 'Ethical research with adult migrant language learners'. In P. I. De Costa, A. Rabie-Ahmed and C. Cinaglia (eds), *Ethical Issues in Applied Linguistics Scholarship*. Amsterdam: John Benjamins, pp. 137–55.

Speak to Me Project. 2021. *https://gallery.southwales.ac.uk/past-exhibitions/speak-me/*

Travis, A. 2013. 'Theresa May defends plans to create "hostile environment"'. *The Guardian*, 10 October 2013.

Welsh Government. 2019. Nation of Sanctuary Delivery Plan, *https://sanctuary.gov.wales/glossary/nationofsanctuaryplan*

Links to YouTube Videos

TESOL Research USW | USW's Speak to Me project goes to Tenby, Wales – YouTube *https://www.youtube.com/watch?v=pMKtsn8orys*

USW Research Impact | Speak to Me, Using Creativity to Aid Language Acquisition for Refugees – YouTube *https://www.youtube.com/watch?v=TftlxKyvfYg*
English Research at USW | Speak to Me Too – YouTube *https://www.youtube.com/watch?v=LWT6nsZmMV4*

Links to Organisations/Projects
City of Sanctuary charity: *www.cityofsanctuary.org*
English for Action: *www.efalondon.org*
Hearts and Parcels: *www.heartsandparcel.org*
Oasis: *www.oasiscardiff.org*
Trinity Centre: *www.trinitycentre.wales*
Student Action for Refugees (STAR): *www.star-network.org.uk*

CHAPTER 4

From City to Nation of Sanctuary? Moving Scalar Imaginaries of Citizenship and National Identity in Wales

Franz Bernhardt, Catrin Wyn Edwards and Rhys Dafydd Jones

Introduction

Narratives of Wales as a nation of welcome often draw on distinct migratory moments, particularly throughout the twentieth century. Stories of migration during this period often refer to the warm welcome extended to the Belgian refugees in Rhyl and Swansea during the First World War, the refugees and *Kindertransportees* fleeing persecution during the Second World War and the Basque child refugees escaping Nationalist forces during the Spanish Civil War. During the second half of the twentieth century, Wales also became home to refugees fleeing Uganda, Somalia and Vietnam. Since the beginning of the twenty-first century, refugees arriving from Afghanistan, Iran, Yemen, Syria, Libya and beyond have settled in Wales, often after navigating the UK's inefficient, merciless and inhumane immigration system (Ngalle Charles, 2016). Painters Josef Herman and Karel Lek, Welsh-language author and campaigner Kate Bosse-Griffiths, poet Eric Ngalle Charles and linguist and Welsh language-campaigner Joseff Gnagbo are but a few Wales-based individuals with lived experience that have become part of the national imaginary with their contributions to Welsh society and culture celebrated. In recent years, the Nation of Sanctuary (NoS) vision has become increasingly familiar in Wales, which has further bolstered the image of a welcoming Wales and distinguishing the Welsh approach to asylum from Whitehall's 'hostile environment'.

This chapter explores the NoS approach by drawing on two complementary research projects that have focused on understanding the NoS vision and its emergence on a national (i.e., Welsh) scale. The first project, 'Between City and Nation of Sanctuary: Examining Political Geographies of Asylum and Hospitality in Wales' (Bernhardt, 2020), examined the idea of a Welsh NoS, what it does and means, and how the discourses and narratives of a 'Nation of Sanctuary' provide new ways of revisiting the metaphor of hospitality, and its role in sovereign framings of migration. This research project collected data material from twenty-five semi-structured interviews with individuals working for non-governmental organisations in refugee support conducted over a period of ten months between August 2017 and May 2018 along with archival research (newspaper and grey literature), ethnographic fieldnotes and participant observation. Most of the interviews were undertaken with participants, volunteers and campaigners of refugee support organisations on an urban and national scale in Wales. These included groups based in Cardiff and Swansea, as well as in smaller and more rural settings, and those with a Wales-wide presence. To find out more about the work of the Welsh Parliament's Equality, Local Government and Communities Committee (ELGCC) and the NoS vision, interviews were conducted with a committee member and a civil servant involved in the work of the ELGCC. Interviews were all conducted face-to-face and lasted around one hour (Bernhardt, 2020).

In addition to the archival research, the project also analysed a range of grey literature (policy and parliamentary papers and discussions, and meeting minutes) selected because the content related to the NoS vision, specifically the ELGCC's first major policy inquiry into refugees and asylum seekers in Wales, which culminated in the report '"I used to be someone": Refugees and asylum seekers in Wales' (2017). This report, along with consultation data, was analysed in-depth due to its significance in the development of the vision.

The second project, which focused on national understandings of sanctuary in Wales, drew on four types of sources: parliamentary debates on sanctuary in the Welsh Parliament between 2015 and 2020; written responses to the ELGCC's 2016 consultation on refugees and asylum seekers; grey literature pertaining to sanctuary including governmental and non-governmental strategies and plans published between 2015 and 2021 (a significant period in the emergence and development of the NoS vision); and nineteen semi-structured interviews with Wales-based politicians, policy-makers and practitioners involved in sanctuary between September 2021 and January 2022. Given the size of the sanctuary sector in Wales, identifying key interviewees was straightforward and undertaken by contacting leading individuals in the field in combination with snowballing sampling. Interviews were conducted online and lasted between forty-five and ninety minutes. While most interviewees were Cardiff- or Swansea-based, the nature of their responsibilities and/or remit of their organisation meant that their insights drew on the opinions of individuals – whether with or without lived experiences – throughout Wales. Data were analysed thematically with a specific focus on key themes such as belonging, welcome, integration, citizenship and identity.

Building a Nation of Sanctuary

On 17 September 2015, the Welsh Government, under a Welsh Labour administration, held an emergency refugee summit, partly as a response to the UK government's 'hostile environment' approach, and partly to what has been termed either the 'European refugee crisis' of 2015 or the 'long summer of migration' (Hess et al. 2016): people seeking sanctuary in Europe following conflict in Syria, Iraq and elsewhere. The summit focused on the Welsh response to resettlement, notably the Syrian Vulnerable Persons Relocation Programme (SVPRP) and brought together representatives from local government, the third sector and the Welsh Government. Yet, it was three years earlier, in 2012, that Carwyn Jones, then First Minister, stated his support for the City of Sanctuary movement and welcomed, in principle, Wales becoming the world's first Nation of Sanctuary (Wales Online, 2012; Evangelical Alliance, 2015). The notion of a (devolved) national administration framing the City of Sanctuary concept in national terms was influenced by discussions between two individuals: Inderjit Bhogal, one of the founders of the UK City of Sanctuary movement, and Reverend Aled Edwards, then Chair of Cytûn and Displaced People in Action (DPIA) (Interview, NGO, 2021).[1] Together, they influenced Jones:

> They just said it would be amazing if Wales became a Nation of Sanctuary, that's how we came about, and then Carwyn Jones jumped on it and the next thing it was in the Wales Online. And it, kind of, nobody did a piece of work on what, I mean this is Inderjit and Aled traditionally, you know, as our wonderful leaders they have the idea and then the rest is going to come to the work. (Interview, NGO, 2021)

Significant collaboration between third sector charities working in the refugee sector bolstered by an outpouring of support from local communities and individuals in Wales resulted in the formation of the Welsh Refugee Coalition (WRC), which was influenced by the NoS vision for Wales. A significant step in the NoS gaining political traction was the priority given to 'supporting Wales to become the world's first Nation of Sanctuary' in the WRC's Seven Steps to Sanctuary Manifesto (Welsh Refugee Coalition, 2016). By the time the Welsh Parliament's ELGCC undertook their first substantial piece of work in 2016, which was on the treatment of refugees and asylum seekers in Wales, the NoS had already gained some momentum and members of the committee were already familiar with the vision (Edwards and Wisthaler, 2023). According to a member of the ELGCC, adopting the idea of NoS as a national ambition 'sent such a strong message', set the tone for subsequent work and helped 'really move things forward in terms of the way we approach these matters in Wales' (Interview, Welsh Parliament, 2022):

> The all-encompassing nature of the concept appealed to the Senedd's ELGCC, as did the fact that it would provide a focal point for the Welsh Government. I think there was a discussion in terms of the power of the term really, capturing. It sort of speaks for itself in many ways, in terms of popular un-

derstandings, I think, doesn't it? … We would provide such a strong focus for government and other agencies and hopefully make asylum seekers and refugees, you know, feel that it did mean something and, you know, they actually were in a country that was welcoming, and we did want to help them. (Interview, Welsh Parliament, 2022)

The ELGCC's published report, "'I used to be someone": Refugees and asylum Seekers in Wales' (Welsh Parliament, 2017) included several recommendations to the Welsh Government, one of which included the aim of establishing Wales as an NoS by drawing on devolved competency (Welsh Parliament, 2017: 57–8). In 2019, the Welsh Government, committed to the aim of establishing Wales as a 'true' NoS in its 'Nation of Sanctuary – Refugee and Asylum Seeker Plan' (Welsh Government, 2019a: 3, 6). In a few years, the concept had gone from being 'little more than a pipedream' (DPIA, 2016: 2) to being adopted by the Welsh Government as a declaration of intent.

Another significant step in the process of creating a national imaginary of 'Welsh' sanctuary was the establishment of the SVPRP that followed the 'long summer of migration' of 2015 (Hess et al., 2016) and subsequent geographical dispersal of refugees throughout Wales, including in rural or semi-urban localities that had little or no previous experience with refugee resettlement or migration, more generally (Challinor, 2018 in Guma et al., 2019: 97).[2] While most asylum seekers continued to be distributed via the established dispersal policy, and thus limited to Cardiff, Swansea, Newport and Wrexham, Syrian refugees arriving through the SVPRP were dispersed to volunteering local authorities. This meant that, by the end of 2017, twenty of the twenty-two local authorities in Wales had agreed to accepting Syrian refugees as part of the programme, which consisted of 725 individuals (Houghton, 2017 in Guma et al., 2019: 99). This geographical influence of refugee resettlement is particularly important for the 'national' idea of the Welsh NoS:

I think one of the things since 2015, that has made that more possible, paradoxically, is the Syrian Resettlement Programme, which required all the local authorities in Wales to have a view on receiving Syrian refugees. So, where you got those four distinct bubbles of the dispersal areas, you are now getting places like Aberystwyth … So, those areas now have acquired, or began to acquire, an expertise and an experience base in receiving asylum seekers and refugees … So, I think what we found since 2015 is that there is now a genuine, all-Wales experience of receiving asylum seekers and refugees, that wasn't there before … (Interview, Welsh public advisory body, 2017)

For individuals long active in the sanctuary movement, establishing a Welsh NoS was initially based on the creation and presence of local sanctuary groups beyond urban dispersal cities. In other words, it became possible to talk of a 'Welsh' sanctuary movement with various sanctuary groups across varying levels in Wales. Thus, in Wales, the sanctuary discourse has been 'levelled up' from urban and grass-roots scales to the national level.

However, the meaning of NoS underwent some transformation from one where NoS was synonymous with the establishment of sanctuary towns and cities across Wales, thus 'rolling-out' the City of Sanctuary vision throughout Wales, to one where the 'national' became the locus of sanctuary. One interviewee noted that the NoS concept changed before and after the 'long summer of migration', from one based on numerous cities or towns of sanctuary throughout Wales, to concerted action on a Wales-wide scale:

You could think of that [sanctuary] on the Welsh level, not just in each city separately … That's simply the picture I got about it. Because now, suddenly within two years, there are not two, but ten City of Sanctuary groups in Wales. And obviously, the majority of them are not urban … So, not only have you got this people wishing to help somehow, you also got David Cameron's scheme for resettling … refugees from Syria, which means that the whole of Wales … so everywhere in Wales, there will be some Syrian refugees, in the same council, not necessarily in the same place. (Interview, NGO, 2017)

This shift has highlighted a disconnection between the discourses of the urban and third-sector movement and process of movement-building on a local, UK and devolved scales, as high-lighted by an interviewee:

> You know, I don't think sanctuary should lead to governance, it's about movement building, it's about grassroots involve-ment ... to embed welcome across mainstream and society. (Interview, NGO, 2021)

Another theme that emerged in analysing the 'levelling-up' of sanctu-ary discourses from one scale to another is the lack of concrete defi-nition of the concept across various scales: 'all of a sudden it's this big concept that everybody kind of thinks they know what it is, but everyone's got a slightly different kind of understanding of it' (Inter-view, NGO, 2021). This has allowed for multiple definitions loosely based on being welcoming, providing support, and facilitating inte-gration (Edwards and Wisthaler, 2023).

'We're Wales versus the Rest of the UK': Shifting to New Scales of Hospitality

In this section, we explore the shift from urban discourses based on a 'culture' of welcome and hospitality to national understandings of hospitality. It is argued that the Welsh Government's announcement to become a NoS constitutes a new phenomenon that represents both a practical and theoretical shift for the notion of hospitality.[3] The-oretically, this represents a novel dynamic to the critical migration literature, which has tended to focus on the limits of hospitality and the exclusionary politics of asylum from the city/state dichotomy (Edwards and Dafydd Jones, 2024). The UK as a sovereign state, for example, constructs and frames itself as a 'firm but hospitable nation', a generous host to some 'genuine' refugees as a means of categorising, classifying and securitising migrants. Yet, it creates imaginaries of itself as a host to guests, however small that number may be, which carries with it obligations and moral duties of hospitality. What happens then, when a devolved political entity such the Welsh Government uses the metaphor of hospitality to frame their responses to migration? Can this self-framing as an independent host challenge the legitimacy of the UK sovereign state and its exclusionary politics of asylum? What does it mean to offer hospitality as a nation without its own legislative control for immigration? Our focus now turns to exploring these questions.

The increasing involvement of actors across scales in Wales in sanctuary efforts such as the SVPRP engendered a 'Wales-wide' image of sanctuary and, thus, a 'national' culture of hospitality that comprised non-urban local authorities. Within the NoS discourse, Wales is constructed as generous 'host' to arriving refugees ('guests') whereby the provision of hospitality beyond the city scale and the notion of Wales as a 'host' is embedded in a form of 'moral nationalism' (Bernhardt, 2022: 234). This 'moral nationalism' consists of the Welsh Government positioning itself as a hospitable host in contradistinction to the 'hostile environment' put in place by the UK government and portraying the Welsh nation as 'a generous and welcoming nation state-host in opposition to the putatively more inhospitable sovereign British asylum regime' (Bernhardt, 2022: 232). The fact that the Welsh executive does not possess full legislative powers allows the Welsh Government to strategically frame itself as a 'moral agent' in opposition to the UK government, and a defender of sanctuary against adversarial state policies (Edwards and Wisthaler, 2023; Edwards and Dafydd Jones, 2024).

Thus, the Welsh Government and Parliament use the NoS concept to emphasise Wales's moral standpoint and often link it to its openness as a nation, juxtaposing it with the UK state's approach to asylum (Edwards and Dafydd Jones, 2024).[4] Interviewees (Welsh Government, 2021; Welsh Government Agency, 2021; Welsh Parliament, 2021) argued that the Welsh Government was taking a stance against the inhospitable approach implemented by the UK government and, by adopting a more open, inclusive stance on refugees and asylum seekers via the NoS declaration, they were:

> trying to say, 'we're trying to do something that signals that we're Wales versus the rest of the UK. We're different, we're doing this. Join with us, we want to be the first Nation of Sanctuary'. (Interview, Welsh Government Agency, 2021)

The act of taking a stance in response to the wider 'hostile environment' approach also influenced the work of the ELGCC, which played a significant role in putting the NoS concept on the Welsh Government's agenda, as highlighted by a committee member:

> We were very aware of UK government policy in terms of the rhetoric, but also, you know, their practical policies. It did create many difficulties for refugees and asylum seekers in Wales. So, at one level, we obviously wanted Welsh Government to make the right statements and raise the right points in meetings and conversations with their UK counterparts and, similarly, at an official level. But you know, as a Committee as well, we wanted to make clear our own opposition really to UK government in terms of the tone that they were setting. (Interview, Welsh Parliament, 2021)

However, within this host versus guest dichotomy present in Wales, the Welsh Government is currently reluctant to overstep its legislative competency (Edwards and Wisthaler, 2023: 14, 18; Welsh Parliament, 2021), which highlights the limitations of a hospitable approach:

> There's always a tension between UK government and Welsh Government that we have to understand the powers that we have and operate within them and use them, rather than constantly seeking to transgress on the edges, as it were. (Interview, Welsh Parliament, 2021)

Further, it also reveals the strategic nature of this 'host/guest' relationship at a national governmental level (Edwards and Wisthaler, 2023). For example, interviewees noted that, in the absence of formal legislative competency, the Welsh Government was more likely to support the NoS concept:

> Because they don't have primary responsibility for dealing with the controversial issues around asylum and immigration, and only have, kind of, responsibility for what you could term 'secondary' ... issues, you have a general level of sympathy and support, which is never tested at the level of making difficult decisions. (Interview, NGO, 2018)

Yet, the executive is not attempting to gain legislative competency in immigration policy areas that are reserved for the UK government, and there is 'no aspiration to have any more power around that system' (Interview, Welsh Government Agency, 2021).

Interviewees criticised the Welsh Government for not doing more within their devolved policy areas (NGO, 2018) and for the need to go further in emphasising how the sovereign politics of asylum impacts upon devolved areas of control. This draws an implicit discursive distinction between a hospitable Wales, in which such hostility would be deemed morally unacceptable, and a more inhospitable other (UK) where it is morally accepted. The 'moral nationalism' of the Welsh devolved polity is not only constructed regarding the refugee-guest-other, but also regarding the UK as the sovereign host-state-other, a form of double othering (Bernhardt, 2022). A positive national self-image is constructed around the affective language of hospitality vis-à-vis their own relationality to migrants and to an imagined (un)hospitable sovereign host-state. In the case of the Welsh Government, it is often more concerned with the creation of national self-imaginaries as a generous host to refugees rather than challenging the exclusionary politics of asylum of the sovereign *other*. In this respect, it is fundamentally not an antagonistic form of politics.

'Just People That Live in Wales': Shifting the Scales of Citizenship Rights

In this section, we focus on the re-scaling of citizenship and what this means for understandings of citizenship as a set of legal rights and as a practice and culture of claiming such rights. While much of the responsibility relating to asylum policy is reserved to the UK government, Wales has adopted specific policies for refugees and asylum seekers representing forms of national citizenship that are beyond city-scale or state citizenship, which exist within Wales's boundaries (Edwards and Dafydd Jones, 2024).

The schism between *de jure* citizenship policies and the growing *de facto* presence and residence of non-citizens in territorial states has led scholars of migration and citizenship to consider the possibilities of re-scaling citizenship, and the connection between the city and citizenship (Varsanyi, 2006: 230). To avoid neglecting other forms of spatial politics and escape the 'territorial trap' (Agnew, 1994) of the nation-state in political theory, critical scholars started to (re)explore connections between the city and citizenship. No longer 'subservient to the nation-state', the city has been reconsidered as a legitimate and new locus for citizenship in an increasingly globalised world (Varsanyi, 2006: 230). Moreover, cities have increasingly come to be essential mediators in a more global and migratory field of politics and economics, as well as for the tensions that can emerge in living with diversity (see Amin, 2012; Sassen, 2006). When citizenship is no longer bounded, in the sense of it assuming *a priori* existing community, but instead grounded, it provides spaces for a form of citizenship in which full membership is not dependent upon explicit (legal) consent to enter and remain, but rather on the reality of residence and presence in a place (Varsanyi, 2006: 239).

While Varsanyi (2006) elaborates on this idea by describing emerging examples of local 'citizenship' policies for undocumented residents in the United States, the notion of localised citizenship policies is also relevant to Wales and the Welsh NoS: the extent to which such a re-scaling of the politics of migration and belonging can assert a form of power and NoS and the (devolved) politics of hospitality. The scholarship on sanctuary and sanctuary-seeking people's presence is tackled from urban citizenship. Urban spaces as cities of sanctuary are, as Darling (2010: 133) argues, ways of 'developing an ethics or responsibility' to those beyond city boundaries, as well as a way of developing an outward-looking civic culture within.

In Wales, new actors have emerged on this scene in the form of civil society organisations, and the Welsh Parliament and Welsh Government. As argued above, together they frame the Welsh nation as 'welcoming' and poised to challenge aspects of the UK asylum regime, thereby establishing new sites and scales for mounting a challenge to the UK's 'hostile environment'. Yet, challenging the exclusionary politics of asylum using this national frame has its limits; whilst it promotes a welcoming narrative, it also reinforces the territorial logic that produces the very idea that those populations without territory (asylum seekers and refugees) are not fully political actors.

Exploring discussions around (national) citizenship in Wales reveals an approach that is based on citizenship as a practice and

culture of claiming rights rather than a set of legal rights. The notion of refugees and asylum seekers as 'just people that live in Wales',
that is, Welsh residents like any other, means that access to services
and rights is not synonymous with legal status. For members of the
ELGCC tasked with researching the experiences of refugees and asylum seekers in Wales and advancing recommendations to the Welsh
Government, this vision was particularly important:

> And if you look at refugees and asylum seekers as just peo-
> ple that live in Wales, and, you know, lots of the things that
> they … their interactions with the state: education, hous-
> ing, transport, healthcare: that's all devolved. So, when we
> were designing this enquiry, that was forefront in my mind.
> (Interview, Welsh Parliament 2018)

The ELGCC worked on the basis that, regardless of their migration
status, they are individuals who require various services in devolved
fields such as housing, healthcare and education. Decoupling access
to services and rights from legal status is reminiscent of Squire and
Darling's (2013) 'rightful presence' conception.[5] Investigating hospitality through the 'rightful presence' lens brings into focus practices
of hospitality and expectations of what it means to be a host to the
other. Yet, it often remains the focus of limited debate on what exact
'responsibilities' the different 'hosts' hold. This resonates with Hill's
(2016: 194) caution that the hospitality is often used as a 'proxy for
expressing anxieties about national identity for the gain of political capital and at the expense of immigrants themselves'. The Welsh
Government, while espousing a positive discourse on refugees and
asylum seekers in contradistinction to the UK government's 'hostile
environment' approach (Bernhardt, 2020, 2022; Edwards and Wisthaler, 2023), still uses the affective language of hospitality on migration mainly for the creation of national self-imaginaries. Rather than
fully challenging the exclusionary asylum regime by emphasising
what it could do to mitigate its effects, there is a tendency to reiterate
what it cannot do due to institutional limitations.

A key area that reveals how individuals seeking sanctuary in
Wales are perceived as Welsh citizens is voting rights. Two pieces of
recent legislation, the Senedd and Elections (Wales) Act 2020 and the

Local Government and Elections (Wales) Act 2021, allow individuals who have been granted refugee status or leave to remain in the UK to vote in the Welsh Parliament and local elections (Welsh Parliament, 2020; 2021). While this contrasts with the inability of refugees in England to vote in local elections, and refugees and asylum seekers are excluded from voting in the UK parliamentary elections, individuals in Wales with a pending asylum application are ineligible to vote in elections. In 2019, Leanne Wood MS challenged this, noting that, as 'qualifying foreign citizens', people seeking asylum should also be included in the franchise. She went to on to argue that:

> everyone who lives in Wales has a stake in our nation's future and has the right to help shape it … As this is a move towards residency-based, rather than citizenship-based, franchise, why are some people who are legally resident in Wales intended to be excluded from it, and how is this intention compatible with the Welsh Government's stated aim to make Wales the first world nation of sanctuary for refugees and asylum seekers? Immigration status should not be a barrier to political participation. On the understanding that these amendments are seeking to ensure that everyone who lives in Wales can participate politically, there is no moral or practical argument in my view for excluding people who are seeking asylum. There will be a gap between the intent of these amendments and their effect unless we take them in their most expansive sense to truly include all people living in Wales. (Leanne Wood MS, Welsh Parliament debate, 13 November 2019)

In addition to voting rights for refugees, the Welsh Government has also implemented initiatives in devolved policy fields such as health, education, welfare, and access to the labour market. In terms of healthcare, refugees and asylum seekers in Wales can access free National Health Service (NHS) services once they have formally applied for leave to remain, along with individuals whose application has been refused, as long as they stay in Wales.[6]

Another initiative which influenced the lives of migrants in Wales was the Welsh Government's decision in 2019 to extend its financial hardship fund, the Discretionary Assistance Fund, to all individuals in Wales experiencing destitution regardless of their migration status (Welsh Government, 2019b). While refugees were already able to access this fund, the ELGCC's consultation and subsequent report recommended that the administration should include specific actions to help asylum seekers and people with no recourse to public funds avoid destitution through the Discretionary Assistance Fund (Welsh Parliament, 2017: 48).

Also of significance is the Welsh Government's emphasis on integration as a process that begins 'on day one' of arrival in Wales irrespective of immigration status. This forms part of a 'holistic' approach to support for individuals and communities in Wales adopted in the 2019 Refugee and Asylum Seeker Plan (Welsh Government, 2019a: 6):

> We believe in the fair treatment of every person, especially those who are most marginalised and have most difficulty accessing the help they need to meet their basic needs. The Welsh Government firmly believes that the integration of refugees and asylum seekers should begin on day one of their arrival. This approach is essential in ensuring the best possible outcomes for individuals and communities. We know there is strong public support for recent arrivals to learn English or Welsh – or both, bearing in mind that many refugees have excellent language skills – and we want to support them to do this. Supporting volunteering schemes for asylum seekers and refugees would contribute to Welsh society whilst also supporting language acquisition, improving mental health and increasing the employability of individuals. (Julie James MS, *Trefnydd* ('Leader of the House') and Chief Whip, Welsh Parliament debate, 19 June 2018)

During discussions in the Welsh Parliament on the 2019 NoS plan, Jane Hutt MS highlighted the importance of 'putting people first and not using immigration status as a barrier to support' (Welsh Parliament debate, 29 January 2019) and providing, within their powers, essential support to refused asylum seekers:

> We continue to ensure that refused asylum seekers are not denied healthcare; they're entitled to the same services as any

other citizen. The plan does contain the action to work towards preventing people seeking sanctuary, including those with no recourse to public funds, becoming human trafficking or modern slavery victims. So, this is a point where we have to look at the holistic approach, within our powers, to the circumstances of refugees in terms of their needs, particularly if they have been refused in terms of their situation. (Jane Hutt MS, Welsh Parliament debate, 29 January 2019)

Given that health is a devolved matter, the Welsh Government is responsible for the NHS in Wales. Reflecting the above statement, asylum seekers in Wales can access free NHS healthcare once they have made a formal application for leave to stay as a refugee in the United Kingdom. The Welsh Government has legislated to extend this exemption from charging to those whose application to remain in the UK had been refused whilst they remain living in Wales, which differs from the situation facing asylum seekers in England. As noted by Eluned Morgan MS, then Minister for Health and Social Services, 'far from being a hostile environment for charging' (correspondence between the Minister for Health and Social Services and Patients not Passports, 20 September 2021), there are in Wales several exemptions for overseas visitors, particularly for those patients from vulnerable groups, to ensure that they can access the NHS treatment they require without charge. Some NHS services are also free of charge to everyone regardless of a patient's residency status.[7] This is not to say that the system is without its issues. Language barriers (and lack of mental health services – see Khanom, 2021) are but a few problems that need tackling. Furthermore, the current set-up means that undocumented migrants, who live their lives 'under the radar' (Interview, NGO, 2021) continue to be rendered invisible:

The people who are kind of, you know, less … I guess supported, are sort of undocumented migrants outside of the asylum process and those are the people for whom NHS care won't be free. Those are also the people for whom there are the least services or organisations working in Wales. You know, we've spoken to people who were claiming asylum and their kind of challenges in terms of accessing healthcare has been, in terms of my understanding of how the system works, sometimes accessing sort of translation and you know the same problems that, you know, everyone has in terms of waiting lists for services, particularly like mental health services, rather than actually not being able to access the services at all. (Interview, NGO, 2021)

While the UK government's hostile approach to asylum and the fact that some aspects remain 'reserved' mean immigration and asylum policy continue to impact upon the lives of migrants in Wales, restricting their day-to-day lives and ability to fully integrate (Parker, 2021: 77), the Welsh administration's actions show how citizenship rights can be re-scaled from the UK state to the Welsh nation as a devolved sub-state polity.

Limitations to the Nation of Sanctuary Approach

While the NoS vision has taken root politically, ensuring a Wales-wide approach to sanctuary is far from fully achieved. Recent anti-migrant protests have highlighted a disconnection between the NoS on a policy-practitioner level and the reality where there is opposition targeted towards people seeking sanctuary on a lived level. While attracting only small numbers, it nevertheless compels a closer analysis of local-level tensions and attitudes towards people seeking sanctuary along with questions of belonging, welcome, inclusion (or rather, exclusion) and the presence of discrimination and racism on a local level. These far-right protests illustrate the limits and contradictions of the Welsh Government's NoS discourse and the need for greater work at the level of the community to tackle the pervasive 'hostile environment' rhetoric.

The UK government's decision to house approximately 250 asylum seekers in an ex-military camp in Penally, western Wales in September 2020 led to protests and counter-protests. Arrangements were made without consulting the Welsh Government, local authorities, health boards or residents, and without providing additional funds for either Pembrokeshire council or Hywel Dda University Health Board

(Joyce Watson MS, 18 November 2020). While pro-migrant protesters argued that the camp was unsuitable and its conditions a breach of human rights, it was also a target of far-right protesters who sought to challenge the UK government's decision to house asylum seekers in western Wales. The Welsh Government's response to the use of the ex-military camp highlights the strength of the NoS rhetoric and its ability to initiate concerted action along with the Welsh Government's capacity to provide leadership (Edwards and Wisthaler, 2023) and reveals differences between the perceptions of Welsh and UK governments of how refugees and asylum seekers should be treated (Closs Stephens and Bernhardt, 2024). The latter, in particular, shows how understandings of 'us and them' can 'animate the nation' (Closs Stephens and Bernhardt, 2024). Together, they represent a contrasting national narrative and imaginary of welcome and hospitality from the state-espoused 'hostile environment' approach. Yet, there is no doubt that the protests against the presence of asylum seekers in west Wales highlights the work that needs to be undertaken to achieve a true NoS:

> You had people, and I have to say, coming in from other parts of the UK, not necessarily from Wales, who tried to turn it into a political circus around hate, and around all that stuff. Less strong on that, I would have to say, but you could argue that we were importing these people, we were importing the right-wing problem, and it just fuelled a fire. Are we fundamentally addressing that? No. Do we then need to think about who these people are and how people in those communities felt, not in my back yard, kind of stuff, counterbalance with the strong, 'you're welcome here' message. But just not welcome quite 'here'. 'You'd be welcome somewhere else, maybe'. And that's the bit that was lost a little bit in terms of, yes it was a horrible place, no we should never have put people in it. Tenby, jewel of tourist crown. (Interview, Welsh Government Agency, 2021)

Despite the counter-protests and 'outpouring of support from local people, who have shown that Wales can be an understanding and compassionate country' (Leanne Wood MS, Welsh Parliament debate, 18 November 2020), the protests were 'taken over by far-right, out-of-town racists' (Mick Antoniw MS, Welsh Parliament debate, 18 November 2020). One interviewee noted that the fact that alternative locations in Wales were 'vetoed' highlights the limitations of the NoS approach, revealing that the offer of sanctuary and welcome is conditional, and dependent on whether individuals in Wales feel as if sanctuary provision 'works for them' (Interview, Welsh Government Agency, 2021). Such reluctance is 'not really in the spirit of sanctuary' (Interview, Welsh Government Agency, 2021). Discussions around Penally and the presence of the far-right reveal the existence of a narrative that the far-right in Wales is imported. There's also a sense that the NoS discourse has been appropriated by the far-right to boost their anti-migrant rhetoric:

> It's been used I suppose by more far right kind of groups hasn't it, to kind of as if it's kind of opening the door to thousands and thousands and thousands of people. So, a lack of understanding of what it actually means I suppose is a bit of a barrier. (Interview, NGO, 2021)

This is reflected in the dialogue of UKIP MS, Neil Hamilton, on using the Penally military base in the Welsh Parliament:

> There are two Governments responsible for this debacle in Penally. First of all, of course, and principally, the Conservative government at Westminster that's responsible for dumping these people in a wholly unsuitable location ... But the second Government – the one in Cardiff: the Welsh Government – is also partly responsible because they've been virtue-signalling about Wales as a nation of sanctuary – that we're open to all-comers – while there are hundreds of millions of people around the world who'd like to come to Britain, no doubt, in order to better their lives and who can blame them? (Welsh Parliament debate, 18 November 2020)

However, the protests in Penally against migrants was not an isolated incident. In February 2023, the far-right group, Patriotic Alternative, started leafleting Llantwit Major residents, calling for support to a planned protest in the town after the Vale of Glamorgan Council announced its plans to build housing for Ukrainian refugees on the site of a closed-down primary school. Rather than organising a full-scale counter-demonstration, the local community instead opted for twenty-four hours of action, which included an overnight vigil for interfaith reflection at a church the night before the protest, music and readings, a Welsh cake giveaway, a football match co-organised with Show Racism the Red Card and the involvement of the local team, guided prayer and refreshments at a local church and a talk about the German philosopher Paul Tillich and his experience of being thrown out of Nazi Germany (Hope Not Hate, 29 March 2023). Much attention was given in the media about the power of the Welsh cake in challenging hate and anti-migrant rhetoric and as a symbol of Welsh hospitality and anti-fascism (Hope Not Hate, 29 March 2023; BBC, 2023).

Then, in June 2023, approximately one hundred people protested plans to house asylum seekers in Stradey Park Hotel in Furnace, Llanelli. Unlike in the Penally case, where the anti-migrant voice was perceived as 'imported', the protest group, 'Furnace Action Committee' consisted of local residents who wrote letters and threatened court action. Yet, the protest escalated to leafleting and conspiracy theories, protesters camping outside the hotel and storming the building, and the harassment of the leader of the original protest for not adopting an extreme enough position. In addition to involving the police, it also gained the attention of Patriotic Alternative and individuals such as Katie Hopkins and Anne Marie Waters, known for their far-right views and links to such far-right movements. For Hope not Hate, the events at the Stradey Park Hotel is a matter of 'far-right radicalisation in real time' (*The Guardian*, 2023). Together, the local level protests to housing people seeking sanctuary in Penally, Llantwit Major and Llanelli not only highlight the radicalisation of Wales, but also the tensions with the NoS approach, the possible gap between the NoS vision and rhetoric and the lived experiences of people seeking sanctuary, and the extent to which Wales is and can be a true NoS and tolerant nation.

Conclusion

This chapter has explored the NoS vision and the implications of a national sanctuary discourse on scalar imaginaries of hospitality and citizenship. It started by tracing the emergence of the NoS vision from the embryonic phrase to its adoption by the Welsh Government in 2019, and, in doing so, highlighted the crucial role that third-sector organisations and the urban grassroots movement played in introducing and embedding this vision and NoS concept within national-level discussions. These efforts were supported by additional factors such as the establishment of the SVPRP and the subsequent geographical dispersal of refugees throughout Wales, along with the ELGCC's decision to recommend that Wales should become a NoS in its influential report. Together, these factors helped engender a 'national' sense of the Welsh NoS.

The chapter then traced a shift around a 'culture' of welcome and hospitality from the city scale to the national level and, in identifying this move, argued that sanctuary discourses can be 'levelled up' from the city to impact on national discourses. In the case of Wales, arguments on the importance of extending a Welsh welcome to guests are bound up in notions of morality and, in the case of the Welsh Government, juxtaposed with the UK government's hostile environment approach. This can be understood as a form of 'moral nationalism' (Bernhardt, 2022: 234) where the Welsh nation is portrayed as generous and welcoming. The lack of competencies held by the Welsh executive enables this position. Given that it does not possess full legislative powers, the Welsh Government is able to strategically frame itself as a 'moral agent' in opposition to the UK government, and a defender of sanctuary against adversarial state policies (Edwards and Wisthaler, 2023; Edwards and Dafydd Jones, 2024).

It was also shown how the NoS concept is tied to a form of citizenship beyond a set of legal rights. In Wales, several initiatives and measures implemented in devolved areas such as health, voting and education highlight citizenship as a practice and culture of claiming such rights. Despite much of the responsibility relating to asylum policy being reserved to the UK government, it was demonstrated how the Welsh Government has been able to carve out specific policies for refugees and asylum seekers. Inspired by an understanding that refugees and asylum seekers are citizens in Wales 'like any other', Welsh Government measures highlight how national citizenship can exist beyond city-scale or state citizenship, that is, existing within Wales's boundaries (Edwards and Dafydd Jones, 2024).

Together, findings on the re-scaling of hospitality and citizenship that has taken place in Wales and been facilitated by the NoS vision have allowed the problematisation of a simplified scalar thought on sanctuary, namely that dichotomy between the 'hostile' state and the 'inclusive' city. Examining the significant role played by a devolved government that is both national and sub-state allows more nuance in interrogating sanctuary politics and practice, revealing the complexities of multi-scalar governance and moral nationalism. More broadly, such studies allow for further thinking around scale and relationality, as the NoS is both a scalar and relational response. However, recent events in Wales have demonstrated a gulf between the NoS as a governmental policy and vision, and its reception in communities. This is not to say that there is wholesale hostility or majority opposition to the NoS, and nor should grassroots sanctuary movements be overlooked, and specific factors (such as job losses among hotel staff) may have a role in mobilising opposition. Nonetheless, there is a distinction here to be made, as well as a question to the extent that the Welsh Government is ready to challenge the UK government compared to the Scottish Government (Bernhardt, 2022). There is still some way to go before Wales can claim to be a hospitable and welcoming nation.

Notes

1 The DPIA co-ordinated the 'Wales Cities of Sanctuary' project, with the aim of spreading the City of Sanctuary vision throughout Wales and establishing Wales as a 'Nation of Sanctuary'.

2 The UK government's invitation to local authorities to participate in the SVPRP marked a shift from settling refugees and asylum seekers in urban dispersal areas alone (Piacentini, 2012, in Guma et al., 2019).

3 It is not claimed that Wales's approach to sanctuary or its positionality vis-à-vis the UK government's hostile environment is exceptional; analyses of the Scottish approach reveal that the Scottish Government also employs pro-immigration discourses and strategies that contrast with the position of the British state (Mulvey, 2023; Parker, 2019). Rather, this chapter seeks to evaluate the emergence of policies and programmes in Wales alongside or as a result of the NoS principle, which is a political position that differs substantially from the UK government's more restrictive approach.

4 Nevertheless, there was some hesitancy amongst third sector organisations that endorsing resettlement schemes would lead the UK Home Office to

further prioritise settlement or sponsorship schemes at the expense of
spontaneous arrivals, thus reinforcing a tiered system.

5   Squire and Darling (2013: 69–70) argue that the concept of welcoming both
    privileges some subjects as being able to welcome others and creates an im-
    plied indebtedness of 'guests' to their 'hosts'.

6   Scholarship on asylum in Wales highlights the existence of a two- or multi-
    tier system exists where individuals seeking sanctuary receive varying levels
    of treatment or care depending on their status, meaning that not all mi-
    grants in Wales have access to the same rights, protection, and services (Ed-
    wards and Wisthaler, 2023: 3619). Scholarship also highlights the lack of
    infrastructure, challenges of connectivity and potential for greater isolation
    in non-urban spaces (Schmid-Scott et al., 2020: 147).

7   In 2021, this included: treatment in an accident and emergency depart-
    ment, family planning services (but not abortions or infertility treatment),
    treatment deemed necessary to protect wider public health, including STIs
    and Covid-19; treatment under the provisions of the Mental Health Act
    1983; and treatment for mental health problems as part of a court probation
    order (correspondence between the Minister for Health and Social Services
    and Patients not Passports, 20 September 2021).

This chapter has benefited from financial support from various funding bodies: the Coleg Cymraeg Cenedlaethol (*Grant Bach*), the Economic and Social
Research Council, and the UK Research and Innovation through a Type 2 Postgraduate Research Studentship (Award Number: 1799836).

Bibliography

Agnew, J. 1994. 'The Territorial Trap: The Geographical Assumptions of Internation-
    al Relations Theory'. *Review of International Political Economy*, 1/1, 53–80.
Amin, Ash. 2012. *Land of Strangers*. Cambridge: Polity Press.
Antoniw, M. 2020., Welsh Parliament, Plenary, Fifth Senedd (18 November
    2020): *https://record.assembly.wales/Plenary/6677*
BBC. 2023. 'Patriotic Alternative: The town fighting the far-right with Welsh
    cakes', *https://www.bbc.co.uk/news/uk-65057093*
Bernhardt, F. 2020. 'Between City and Nation of Sanctuary: Examining the Po-
    litical Geographies of Asylum and Hospitality in Wales'. Unpublished PhD
    thesis, Swansea University.
Bernhardt, F. 2022. 'Othering the sovereign host: Welsh responses to the British
    politics of asylum and resettlement after the 2015 European refugee "crisis"'.
    Hospitality and Society, 12/2, 223–41.
Challinor, E. 2018. 'Refugee hospitality encounters in northern Portugal: "Cultural
    orientations" and "con-textual protection"'. *Migration and Society*, 1/1, 96–110.
City of Sanctuary UK & Ireland and Wales Cities of Sanctuary project. 2016. Sub-
    mission to the Welsh Parliament's Committee on Equality, Local Government

and Communities – Inquiry on Asylum Seekers and Refugees in Wales: *https://business.senedd.wales/documents/s57745/RAS 21 - City of Sanctuary. pdf#:~:text=In%20Wales%2C%20it%20currently%20supports%20the%20 %E2%80%98Wales%20Cities,have%20the%20largest%20populations%20 of%20dispersed%20asylum%20seekers* (accessed 22 June 2023).

Closs-Stephens, A. and Bernhardt, F. 2024. 'Nationalism and Nation-States'. In K. Dombroski, M. Goodwin, J. Qian, A. Williams and P. Cloke (eds), *Introducing Human Geographies*, 4th edn. London: Routledge, pp. 637–50.

Darling, J. 2010. 'A city of sanctuary: the relational re-imagining of Sheffield's asylum politics'. *Transactions of the Institute of British Geographers*, 35/1, 125–40.

Darling, J. 2013. 'Moral Urbanism, asylum, and the politics of critique'. *Environment and Planning*, 45/8, 1785–801.

Derrida, Jacques. 2000. *Of Hospitality: Anne Dufourmantelle invites Jacques Derrida to Respond*, trans. R. Bowly. Stanford: Stanford University Press.

Edwards, C. W. and Dafydd Jones, Rh. 2024. 'Reconceptualising the Nation in Sanctuary Practices: towards a progressive, relational national politics?'. *International Political Sociology*, 18/2, olae006.

Edwards, C. W. and Wisthaler, V. 2023. 'The power of symbolic sanctuary: insights from Wales on the limitations and potential of a regional approach to sanctuary'. *Journal of Ethnic and Migration Studies*, 49/14, 3602–28.

Evangelical Alliance. 2015. 'Wales – towards a nation of sanctuary'. *https://www. eauk.org/current-affairs/politics/wales-towards-a-nation-of-sanctuary.cfm* (17 September).

The Guardian. 2023. 'This horror story visited on South Wales by Suella Braverman could be coming to a street near you' (24 August), *https://www.theguardian.com/commentisfree/2023/aug/24/south-wales-suella-braverman-welsh-stradey-park-hotel*

Guma, T., Woods, M., Yarker, S. and Anderson, J. 2019. '"It's that Kind of Place Here": Solidarity, Place-Making and Civil Society Response to the 2015 Refugee Crisis in Wales, UK'. *Social Inclusion*, 7/2, 96–105.

Hamilton, N. 2020. Welsh Parliament, Plenary, Fifth Senedd (18 November 2020): *https://record.assembly.wales/Plenary/6677*

Hess, S., Kasparek, B., Kron, S., Rodatz, M., Schwertl, M. and Sontowski, S. (eds). 2016. *Der lange Sommer der Migration-Grenzregime III*. Berlin: Assoziation A. Universität Göttingen.

Hill, E. 2016. 'Welcoming Nations? Hospitality as a Proxy for National Identity: A Consideration of British and Scottish Contexts'. In A. Haynes, M. J. Power, E. Devereux, A. Dillane and J. Carr (eds), *Public and Political Discourses of Migration: International Perspectives*. London: Rowman & Littlefield, pp. 193–206.

Home Office. 2017. *The Syrian Vulnerable Persons Resettlement Scheme (SVPRS) Guidance for Local Authorities and Partners*. Home Office: London (July).

Hope Not Hate. 2023., 'How a town in South Wales said no to fascism – and yes to Welsh cakes – HOPE not hate' (29 March).

Houghton, T. 2017. 'This is how many refugees have been resettled in Wales over the past year'. *Western Mail* (26 December): *https://www. walesonline.co.uk/ news/wales-news/how-many- refugees-been-resettled-14055878*

Hutt, J. 2019. Welsh Parliament, Plenary, Fifth Senedd (29 January 2019): *https:// record.assembly.wales/Plenary/5421*

James, J. 2018. Welsh Parliament, Plenary, Fifth Senedd (19 June 2018): *https:// record.assembly.wales/Plenary/4991*

Khanom A., Alanazy, W., Couzens, L., Evans, B. A., Fagan, L., Fogarty, R., John, A., Khan, T., Kingston, M. R., Moyo, S., Porter, A., Rhydderch, M., Richardson, G., Rungua, G., Russell, I. and Snooks, H. 2021. 'Asylum seekers' and refugees' experiences of accessing health care: a qualitative study'. *BJGP Open*, 5/6, BJGPO.2021.0059.

Local Government and Elections (Wales) Act 2021, *https://www.legislation.gov. uk/asc/2021/1/contents*

Mulvey, G., Skleparis, D. and Boyle, B. 2023. 'Territorial variance in the UK's refugee politics and its consequences: Young Syrian refugees in England and Scotland'. *Environment and Planning C: Politics and Space*, 41/5, 958–75.

Ngalle Charles, Eric. 2016. *Asylum*. Swansea: Hafan Books.

Parker, S. 2019. '"A proud history of protecting refugees": Ambivalent responses to refugee integration in government policy documents'. *Critical Approaches to Discourse Analysis across Disciplines*, 11/1, 20–40.

Parker, S. 2021. 'Inhibiting integration and strengthening inequality? The effects of UK policy making on refugees and asylum seekers in Wales'. *People, Place and Policy*, 15/2, 72–84.

Piacentini, T. 2012. 'Solidarity and struggle: An ethnography of the associational lives of African asylum seekers and refugees in Glasgow'. Unpublished PhD thesis, University of Glasgow.

Sassen, Saskia. 2006. *Territory, Authority, Rights: From Medieval to Global Assemblages*. Princeton: Princeton University Press.

Schmid-Scott, A., Marshall, E., Gill, N. and Bagelman, J. 2020. 'Rural Geographies of Refugee Activism: The Expanding Spaces of Sanctuary in the UK'. *Revue européenne des migrations internationales*, 36/2–3, 137–60.

Senedd and Elections (Wales) Act 2020, *https://www.legislation.gov.uk/ anaw/2020/1/ contents/enacted*

Squire, V. and Darling, J. 2013. 'The "Minor" Politics of Rightful Presence: Justice and Relationality in City of Sanctuary'. *International Political Sociology*, 7/1, 59–74.

Varsanyi, M. W. 2006. 'Interrogating "Urban Citizenship" vis-à-vis Undocumented Migration'. *Citizenship Studies*, 10/2, 229–49.

Wales Online. 2012. 'Welsh Government backs bid for Wales to become the first "nation of sanctuary" – Wales Online', *https://www.walesonline.co.uk/ news/ wales-news/welsh-government-backs-bid-wales-2035024*

Watson, J. 2020. Welsh Parliament, Plenary, Fifth Senedd (18 November 2020): *https://record.assembly.wales/Plenary/6677*

Welsh Government. 2019a. 'Nation of Sanctuary: Refugee and Asylum Seeker Plan', Nation of Sanctuary Refugee and Asylum Seeker Plan, *https://www.gov.wales/sites/default/files/publications/2019-03/nation-of-sanctuary-refugee-and-asylum-seeker-plan_0.pdf*

Welsh Government. 2019b. 'Written Statement: Progress Towards Wales becoming a Nation of Sanctuary', *https://www.gov.wales/written-statement-progress-towards-wales-becomingnation-sanctuary.*

Welsh Government. 2021. 'Correspondence. Response to Patients not Passports Request for Data', 20 September 2021.

Welsh Parliament. 2017. Equality, Local Government and Communities Committee, '"I used to be someone": Refugees and asylum seekers in Wales' (April), *https://senedd.wales/laid%20documents/cr-ld11012/cr-ld11012-e.pdf*

Welsh Refugee Coalition. 2016. 'Seven Steps to Sanctuary Manifesto', *https://cdn.cityofsanctuary.org/uploads/sites/74/2019/10/Welsh-Refugee-Coalition-Manifesto-CYM-16-English.pdf* (accessed 22 June 2023).

Wood, L. 2019. Welsh Parliament, Plenary, Fifth Senedd (13 November 2019): *https://record.assembly.wales/Plenary/6042*

CHAPTER 5

Creating a Welcoming Nation in a Hostile Environment: LGBTQ+ Precarious Experiences

Ourania Vamvaka-Tatsi

Introduction

The European refugee 'crisis' has spurred discussions around the terms 'asylum seekers' and 'refugees', which often oversimplify the complexities of migration pathways and legal processes (Crawley and Skleparis, 2017). In 2012, the UK government adopted the 'hostile environment' strategy, designed to make life difficult for individuals lacking legal residency, including asylum seekers. The more recent Immigration Bill: An End to Free Movement (2020) further complicated the legal landscape, aiming to consolidate immigration control solely under the UK government, reminiscent of historical anti-immigration measures such as the 1905 Aliens Restriction Act and 1919 Amendment Act.

The trajectory of UK migration policy has seen fluctuations, notably relaxed after the Second World War with the 1948 British Nationality Act to address labour shortages, allowing Commonwealth citizens to join the UK workforce. Subsequent legislation, such as the 1971 Immigration Act and later amendments, ignited discussions on race and multiculturalism in Britain, ultimately leading to anti-discrimination measures. The 1981 Nationality Act, by removing *jus soli* ('right of the soil'), reduced eligibility to British Citizenship, and was designed to exclude (Tyler, 2010: 61).[1] Subsequent laws, such as the 1993 Asylum and Immigration Act, created a dichotomy between refugees and asylum seekers, restricting the latter's access to work and education while imposing harsh measures on social rights.

The implementation of the 1999 Immigration and Asylum Act centralised housing and welfare assistance for asylum seekers through the National Asylum Support Service (NASS), often resulting in subpar housing conditions and limited choice for asylum seekers. Upon receiving refugee status, individuals are given a brief period to find new accommodation and enter the job market, facing eviction and potential homelessness, if unsuccessful. Challenges persist during the asylum process, including difficulty saving money for private accommodation and uncertainty surrounding employment due to employer reluctance and lack of clarity from the Home Office.

Refugees and asylum seekers are often viewed collectively in policy and integration frameworks, defined primarily by their legal status and spatial location (Lems, 2016). Their displacement transforms notions of home from a place of origin to a socio-cultural space negotiating various communities, symbolising global mobility and transition from citizenship to non-citizenship (Castles and Davidson, 2000). Displacement disrupts social ties, impacting access to networks and community integration, which is particularly challenging for LGBTQ+ individuals from specific ethnic backgrounds (Al-Ali, 2007; Al-Ali and Tas, 2017). Despite the agency acquired through social interaction, displacement often results in emotional and material fractures, hindering the formation of meaningful community ties (Atkinson, 2015; Hubbart and Lees, 2018).

In addition to the structural challenges posed by immigration and asylum policies, LGBTQ+ refugees face unique hurdles due to their intersecting identities. The complexities of their experiences are often overlooked within broader policy frameworks, leading to inadequate support and increased vulnerability. Discrimination and marginalisation based on sexual orientation and gender identity compound the already daunting journey of forced migration, amplifying feelings of isolation and alienation.

Furthermore, the intersectionality of LGBTQ+ identities with other marginalised aspects such as race, ethnicity and religion add layers of complexity to their experiences. For LGBTQ+ refugees from minority ethnic backgrounds, navigating cultural norms and expectations within both their home and host communities can be particularly challenging. They may face prejudice and exclusion not only based on their sexual orientation or gender identity but also due to racial or ethnic stereotypes, further exacerbating feelings of otherness and isolation. Despite these challenges, LGBTQ+ refugees demonstrate resilience and agency in their pursuit of safety and acceptance. Their narratives offer valuable insights into the shortcomings of current immigration and asylum policies and underscore the importance of adopting a more inclusive and intersectional approach to refugee protection. By centring their voices and experiences, we can better understand the barriers they face and work towards creating more equitable and supportive systems that uphold their rights and dignity.

This chapter expands existing research on queer asylum policy, specifically examining the intersectional identities experienced by LGBTQ+ forced migrants within the framework of UK asylum policies. Through a focused exploration of their lived experiences on arrival and settlement in Wales, this chapter delves into themes of otherness, belonging, community and the expression of sexual orientation and gender identities whether imposed by Home Office procedures or encountered within their new resettlement communities, prompting critical reflections on acceptance, belonging, and everyday expressions of identity. By centring the narratives of participants, this chapter contributes to a broader dialogue on the necessity for sustainable and inclusive asylum policies. It shows how UK asylum policies both construct and shape the experiences of a marginalised group, while simultaneously perpetuating social barriers for vulnerable populations. Additionally, this study contributes to broader discussions within academia and activism regarding the importance of amplifying marginalised voices and advocating for social justice and equity for all members of society.

The precarious journey of LGBTQ+ forced migrants highlights the complex interplay of identity and policy within the asylum system. The findings of this study have implications for policy and practice, particularly within the realms of immigration, housing and mental health services in Wales whereby policy-makers and service providers can develop more responsive and inclusive approaches that recognise the unique challenges faced by this population. Furthermore, this research underscores the urgent need for policies that recognise and address the unique vulnerabilities faced by LGBTQ+ individuals within the asylum process. Through a comprehensive analysis of these experiences, this chapter contributes to ongoing efforts to advocate for more equitable and inclusive asylum policies that uphold the rights and dignity of all forced migrants, regardless of their sexual orientation or gender identity.

Methodology and Fieldwork

A qualitative case study was conducted to delve deeply into the experiences of groups often perceived as 'hard-to-reach' as outlined by Silverman (2014). Given the sensitivity of the topic, one-on-one interviews were chosen, employing Dervin's (1976) reflexive interviewing strategy. To enhance researcher reflexivity, Guba's (1981) approach was followed, providing commentary during data analysis and identifying emerging patterns in the collected data.

The present writer's positionality holds particular significance in this study, as contextual factors shape subjectivity, which manifests through lived experiences (hooks, 1984). Leveraging their position as a social scientist and LGBTQ+ activist, the writer aimed to amplify the voices of marginalised LGBTQ+ forced migrants within academic discourse. The genesis of this study traces back to involvement, in an activist capacity, with a grassroots LGBTQ+ community group in southern Wales since 2016, through which participants were recruited by the writer. Building trusting relationships with participants prior to fieldwork allowed both an insider's and an outsider's perspective (Labaree, 2002), affording the opportunity to critically assess the writer's insider knowledge while accessing otherwise guarded truths (Merton, 1972). As the study progressed, there was intentional distancing by the writer from group activities to prevent undue pressure on members to participate.

This unique positioning enabled a nuanced understanding of the experiences and perspectives of LGBTQ+ forced migrants in Wales. By navigating the complexities of dual roles as researcher and activist, the writer aimed to ensure the integrity and ethical conduct of the study while honouring the voices and agency of the participants. Through reflexive engagement with the data, they strove to shed light on the intersectional challenges faced by this marginalised group and advocate for more inclusive policies and support mechanisms.

Moreover, the adoption of a reflexive interviewing strategy allowed for a dynamic and responsive approach to data collection, enabling participants to share their narratives authentically. By acknowledging positionality as both a researcher and LGBTQ+ activist, the writer aimed to create a safe and supportive environment for participants to express their experiences openly. This reflexivity also guided the interpretation and analysis of the data, fostering a deeper understanding of the nuanced complexities within the narratives shared.

As the study unfolded, it became evident that the intersectionality of identities played a significant role in shaping the experiences of LGBTQ+ forced migrants in Wales. Factors such as race, ethnicity, socio-economic status, health and immigration status intersected with sexual orientation and gender identity to influence access to services, experiences of discrimination, and opportunities for integration. These insights underscored the importance of adopting an intersectional lens in both research and policy-making to address the diverse and multifaceted needs of LGBTQ+ forced migrants.

This chapter is based on the experiences of three single asylum seekers who arrived in the UK and applied for refugee status. Participants were selected based on their identification as LGBTQ+ refugees who had recently been granted refugee status.[2] Gora hails from Mauritania, where being gay is punishable by death. He experienced severe physical and emotional violence due to his sexuality. Currently employed as a mental health support worker for vulnerable young adults, Gora maintains a relatively low profile within the LGBTQ+ community. Aasar, originally from Afghanistan, faced similar persecution due to his sexual orientation, as being gay is also punishable by death in his home country. Aasar is actively engaged in LGBTQ+ activism, balancing his role as a PhD researcher with organising fundraisers for LGBTQ+ causes and providing financial support to initiatives in Afghanistan. Medhi, born in Tunisia, fled persecution owing to his sexuality, experiencing expulsion from his family home after being involuntarily 'outed'. As an actor, Medhi utilises theatre as a platform to advocate for LGBTQ+ rights in northern Africa.

The research involved conducting a series of three one-to-one, in-depth, re-occurrent interviews with each participant over the course of three months. Each interview lasted between forty-five minutes to two-and-a-half hours, allowing for an in-depth exploration of the participants' experiences. All conversations were recorded (with consent), ensuring accuracy and facilitating a comprehensive analysis. Additionally, a researcher diary was maintained throughout the engagement period to document observations, reflections and insights that emerged outside the recorded interviews. This approach enabled an in-depth understanding of the participants' narratives and allowed for reflection and rapport-building over time.

Through these interviews, the study aimed to capture diverse experiences within the LGBTQ+ refugee community, highlighting the challenges faced by individuals from different cultural backgrounds and geographical regions. By amplifying their voices, the study seeks to inform policy and advocacy efforts aimed at supporting LGBTQ+ refugees in their resettlement journey.

One notable weakness of this study is the limited demographic representation, as it primarily focuses on single forced migrant men within the LGBTQ+ community. Unfortunately, single male forced migrants comprise the vast majority of LGBTQ+ forced migrants, further narrowing the sample pool.[3] Additionally, within this already limited group, those willing to come forward and discuss their traumatic experiences may be even scarcer. This limitation underscores the challenge of accessing and amplifying the voices of marginalised communities, particularly within the context of forced migration.

Despite efforts to recruit participants from diverse backgrounds, there was a lack of representation among queer forced migrant women willing to share their experiences. This gap in representation highlights the need for more inclusive research approaches and greater visibility for the experiences of LGBTQ+ forced migrant women. Their perspectives are essential for gaining a comprehensive understanding of the challenges faced by LGBTQ+ individuals within the asylum process. Moving forward, efforts should be made to create spaces and platforms where LGBTQ+ forced migrant women feel safe and empowered to share their stories. By amplifying their voices and experiences, we can develop more responsive and inclusive policies and support mechanisms that address the diverse needs of all members of the LGBTQ+ forced migrant community.

Ethical considerations were paramount in the design of this study, with measures implemented to safeguard the well-being and privacy of participants. Pseudonyms were consistently used, and demographic details were altered to protect anonymity. Recognising the potential for blurred boundaries in the researcher–participant relationship, especially within a context of social trauma, the writer made a concerted effort to clarify their role as a researcher prior to conducting interviews, ensuring transparency and trustworthiness. Additionally, to mitigate power imbalances, self-disclosure was employed as an interviewing technique, allowing participants to feel more comfortable sharing their stories (Birch and Miller, 2010). Furthermore, post-interview care was made available to participants should they require support (Boser, 2007).

Conducting research involving small LGBTQ+ forced migrant populations in Wales presents unique ethical challenges that necessitate careful consideration of participant anonymity and confidentiality. Given the sensitive nature of their experiences and the potential risks they face, protecting participants' identities is paramount to ensure their safety and well-being. Anonymisation techniques were used, including the use of pseudonyms as well as altering demographic details such as age and nationality, and removing any identifying information from transcripts and data sets. Additionally, the researcher chose to aggregate certain characteristics to further safeguard participants' identities while still maintaining the integrity of the data. These measures are essential in mitigating the risk of participants being identified and experiencing harm or discrimination as a result of their involvement in the study.

The act of sharing trauma can be profoundly impactful for LGBTQ+ forced migrants, providing a cathartic release and a sense of validation for their experiences. However, it also places a significant responsibility on the researcher to handle this information with care and sensitivity. Listening to and bearing witness to traumatic narratives requires a delicate balance of empathy and professionalism. Ultimately, the ethical imperative to conduct research with integrity and compassion underscores the importance of upholding the dignity and agency of LGBTQ+ forced migrants throughout the research process, and extensive training on ethical research practices, particularly in the study of trauma, was integral to the preparation for this study.

A Welcoming Nation: 'Requires LGBTQ+ Asylum Housing' – Advocating for Inclusive Policies in Wales

Despite Wales having devolved powers over housing, the issue of asylum accommodation remains non-devolved, leading to inconsistencies in policy and support. The UK's NASS designates twelve dispersal areas across the country, including Cardiff. Upon reaching Cardiff, asylum seekers are directed to dispersal hostels like 'The House'. While efforts have been made to address the housing needs of LGBTQ+ forced migrants, such as the proposed LGBTQ+ Housing initiative in the Glitter Cymru LGBTQ+ Action Plan (Welsh Government, 2023), progress has been slow, with little tangible action from the Welsh Government, This highlights the broader challenges faced when navigating the intersection of devolved and non-devolved matters, particularly concerning vulnerable populations such as LGBTQ+ forced migrants.

All participants arrived in the UK after fleeing violence and persecution in their home countries due to their sexual orientation. Their shared experiences upon arrival in the UK highlight the urgency of seeking asylum, coupled with the lack of choice in determining their place of residence, a policy known as 'no-choice dispersal'.[4] This policy aims to discourage asylum seekers from entering the UK but can exacerbate stress during the asylum process, particularly for individuals who have previously experienced human rights violations. The participants' accounts reveal feelings of powerlessness and social isolation resulting from this policy, underscoring its detrimental effects on mental health.

Gora recounts:

> I landed at Heathrow and claimed asylum. I was kept in the airport for hours in a small room. They did not give me any information, and I was so scared they were going to send me back. I wasn't given a choice of where I can live but I didn't care, I would have gone anywhere, if they allowed me to stay in the UK. If they sent me back to Mauritania, I'd probably be dead.

Mehdi explains:

> Back then my English was limited so when I claimed asylum, I thought I was going to stay in London. To be honest with you, I wanted to stay in London because of the great gay scene. I agreed to come to Wales because I didn't realise how far from London it is, I thought Wales was a neighbourhood in London. I was very shocked when the driver told me Wales is basically another country.

Those responsible for managing dispersal hostels often display indifference to socio-cultural differences, religious beliefs and LGBTQ+ identities, resulting in tense and sometimes violent living conditions. As a result, participants report minimal interaction with roommates and others due to concerns for their safety. They describe the atmosphere at these hostels as toxic, perilous, and rife with homophobia. Consequently, participants felt unsafe and marginalised, forcing them back into the closet out of fear for their lives.

Gora elaborates:

> The House staff did not ask if I am comfortable with sharing a room. I was sleeping in a room with five men. That gave me serious anxiety and I was afraid to speak because I did not want people to know I am gay.

Aasar explains:

> There were some men at the House and I think they understood by my manners that I'm gay. Even though they never blatantly asked me if I'm gay, they were making homophobic jokes loudly outside my room so I can hear them, they were eyeing me up and down in the corridors, whispering abuse, or making sexual hand gestures. They refused to sit and eat with me like I have cholera or something. I was crying myself to sleep every night. I left my home country to escape all of this. I came to the UK to be free and be myself. The moment I entered the House, I was back in the closet.

The participants emphasise feeling profoundly unsafe and subjected to abuse while residing in the dispersal accommodation. Their experiences force them to revert to concealing their sexual orientation out of fear for their safety, leading to severe negative impacts on their mental well-being. Milne and Travis (2003) argue that the housing and mental health requirements of asylum seekers pose significant challenges, with incidents of racism escalating due to ethnic tensions, backgrounds and religious disparities. LGBTQ+ asylum seekers face heightened risks of sexual harassment, violence and victimisation in such accommodations, often resulting in suicide attempts and post-traumatic stress (Hobbs et al., 2002). Additionally, factors like internalised homophobia and avoidance further compound the challenges faced by LGBTQ+ asylum seekers in dispersal accommodation (Blackaby, 2004). After enduring over sixty days at 'The House', the men were relocated to alternative dispersal accommodation.

Gora remembers:

> The move increased my anxiety. I was embarrassed to bring friends over because the new house was a mess. My room was so small that when I stretched my arms I could almost touch both walls. The furniture was old and destroyed, the walls were dirty and full of holes and the carpet had stains. My room had only one window, but it had bars, so I don't jump out. Apparently, it happened a lot.

Mehdi explains:

> I was just settling in the new house when the manager came and said, 'on Monday you are moving to Swansea'. That was on a Saturday morning. That is not even two days' notice. I had no choice; you are not allowed to argue. That move knocked me down. I did not know anybody in Swansea. I had to start again from zero. It took me a long time.

The transition to the new accommodation emerges as a tumultuous experience for the participants, marked by challenges in adapting to unfamiliar surroundings. Research indicates that asylum seekers residing in displacement accommodation exhibit notably higher levels of mental health issues compared to those living with friends or family (Carter and El-Hassan, 2003). Moreover, the harsh living conditions prevalent in such accommodations serve as significant predictors of depression (Pearl and Setter, 2002). Studies have shown that the lack of affirming and inclusive housing options can lead to profound feelings of isolation, anxiety and depression among LGBTQ+ asylum seekers (Hobbs et al., 2002). Asylum seekers living in displacement accommodation are disproportionately affected by mental health issues, exacerbated by substandard housing conditions and abrupt relocations. These challenges underscore the urgent need for improved support and resources for LGBTQ+ forced migrants in Wales.

Private accommodations utilised under the displacement policy often fail to meet acceptable standards and are typically situated in areas with low demand, which are frequently plagued by elevated crime rates (Carter and El-Hassan, 2003). D'Onofrio and Munk (2003) further underscore the substandard housing conditions faced by asylum seekers, highlighting the heightened risk of fire hazards.

The absence of safe and supportive housing specifically tailored to LGBTQ+ asylum seekers exacerbates the already precarious mental health challenges faced by this vulnerable population. The hostile and homophobic environments prevalent in many displacement accommodations not only subject LGBTQ+ individuals to heightened risks of discrimination and abuse but also contribute significantly to their psychological distress. Additionally, the constant fear of violence or harassment within these accommodations further compounds the mental health burden carried by LGBTQ+ individuals, hindering their ability to heal and rebuild their lives in a safe and supportive environment.

A Welcoming Nation: Should Not Require Proof of Sexual Orientation

Since March 2007, the UK has implemented the New Asylum Model (NAM) to streamline the processing of asylum applications, aiming to expedite initial decision-making procedures. Under the NAM framework, each asylum claim is assigned a dedicated case

owner responsible for maintaining ongoing communication with
the claimant throughout the asylum process (Home Office, 2008).
As part of this process, asylum seekers undergo interviews conducted by their allocated NAM case owner, during which they are
required to disclose the reasons for fleeing their home country,
detail any experiences of persecution, and present arguments supporting their eligibility for refugee status (Laban et al., 2005; Fasel
et al., 2014). While NAM itself does not directly encompass the
hostile environment policies, they intersect in the asylum process
through restrictions on accessing essential services like healthcare
or housing. It is crucial to consider both the NAM framework and
the broader immigration policy landscape, including the hostile
environment, when discussing asylum processes and experiences
in the UK.

Research indicates that the Home Office interviews conducted as
part of the asylum process can have severe detrimental effects on asylum seekers' mental health, with studies reporting increased rates of
post-traumatic stress disorder following these interviews (Llosa et al.,
2014; Fasel et al., 2005). This impact is exacerbated for asylum seekers
who are not proficient in English and do not receive adequate psychological support during the interview process (Priebe et al., 2012).
Despite claims by the Home Office regarding the transparency of the
interview process, it has faced ongoing criticism for its role in pro-
longing the appeals process, often perceived as a tactic to identify and
reject perceived illegitimate claims (Stevens, 2004). LGBTQ+ asylum
seekers face significant challenges during these interviews, as they are
required to provide detailed accounts of their experiences of sexual
violence and justify the authenticity of their sexual orientation, often
facing scepticism and disbelief from interviewers.

Mehdi remembers:

I was allocated my asylum interview after a month. It was
an awful interview. The guy was asking me unnecessary
questions like 'when did you find out you are gay? How did
you know you are gay? When were you first sexually harassed? How were you sexually harassed?' I said to him, 'how
do these questions help? Why are they important?' and he
said, 'because lots of people lie about their sexuality and if

the Home Office does not believe you are gay, you are not gay'. He was explicit. He told me he judged the way I look to make the decision, and he said, 'you do not look too gay, you can be discreet in your country'. He said that to my face. As I expected, I got rejected the first time. I was a mess when I found out. My court was a month later. That month I was emotionally suffering. My court appeal was successful, but it was horrible to be interrogated about my sex life.

Aasar says:

The paperwork was relatively straightforward, but the interview was very intense. I had no boyfriend then, and I was not part of any LGBTQ+ organisation, so all I had was my story. If the Home Office sent me back to Afghanistan I would be persecuted because being gay is a criminal offence. In the month leading up to my interview, I read as many asylum cases as I could, so I knew what questions to expect. I was not going to be intimidated, but when I entered the room, I saw a chair with an ankle chain and my heart started beating so fast. I was an asylum seeker, not a murderer.

LGBTQ+ asylum seekers are tasked with presenting deeply personal narratives to convince interviewers of the authenticity of their sexual orientation, which is not merely a matter of group membership but a fundamental aspect of self-identity. Unlike other forms of membership that can be verified through group affiliations or documentation, LGBTQ+ claims are often more complex and subjective. As such, claimants are frequently asked to provide evidence of involvement in LGBTQ+ community groups or proof of same-sex relationships, which may not always be feasible. Consequently, asylum seekers often rely solely on their own narratives of self-identity, which are then subjectively assessed by Home Office decision-makers who scrutinise their sexual experiences for authenticity.

To establish the legitimacy of their claims, asylum seekers are expected to present well-constructed and articulate narratives, often rehearsed in advance. However, this process can be highly intrusive and uncomfortable for claimants, who may find themselves compelled to disclose intimate details about their personal lives to strangers. Despite the discomfort, asylum seekers understand that failure to provide satisfactory responses or avoidance of questions could jeopardise the success of their claims. Thus, they must navigate a delicate balance between maintaining their privacy and providing the necessary information to support their case.

Mehdi says:

> Back in Tunisia I was trying to 'pass' but when I went out with my friends, I always had with me money for beer and for a bribe in case the police stopped me for 'acting gay'. I can't even tell you how many times policemen said, 'if you do with X and Y with me in the car, I won't jail you for homosexuality'. And the Home Office guy kept asking me to trust him because he's on my side. Really queen? I know his type.

During the Home Office interview process, there is an implicit expectation that asylum claimants can provide a linear and coherent account of their life experiences, which poses significant challenges, particularly for LGBTQ+ individuals. Discussing matters of self-identity amidst experiences of persecution, trauma, sexual violence, assault and torture is inherently difficult and can evoke feelings of repression, denial and shame. Many LGBTQ+ claimants have developed coping mechanisms, such as attempting to pass unnoticed by conforming to societal norms, as a means of avoiding stigmatisation. Consequently, openly disclosing and discussing their sexual orientation during interviews becomes a threatening and uncomfortable prospect, particularly for those hailing from oppressive societies.

In many societies, the relationship between LGBTQ+ individuals and authority figures is fraught with tension and hostility, further complicating their willingness to disclose their homosexuality to Home Office decision-makers. Fear of reprisal or further persecution often leads LGBTQ+ asylum seekers to conceal or downplay aspects of their identity during interviews, as they grapple with the uncertainty of how their disclosures may be perceived and the potential consequences they may face as a result.

Gora says:

> I had to go all the way back and re-live all the good and bad
> moments, remember people I'd forgotten and give the Home
> Office details about my life that nobody else knows. Not sure
> what they will do with all the information, but I hope the
> officer who was asking all these awful questions he finds it
> in his heart to be more compassionate with the next asylum
> seeker that comes through the door.

The LGBTQ+ experiences, presented as life stories, offer a glimpse
into the emotional state and decision-making processes of asylum
claimants at specific moments in their lives, providing valuable
insights into their worldview. These narratives play a crucial role in
the asylum process, yet the success of a claim often hinges on the
understanding of sexual identity and orientation by Home Office
policy-makers, as well as the dynamics between the asylum seeker
and the decision-maker. The outcome of the interview is heavily
influenced by the interviewer's approach – how they engage with
the claimant's sexual identity, what information they consider relevant to the claim, and how they extract it. Consequently, LGBTQ+
asylum experiences are not purely a reflection of the claimant's self-
identification but are rather evaluated based on their alignment with
Western notions of sexual orientation.

This essentialist perception of sexual orientation prevalent within the Home Office interview process operates under the assumption
that sexuality conforms to strict binary categories – either straight or
gay – and is unchanging, thereby disregarding transgender and bisexual individuals (Cossman, 2004). This rigid understanding suggests
that the Home Office expects a singular, authentic queer identity to
be uncovered and validated by the decision-maker, reinforcing the
notion that queer identities must be justified and visible to be deemed
legitimate. Moreover, the interview process often assumes a homoge-
nised experience of sexual identity among claimants, overlooking the
diversity and fluidity inherent in sexual orientations, and failing to
acknowledge that individuals' identities can evolve over time.

Furthermore, within the context of asylum interviews, the stigmatisation and erasure of bisexuality and other non-binary sexualities

are particularly pronounced. Bisexual individuals often face challenges in having their sexual orientation recognised and validated, as
it does not neatly fit into the binary framework of Western notions
of sexuality. Consequently, bisexual asylum claimants may encounter
scepticism or disbelief regarding the authenticity of their sexual orientation, further complicating their asylum claims and exacerbating
feelings of marginalisation and invisibility within the asylum process
(Lasowsi et al., 2023).

'It's One Thing To Be a Refugee and Another To Be Gay': The Enduring Experiences of 'Othering'

The enduring experiences of 'othering', exacerbated by the obstruc-
tive settlement procedures of the Home Office and the lack of adequate information and support services, are of paramount concern.
Instances of feeling marginalised include refugees' encounters with
obstacles in exercising their right to work, particularly the alienating
nature of job applications and interviews. These experiences of 'othering' extend beyond the realm of employment, permeating various
aspects of LGBTQ+ refugees' lives in their host country. From navigating bureaucratic hurdles to accessing essential services, refugees
often find themselves grappling with a sense of exclusion and alienation. The lack of tailored support exacerbates feelings of isolation,
making it challenging for individuals to integrate into their new communities effectively.

Furthermore, the reliance on European and British friends for assistance underscores the importance of social networks in facilitating
the resettlement process. While these connections provide valuable
support, they also highlight the gaps in formal support structures for
LGBTQ+ refugees (Williams, 2006; Squire, 2011). As a result, individuals may feel compelled to rely on informal networks, reinforcing
existing social divides and perpetuating feelings of marginalisation.
Addressing these systemic issues requires a comprehensive approach
that prioritises the unique needs of LGBTQ+ refugees and fosters inclusive environments where all individuals can thrive. The reliance
on social networks among sanctuary seekers, including LGBTQ+ refugees, is a well-documented aspect within the literature on refugee

studies. Studies consistently reveal that the social networks of sanctuary seekers tend to be limited, often extending primarily to other refugees or individuals within refugee support communities (Williams, 2006; Squire, 2011). These networks serve as vital sources of practical assistance, emotional support and information exchange, helping individuals navigate the challenges of resettlement and integration in unfamiliar environments. However, the literature also underscores the inherent limitations of relying solely on informal networks, particularly concerning LGBTQ+ refugees.

Research indicates that LGBTQ+ refugees may face additional barriers in accessing support within traditional refugee networks due to concerns about stigma, discrimination and cultural differences regarding LGBTQ+ identities and experiences. Consequently, LGBTQ+ refugees may find themselves marginalised within these networks or may hesitate to disclose their sexual orientation or gender identity for fear of rejection or persecution (Zierch et al., 2023). This highlights the need for specialised support services and inclusive spaces that cater to the unique needs of LGBTQ+ refugees, providing them with the opportunity to connect with peers who share similar experiences and identities.

By acknowledging the limitations of existing social networks for LGBTQ+ refugees and advocating for the development of more inclusive support structures, policy-makers, service providers and advocacy organisations can better address the specific challenges faced by this marginalised population. Creating spaces where LGBTQ+ refugees feel safe and supported not only enhances their resettlement experience but also contributes to the broader goal of fostering inclusive communities where all individuals can thrive (Zierch et al., 2023).

Aasar explains:

> The job market is tough for refugees. The whole job hunt is so complicated with lots of steps, and I was given no guidance by the Home Office. My friends helped me out by showing me how to fill out the forms and how to present myself in the interviews. Still – it took me a long time to get a job, so many closed doors, so much racism. I was invited for interviews because the companies needed to check a HR box. In

the first couple of interviews, I mentioned my refugee status. You should have seen their faces! They were mortified; like I told them I'm an alien. I bet you they probably thought I was illegal. Obviously, I didn't get those jobs.

Mehdi says:

I was shocked when I realised, I had to fill out an equalities form, I understand why it is important, but I feel very uncomfortable discussing my sexuality with people I don't know, and especially potential employers! I checked the 'prefer not to say' box. I don't want employers to treat me differently and you never know who you are talking to. It's one thing to be a refugee and another to be gay.

These narratives underscore the participants' unfamiliarity with navigating the Welsh labour market, revealing a lack of support and guidance from the Home Office and the Welsh Government in the job application process. The absence of assistance regarding employee rights and pre- and post-interview requirements leaves LGBTQ+ refugees ill-prepared for the competitive job market in Wales. Essentially left to fend for themselves, refugees are compelled to conform to standardised application procedures that fail to account for their unique circumstances. This approach perpetuates their disenfranchisement, reinforcing social exclusion and erecting artificial barriers between 'locals' and 'others', further marginalising LGBTQ+ refugees in both social and financial spheres.

Moreover, the completion of equality monitoring forms serves as another reminder of the participants' sense of 'otherness' within society. These forms, while ostensibly designed to track diversity and inclusion, inadvertently highlight the participants' divergence from societal norms regarding location, sexual orientation and ethnic background. For LGBTQ+ refugees, these forms become symbols of their outsider status, exacerbating feelings of internalised shame and reluctance to disclose personal information due to fears of discrimination and stigmatisation.

The reaction of recruiters to the disclosure of refugee status reflects a broader trend of objectifying and marginalising refugees as a collective 'other'. This objectification not only perpetuates financial insecurity among a vulnerable group but also perpetuates a cycle of discrimination that impedes economic integration and social cohesion. Despite legal provisions granting refugees the right to work in the UK, systemic barriers prevent the recognition and utilisation of their skills and experiences, hindering their ability to achieve financial independence and stability. This economic marginalisation has far-reaching consequences, contributing to elevated rates of depression and social isolation among refugee populations, particularly those from ethnic minority backgrounds.

Despite their affiliations with both LGBTQ+ and refugee communities, participants find themselves excluded from both due to the perceived mismatch between their intersectional identities and the internal membership criteria of these groups.

'I'm a Minority Within a Minority – Within a Minority!'

Despite their affiliations with both LGBTQ+ and refugee communities, participants find themselves excluded from both due to the perceived mismatch between their intersectional identities and the internal membership criteria of these groups.

Gora explains:

> When I arrived, I didn't know any other gay asylum seekers. The refugees I knew were straight and I wasn't going to mix with them because they were homophobic. I wanted to meet people like me, who have gone through similar situations and will understand my struggles. I met a lot of Welsh gays at the clubs but nobody I could call a friend. The club gays are white and I'm tall and black and I stand out. They think I'm 'exotic'; at the club they are friendly, but outside the club I'm just another foreigner on the street.

Mehdi says:

> People who say that Wales is diverse are clearly blind. I'm a gay refugee from Tunisia – I'm a minority within a minority

– within a minority! It's almost impossible to find people like me around here because Cardiff is so small! The gays here are visible but they are not very welcoming, and they don't socialise with ethnic minorities, because they don't take us seriously. And don't get me started with the straight refugees! I can't hang out with them; we are from different universes.

Within the confines of gay clubs, LGBTQ+ refugees find themselves relegated to the periphery, treated as exotic novelties rather than genuine members of the community. This superficial inclusion, driven by a desire to project an image of diversity, fails to address underlying prejudices and further marginalises LGBTQ+ refugees. Consequently, participants feel compelled to distance themselves from both the straight refugee community, with whom they share or perceive as sharing little common ground, and the LGBTQ+ community, which they perceive as unwelcoming and exclusive. Being fetishised within the LGBTQ+ community further underscores the racial dynamics at play, highlighting the insidious nature of racism even within ostensibly inclusive spaces. LGBTQ+ refugees often find themselves objectified and reduced to stereotypes, their identities commodified for the entertainment or satisfaction of others. This objectification perpetuates harmful racial stereotypes and reinforces power imbalances, as LGBTQ+ refugees are stripped of their agency and treated as mere curiosities rather than individuals deserving of respect and dignity. Moreover, the fetishisation of LGBTQ+ refugees based on racial or ethnic characteristics not only diminishes their humanity but also perpetuates harmful narratives of exoticism and racial superiority, ultimately contributing to the marginalisation and dehumanisation of minority communities within the LGBTQ+ community.

The narratives provided by LGBTQ+ refugees underscore a desire for acceptance and integration within the LGBTQ+ community in Cardiff. However, they observe a palpable apprehension among established community members towards 'the other', particularly those perceived as different due to race or ethnicity. This reluctance to embrace diversity suggests that the LGBTQ+ community in southern Wales may prioritise homogeneity and exclusivity over inclusivity, perpetuating social barriers and inhibiting meaningful connections with newcomers. Furthermore, the participants note that the prevailing mindset within the LGBTQ+ community equates membership with whiteness, effectively excluding those who do not fit this mould and reinforcing a narrow definition of belonging.

In navigating their own sense of otherness, LGBTQ+ refugees prioritise their sexual orientation over their legal status as refugees, highlighting the importance of identity in shaping their interactions and sense of belonging. By condemning homophobic behaviours and attitudes, participants assert their agency and reaffirm their commitment to fostering a more inclusive and accepting environment within both LGBTQ+ and refugee communities. However, the prevalence of otherness as a criterion for social categorisation perpetuates divisions and reinforces societal norms, ultimately hindering genuine social cohesion and understanding.

A Welcoming Nation: Should Centre Intersectionality

In addition to navigating the challenges of resettlement, LGBTQ+ refugees also face the complexities of reconciling their intersecting identities within unfamiliar social contexts. The intersectionality of their experiences – incorporating aspects of sexuality, gender identity, refugee status and cultural background – adds layers of complexity to their sense of belonging and self-identity. As they strive to carve out spaces where they can authentically express themselves, LGBTQ+ refugees must contend with societal attitudes, legal frameworks, and cultural norms that may not fully recognise or validate their identities. Despite these obstacles, their resilience and determination to forge meaningful connections highlight the importance of fostering inclusive environments that celebrate diversity and promote equity for all individuals, regardless of background or identity.

Intersectionality plays a pivotal role in understanding the refugee status of queer individuals who belong to ethnic and racial minorities. This framework is essential for grasping how these intersecting identities can both advantage and disadvantage individuals within society. Refugees, particularly those who identify as queer, navigate a complex landscape shaped by their queerness, gender and racial/ ethnic backgrounds, positioning them as distinct social actors with unique experiences and challenges. Within this framework, refugees often find themselves constructed as 'subordinate' in relation to more dominant actors, as their identities intersect and interact within various systems of power and oppression, influencing their access to services and opportunities.

Displacement thrusts forced migrants into a continuous process of adaptation, where they navigate self-imposed and socio-cultural boundaries. Through these interactions, individuals come to realise that difference is not inherently problematic and does not threaten social cohesion. In fact, acknowledging and embracing intersectional identities is crucial for fostering socio-cultural transformation and building a more inclusive and stable society. However, adopting an intersectional societal approach can be fraught with challenges, as it risks oversimplifying or conflating the interconnected categories of identity and structure, potentially blurring the boundaries between different intersectional identities and systems of oppression.

In the context of Wales, participants' experiences reflect stark differences in gender, sexuality and racial/ethnic backgrounds, yet they also transcend multiple social norms. Participants often present their identities as negotiable and flexible, challenging assumptions about the immutability of sexual orientation and racial background while highlighting the influence of legal status and cultural characteristics. Despite these complexities, participants unite as a marginalised community, using their diverse voices to openly discuss their experiences and navigate their intersectional identities. By doing so, they aim to interrogate social identity boundaries and increase visibility and understanding of intersectional experiences within society.

Mehdi explains:

We were a small group of queens, all refugees by the way – from Iran, Morocco, Pakistan, and me and wanted to get in the club. We were just starting the night, we were sober. The bouncer looked at us one by one and asked for our IDs. We gave him the IDs provided by the Home Office. He looked at them with a face of disgust and said, 'we don't accept these here'. We've all been to that club many times and had no issues before. He let all the British in before us in without checking IDs. That moment really broke my heart. All we wanted to do was have fun at a safe LGBTQ+ space and have a drink. I cried all the way back home.

By examining the intersections of multiple categories simultaneously, the complexities of the participants' lived experiences become apparent. It becomes evident that their social interactions are shaped by perceptions of identity limitations, with their intersectionality often perceived as a burden and vulnerability. Participants express conflicting notions regarding their intersectionality, viewing it as both impacting their social status due to their refugee status and as influential in navigating evolving social dynamics.

Significantly, the participants, rather than emphasising the fluidity of their intersectionality and its potential to deconstruct categories of difference, they tend to focus on comparing social group inequality and privilege. This focus overlooks the fluid and dynamic nature of social categories, which are neither fixed nor stable. Perry (2009) emphasises that intersectionality necessitates an examination of the interconnections between social structures, human agency, tensions within lived experiences, and an assessment of social contradictions and interactions.

Mehdi explains:

You know I never had a boyfriend in Wales? I dated a few people, but I got super tired because it was the same story again and again. At first, they were all curious to date a brown fem but then they treat me like their humanitarian deed of the month! This one guy insisted that I meet his friends only after four dates. He introduced and they were like 'So you are the HIV positive refugee from Tunisia!' Who says that! I left early and never saw the guy again.

Aasar mentions:

When I'm at work I wear many hats because I represent so many people, the LGBTQ+, the Afghanis, the single refugee men. I put pressure on myself to be the perfect example. I don't want anyone to turn around and say, 'That gay refugee doesn't work hard' or 'That brown gay is only talk'. I want people who haven't met a gay, Afghan, refugee man to have a great first impression and hopefully this will make them a little more tolerant. I work ten times harder than everyone else, I'm involved with many work-related groups, I'm open about all the different layers of my identity, and I communicate my experiences. But sometimes I feel like I'm acting, like my identity is not real and I'm putting on a show to educate the rest of the LGBTQ community or the white British and Europeans. It is not my job and it's exhausting.

The participants highlight the presence of conflicting dynamics that shape their lived experiences, which are evident in power relations and the diversities within intersecting groups. Interestingly, they note that there seems to be a limitation on the number of intersectional categories a person can navigate based on their specific experiences. While they acknowledge a lack of awareness of many others who share similar intersectional identities, they emphasise the strong bonds formed with those who share intersecting similarities, suggesting a potential reduction in power inequality among intersectional refugees. Furthermore, they discuss the significance of friendships and close connections with individuals from diverse backgrounds, underscoring the transformative potential of intersectionality in fostering meaningful relationships across social boundaries.

Hancock (2007), in building on Crenshaw's (1989) seminal work on intersectionality, elucidates that intersectionality aims to capture the dynamic interplay of social categories and generate knowledge about identities and their cultural interconnections within sociological contexts that shape them. Similarly, Collins (1968; 2004; 2015) proposes that exploring expressions of intersectional interactions introduces additional layers of difference, facilitating the deconstruction of identity categories and highlighting inequalities among social groups. However, the participants express a sense of limited understanding and recognition of their identities, lives and differences within both LGBTQ+ and refugee communities. Intersectional refugees often find themselves positioned outside the norms of each community, rendering their experiences less valid or influential in shaping new social interactions.

Conclusion

This chapter delves into the profound impact of UK immigration and asylum policies on the lives of LGBTQ+ forced migrants in southern Wales. By delving into the participants' everyday experiences of settlement and arrival, it explored how they navigate socio-cultural landscapes and the role of intersectional identities in shaping their community and social interactions.

The narratives shared by LGBTQ+ asylum seekers in Wales shed light on the significant challenges they face in navigating the UK's asylum system and settling into their new lives. From the moment of arrival, these individuals encounter a lack of agency and autonomy, compelled to reside in dispersal accommodations without the opportunity to choose their living arrangements. This policy of 'no-choice displacement' not only exacerbates their vulnerability but also contributes to heightened levels of stress and social isolation, particularly among those who have endured previous human rights violations.

Once housed in dispersal accommodations, LGBTQ+ asylum seekers often find themselves in hostile and unsafe environments, where they must conceal their sexual orientation or gender identity out of fear for their safety. The toxic atmosphere prevalent in these accommodations, coupled with the absence of support for their unique needs, further compounds the mental health challenges faced by LGBTQ+ individuals, leading to increased rates of depression, anxiety and post-traumatic stress.

Moreover, the transition to new accommodation exacerbates the participants' struggles, as they grapple with unfamiliar surroundings and substandard living conditions. Research underscores the detrimental impact of such environments on mental health, highlighting the urgent need for safe and supportive housing options tailored to the needs of LGBTQ+ asylum seekers. However, the lack of such accommodations perpetuates feelings of isolation and vulnerability, hindering their ability to integrate into their new communities and rebuild their lives.

Furthermore, the asylum application process itself presents significant hurdles for LGBTQ+ claimants, who are required to disclose intimate details about their sexual orientation and experiences of persecution. The essentialist approach adopted by the Home Office in assessing LGBTQ+ identities often fails to recognise the complexities of sexual orientation and gender identity, further marginalising and stigmatising these individuals. These policies question the authenticity of their sexuality and life stories, leaving them feeling marginalised and misunderstood. Furthermore, the services offered by NASS during and after settlement periods operate within neo-colonial frameworks, neglecting the multifaceted needs of LGBTQ+ individuals and exacerbating feelings of invisibility and lack of support.

Ultimately, the experiences of LGBTQ+ asylum seekers in Wales underscore the urgent need for systemic reforms within the UK's asylum system. Policies must be reformed to prioritise the safety and well-being of LGBTQ+ individuals, including the provision of safe housing options, culturally competent support services, and fair and sensitive asylum procedures. Only through such reforms can the UK fulfil its obligations to protect the rights and dignity of all individuals fleeing persecution based on their sexual orientation or gender identity.

Indeed, addressing issues related to LGBTQ+ asylum seekers and refugees in Wales requires a multi-faceted approach that extends beyond governance and involves Welsh organisations, the Welsh Government, and the attitudes and behaviours of Welsh citizens.

Welsh organisations, including non-governmental organisations, community groups and charities, play a crucial role in providing support and resources to asylum seekers and refugees. These organisations often offer essential services such as language classes, legal assistance, housing support and access to healthcare. Additionally, they provide valuable advocacy efforts, raising awareness about the challenges faced by asylum seekers and refugees and lobbying for more inclusive policies at both the local and national levels.

The Welsh Government also has a significant role to play in addressing the needs of asylum seekers and refugees within its jurisdiction. This includes implementing policies and initiatives to support integration, providing funding for essential services, and working collaboratively with local authorities and organisations to ensure a coordinated response to the needs of this vulnerable population.

Furthermore, addressing the attitudes and behaviours of Welsh citizens is essential for fostering a welcoming and inclusive society for asylum seekers and refugees. This involves raising awareness about the experiences and backgrounds of asylum seekers and refugees, challenging stereotypes and misconceptions, and promoting empathy and understanding. Education and community engagement initiatives can play a vital role in promoting positive attitudes and fostering social cohesion.

Supporting diverse migrants in Wales requires a compassionate and multi-layered approach, one that sees people beyond their labels and embraces the complexities of their identities. Migrants – especially those from vulnerable groups like LGBTQ+ individuals, women and non-binary people – often face compounded challenges, from discrimination to trauma. To truly help, Welsh migration policy needs to be flexible and responsive to these realities. This means listening to migrant voices and working with their communities to craft policies that reflect their experiences. Stronger protections against discrimination in areas like housing, healthcare and employment are not just policy issues – they are lifelines that can ensure people are treated with dignity and respect.

On the ground, practical support must go beyond paperwork and bureaucratic processes. Legal help, mental health services and safe housing should be readily available, designed with care for the specific needs of migrants who often arrive with heavy emotional burdens or face discrimination in their daily lives. For instance, housing options should ensure safety and inclusivity, particularly for LGBTQ+ migrants who might otherwise face hostility or isolation. Community integration programs – whether language classes, employment support, or cultural training for service providers – can be a bridge to help migrants feel at home, while also equipping the community to better welcome them.

It is also vital to create spaces where migrants can safely report abuses or rights violations without fear of retaliation. Having an independent body overseeing these complaints would provide accountability and offer migrants a sense of security. At the same time, collaboration with NGOs, community groups and migrant-led initiatives is key to shaping policies that are genuinely grounded in people's real-life experiences. Public awareness campaigns that celebrate the contributions migrants make to Welsh society, while challenging xenophobia and homophobia, would help build a more inclusive, compassionate environment. By taking these steps, Wales can not only support migrants in practical ways but also foster solidarity.

This chapter prompts reflection on issues of group membership, belonging and inter-community conflicts, emphasising the urgent need for inclusive community development initiatives. Participants encountered 'othering', discrimination and stigmatisation along with challenges in existing within rigid social boundaries in Cardiff and Swansea, defined by economic status, legal standing and ethnic background. These constraints on their lived experiences of settlement hinder their social integration, exposing the lack of diversity, inclusivity and acceptance of intersectional identities in southern Wales. The intersectional identities of participants underscore the complex interplay between socio-legal status and community affiliations, revealing diverse expressions and understandings of identity within the context of migration and settlement.

Notes

1   Tyler (2010: 62–3) argues that it created several categories of nationality and citizenship to 'define, limit and remove the entitlements to citizenship from British nationals in the Commonwealth (the former colonies) thereby restricting immigration to the British Isles and creating "aliens" within the borders of the nation state.' It included a category of 'Commonwealth citizenship' that 'removed from British nationals in the Commonwealth and Hong Kong their historic rights to residency in the United Kingdom.'

2   Despite initial interest from twelve potential participants, some were unable to participate due to scheduling conflicts, while others withdrew for unspecified reasons.

3   Within the LGBTQ+ community, the concept of 'male' identity is often fluid and may be self-defined or shaped by external perceptions. The boundaries of gender and sex are not binary. For single forced migrant men who identify within the LGBTQ+ spectrum, their 'male' identity intersects with other identities, including non-binary, trans or gender non-conforming identities. These intersections add to the traditional definition of 'male', making it necessary to consider how gender markers and societal expectations influence personal identity. Consequently, the category of 'male' in this context includes a range of experiences that reflect the complex and often contested nature of gender within the LGBTQ+ community.

4   The 1999 Immigration and Asylum Act provided housing on a 'no choice' basis to asylum seekers across the UK as a means of managing their settlement (Phillips, 2006; Robinson et al. 2003).

Bibliography

Al-Ali, N. S. 2007. 'Gender, diasporas, and post-war conflict'. In H. Smith and P. Stares (eds), *Diasporas in conflict: Peacemakers or peace-wreckers*. Tokyo: United Nations University Press, pp. 39–61.

Al-Ali, N. and Tas, L. 2017. '"War is like a blanket": Feminist convergences in Kurdish and Turkish women's rights activism for peace'. *Journal of Middle East Women's Studies*, 13/3, 354–75.

Al-Ali, N. and Koser, K. 2002. *New approaches to migration? Transnational communities and transformation of home*. London and New York: Routledge.

Anthias, A. 2001. 'New hybridities, old concepts: the limits of "culture"'. *Ethnic and Racial Studies*, 24/4, 619–41.

Anthias, A. 2002. 'Where do I belong? Narrating collective identity and translocational positionality'. *Ethnicities*, 2/4, 491–515.

Atkinson, A. 2015. *Inequality – What Can Be Done?* Cambridge, MA: Harvard University Press.

Basedow, J. and Doyle, L. 2016. *England's forgotten refugees: Out of the fire and into the frying pan*. London: Refugee Council.

Baxter, R. and Brickell, K. 2014. 'For Home Unmaking'. *Home Cultures*, 11/2, 133–43.

Birch, M. and Miller, T. 2000. 'Inviting intimacy: The interview as therapeutic opportunity'. *International Journal of Social Research Methodology*, 3/3, 189–202.

Blackaby, B. 2004. *Community Cohesion and Housing: A Good Practice Guide*. London: Chartered Institute of Housing.

Bleich, E. 2002. 'Integrating Ideas into Policy-making Analysis: Frames and Race Policies in Britain and France'. *Comparative Political Studies*, 35/9, 1054–76.

Bloch, A. and Schuster, L. 2005. 'At the Extremes of Exclusion: Deportation, Detention and Dispersal'. *Ethnic and Racial Studies*, 28/3, 491–512.

Boser, S. 2007. 'Power, Ethics, and the IRB: Dissonance Over Human Participant Review of Participatory Research'. *Qualitative Inquiry*, 13/8, 1060–74.

Brah, A. 1996. *Cartographies of Diaspora: Contesting Identities*. London: Routledge.

Browne, I. and Misra, J. 2003. 'The Intersection of Gender and Race in the Labour Market'. *Annual Review of Sociology*, 29, 487–513.

Carter, M. and El-Hassan, A. 2003. 'Between NASS and a Hard Place'. London: Housing Action Charitable Trust.

Castles, S. and Davidson, A. 2000. *Citizenship and Migration: Globalisation and the Politics of Belonging*. Routledge: New York.

Collins, P. H. 1986. 'Learning from the Outsider Within: The Sociological Significance of Black Feminist Thought'. *Social Problems*, 33/6, 14–32.

Collins, Patricia Hill. 1993. *Toward a New Vision: Race, Class, and Gender as Categories*. New York, NY: Routledge.

Collins, Patricia Hill. 2004. *Black Sexual Politics*. New York, NY: Routledge.

Collins, P. H. 2009. 'It's all in the family: intersections of Gender, Race, and Nation'. *Hypatia*, 13/3, 62–82.

Collins, P. H. 2015. 'Intersectionality's Definitional Dilemmas'. *Annual Review of Sociology*, 41/6, 1–20.

Cossman, B. 2004. *Sexuality, Queer Theory, and 'Feminism After' – Reading and Rereading the Sexual Subject*. London: Pluto Press.

Crawley, H. and Skleparis, D. 2017. 'Refugees, migrants, neither, both: Categorical fetishism and the politics of bounding in Europe's "migration crisis"'. *Journal of Ethnic and Migration Studies*, 18/2, 132–45.

Crenshaw, K. 1994. 'Mapping the Margins: Intersectionality, Identity Politics and Violence Against Women of Colour'. In M. A. Fineman and R. Mykitiuk (eds), *The Public Nature of Private Violence*. London: Routledge, pp. 93–118.

Eastmond, M. 2007. 'Stories as Lived Experience'. *Journal of Refugee Studies*, 20/2, 248–64.

D'Onofrio, L. and Munk, K.. 2003. 'Understanding the Stranger'. *Nursing science quarterly*, 16, 305–9. 10.1177/0894318403257124.

Esses, V. M., Bennett-AbuAyyash, C. and Lapshina, N. 2014. 'How Discrimination Against Ethnic and Religious Minorities Contributes to the Underutilisation of Immigrants Skills'. *Policy Insights from the Behavioural and Brain Sciences*, 1/1, 55–62.

Fasel, M., Karunakara U. and Newnham, E. A. 2014. 'Detention, denial, and death: migration hazards for refugee children'. *Lancet Global Health*, 2/3, 313–14.

Fasel, M., Wheeler J. and Danesh, J. 2005. 'Prevalence of serious mental disorder in 7000 refugees resettled in western countries: a systematic review'. *Lancet*, 365/5, 1309–14.

Galarneau, D. and Morissette, R. 2004. 'Immigrants: Settling for less? Perspectives on labour and income'. *Statistics Canada Catalogue*, 75-001-XIE/5, 5–16.

Geddes, A. 2005. 'Europe's border relationships and international migration relations'. *Journal of Common Market Studies*, 43/4, 787–806.

Goodhart, D. 2004. 'Too Diverse?'. *Prospect Magazine*, http://www.prospect magasine.co.uk/magasine/too-diverse-david-goodhart-multiculturalism-britain-immigration-globalisation (accessed 15 October 2021).

Guba, E. 1981. 'Criteria for assessing the trustworthiness of naturalistic inquiries'. *Educational Resources Information Centre Annual Review Paper*, 29/3, 75–91.

Hancock, A.-M. 2007. 'When Multiplication Doesn't Equal Quick Addition'. *Perspectives on Politics*, 5/1, 63–79.

Hobbs, M., Moor, C. and Wansbrough, T. 2002. 'The health status of asylum seekers screened by Auckland Public Health in 1999 and 2000'. *New Zealand Medical Journal*, 115/1160, U152.

Home Office. 2008. *Control of Immigration Statistics 2008*, Issue 10, United Kingdom.

Home Office. 2010. *UK Border Agency, Analysis, Research and Knowledge Management, Survey of New Refugees, 2005–2009*. UK Data Service.

hooks, b. 1984. *From margin to Centre*. Boston, MA: South End Press.

Hubbard, P. and Lees, L. 2018. 'The right to community?' *City*, 22/1, 8–25.

Kaiser, K. 2009. 'Protecting Respondent Confidentiality in Qualitative Research'. *Qualitative Health Research*, 19/11, 1632–41.

Karimi, A. 2018. 'Sexuality and Integration'. *Ethnic and Racial Studies*, 19/8, 1–19.

King, E. B. and Ahmad, A. S. 2010. 'An experimental field study of interpersonal discrimination against Muslim job applicants'. *Personnel Psychology*, 63/9, 881–906.

Krings, F. and Olivares, J. O. 2007. 'At the doorstep to employment: Discrimination against immigrants as a function of applicant ethnicity, job type and raters' prejudice'. *International Journal of Psychology*, 42/5, 406–17.

Kumar, S. and Cavallaro, L. 2018. 'Researcher Self-Care in Emotionally Demanding Research: A Proposed Conceptual Framework'. *Qualitative Health Research*, 28/4, 648–58.

Labaree, R. V. 2002. 'The risk of "going observationalist": negotiating the hidden dilemmas of being an insider participant observer'. *Qualitative Research*, 2/1, 97–122.

Lasowski, P., Moscicki, O., Liu, C. Z., Katzenstein, C., Singer, E. K. and Baranowski, K. A. 2023. 'Persecution and migration experiences of lesbian, gay, bisexual, transgender, queer/questioning, and other sexual and gender minority asylum seekers'. *Journal of Traumatic Stress*, 36/3, 605–16.

Lems, A. 2016. 'Placing displacement: Place-making in a world of movement'. *Ethnos*, 81/2, 315–37.

Lentin, A. and Titley, G. 2011. 'The crisis of "multiculturalism" in Europe: Mediated minarets, intolerable subjects'. *European Journal of Cultural Studies*, 15/2, 123–38.

Llosa, A. E., Ghantous, S., Sousa, R., Forgione, F., Bastin, P., Jones, A., Antierens, A., Slavuckij, A. and Grais, R. F. 2014. 'Mental disorders, disability, and treatment gap in a protracted refugee setting'. *British Journal of Psychiatry*, 204/2, 208–13.

Manso, L. C., Kleit, R. G. and Couch, D. 2008. 'Moving Three Times Is Like Having Your House on Fire Once: The Experience of Place and Impending Displacement among Public Housing Residents'. *Urban Studies*, 45/9, 1855–78.

McCall, L. 2005. 'The Complexity of Intersectionality', *Signs*, 30/3, 1771–800.

Merton, R. K. 1972. 'Insiders and Outsiders: A Chapter in the Sociology of Knowledge'. *American Journal of Sociology*, 78/1, 9–47.

Meyer, D. 2012. 'An Intersectional Analysis of Lesbian, Gay, Bisexual, and Transgender (LGBT) People's Evaluations of Anti-queer Violence'. *Gender and Society*, 26/6, 849–73.

Milne, S. and Travis, A. 2003. 'Safe Havens Plan to Slash Asylum Numbers', *The Guardian*, http://www.guardian.co.uk/uk=news/story/0,3604,889014,00.html

Mulvey, G. 2010. 'When Policy Creates Politics: The Problematising of Immigration and the Consequences for Refugee Integration in the UK'. *Journal of Refugee Studies*, 23/4, 437–62.

Murray, D. 2014. 'Real Queer: "Authentic" LGBT Refugee Claimants and Homonationalism in the Canadian Refugee System'. *Anthropologica*, 56/1, 24–36.

Murray, David A. B. 2015. *Real Queer? Sexual Orientation and Gender Identity Refugees in the Canadian Refugee Apparatus*. London: Pickering and Chatto Publishers.

Nash, J. 2008. 'Re-thinking Intersectionality'. *Feminist Review*, 89/1, 1–15.

Netto, G. 2011. 'Strangers in the city: Addressing challenges to the protection, housing, and settlement of refugees'. *International Journal of Housing Policy*, 11/3, 285–303.

Oakley, Ann. 2013. *Doing Feminist Research*. New York, NY: Routledge.

Phillips, D. 2006. 'Moving towards integration: the housing of asylum seekers and refugees in Britain'. *Housing Studies*, 21/4, 539–53.

Robinson, V., Andersson, R. and Musterd, S. (eds). 2003. *Spreading the 'burden'? A review of policies to disperse asylum seekers and refugees*. Bristol: Policy Press.

Squire, V. 2011. 'From Community Cohesion to Mobile Solidarities: The City of Sanctuary Network and the Strangers into Citizens Campaign'. *Political Studies*, 59/2, 290–307.

Welsh Government. 2023. *LGBTQ+ Action Plan for Wales: progress update* (15 June). Available at: *https://www.gov.wales/lgbtq-action-plan-wales-progress-update*

Williams, L. 2006. 'Social Networks of Refugees in the United Kingdom: Tradition, Tactics and New Community Spaces'. *Journal of Ethnic and Migration Studies*, 32/5, 865–79.

Ziersch, A., Walsh, M. and Due, C. 2023. '"Having a good friend, a good neighbour, can help you find yourself": social capital and integration for people from refugee and asylum-seeking backgrounds in Australia'. *Journal of Ethnic and Migration Studies*, 49/15, 3877–99.

CHAPTER 6

Mothers' Narratives of Transitions and Resilience Through Social Learning

Laura Shobiye

Context and Background

This chapter, which is based on and adapted from a chapter in the present writer's PhD thesis (Shobiye, 2023), explores the educational and learning experiences of mothers seeking sanctuary in Wales. The chapter specifically seeks to address the question: 'What role does learning play during transitional experiences for mothers living as asylum seekers and refugees in Wales?' The research provides an original contribution to refugee education literature through its three interconnected areas of focus: Wales, mothers and social learning. Using Wenger's (2018) theories, social learning is defined as a social process or phenomenon of active participation through which individuals and communities develop individual identities and a shared sense of belonging. By applying this definition to formal education and informal learning, the research could explore the role education plays in journeys of survival, well-being and resilience within Welsh communities. The analysis of three mothers' narratives of active participation in communities as learning is also informed by key theoretical literature that utilises Bourdieu's (1977) concept of social capital as a means of reproduction social hierarchies. Use of both the framework on multi-layered social resilience (Obrist et al., 2010) and feminist scholarship on social reproduction (Bhattacharyya, 2018) provide a nuanced theoretical framework for exploring the specific stories of mothers seeking sanctuary. In this way, the chapter shows that a social learning perspective is vital in understanding how Wales might become a 'true Nation of Sanctuary'(Welsh Government, 2019: 3).

The focus of existing refugee education literature in the UK is generally on routes to employment and social inclusion and exclusion for individuals. At the start of the doctoral project for this research, there was no literature for Wales that studies refugee education in Wales beyond the (significant) topic of English for Speakers of Other Languages (ESOL) and links to employment (Chick and Hannagan-Lewis, 2019; Holtom and Iqbal, 2020) and Welsh for Speakers of Other Languages (WSOL) (Higham, 2014, 2020, this volume). Some work in England has explored learning beyond formal education and the link to employment opportunities. For example, Clarke (2014) argues that refugee community organisations play an essential role in learning, recognition and empowerment. However, the body of literature highlighted above often reduces mothers' roles and experiences to their domestic reproductive and caring roles rather than a more whole person-centred approach. That reductive approach to mothers' experiences is an issue discussed in depth elsewhere in feminist social reproduction literature (Bhattacharyya, 2018). For the present writer, the existing literature, therefore, left potential gaps in knowledge of sanctuary-seeking women's experiences.

A small body of literature explores the specific experiences of women seeking sanctuary in England. Thompson and Nasimi's (2022) research recently investigated the role of community learning to support learning of cultural and social norms and women's rights, reporting positive impacts on integration and self-esteem. Morrice (2007) advocated for greater recognition of informal social learning as necessary for mothers who often build their social capital through relationships with other mothers in local communities rather than in the workplace. Morrice's findings have since been supported by Klenk's (2017) work that explored ESOL classes for refugee women held at a community centre in London. Klenk called for a broader notion of education in policy to better align with refugee women's skills, needs and aspirations and to better reflect the intrinsic benefits for mothers and their children. Both Morrice and Klenk highlight the undervaluing of the role of motherhood as an agentic force for women and their children's futures. Yet, when the present writer's doctoral research commenced, Wales had no equivalent literature. There was a clear gap in understanding the broader role that learning and education can have for mothers seeking sanctuary in Wales, beyond individual routes to employment.

Methods

The qualitative methodological approach was based on exploring participatory and ethically sensitive experiences and used ethnographic, creative and collaborative multi-modal methods. Refugee support communities were visited and data generated through interviews with twenty-six participants from four areas of Wales. Some participants were interviewed twice, with a total of thirty-three interviews conducted. Participants were invited to create drawings to depict their experiences, at the end of each interview. The structure for the interviews, and therefore the direction for the drawings, was very open, with just four question areas. The women who created an image were invited to describe/discuss the item briefly before the interview concluded. This approach was to enable participants to decide what they communicated verbally and/or visually within the overall scope of learning and education. This overall approach was based on auteur theory, focusing on the creator's perspective and intent more than the viewer's interpretation (Rose, 2016). During UK lockdowns for the Covid-19 pandemic, the researcher also remotely elicited photographs via WhatsApp messages. The data generated focuses on the participants' particular subjective experiences and perceptions.

The research approach was influenced by decolonial (Asher, 2017) and representative approaches (Pickering and Kara, 2017a; Manning, 2018; Rhee, 2021), which informed every research stage, including how this chapter was written. The qualitative ethnographical approach that took the researcher into participants' communities and spaces (Gobo and Marciniak, 2016; Hammersley, 2018) provided an ethical option for the comfort and well-being of research participants. Each narrative is discussed using a structure of three short 'episodes', reflecting the temporal nature of some of the women's experiences (Neale, 2017; Mueller, 2019). The women's stories are presented through three 'episodes', one for each sub-section, that relate to the generation of data/research phases and highlight temporality and transitions.

Three Narratives

As outlined in the introduction, this chapter explores the narratives of three individuals – Sarah, Pam and Irene. The interconnections between different areas and moments in their lives are demonstrated in terms of learning experiences. In doing so, it is shown that these experiences do not happen in siloed contexts; and presented findings show how social learning and all its interconnections are vital for mothers rebuilding their lives as sanctuary seekers in Wales.

The presentation of three specific narratives focuses on their perspectives, analysed using specific theoretical frameworks. Wenger's (2018) theory is used to define social learning as a process in which meaning, individual belonging and identity are developed in a community through interaction and active participation. Resilience to the adversities of the asylum system are explored using Obrist et al.'s (2010) multi-layered social resilience framework, which provides a model for exploring interconnected social processes. The analysis is mainly influenced by the multi-layered framework, using its ideas on interactions at different societal levels to explore how the research participants might have built sustainable changes or transitions for themselves. Social and cultural capital development is explored through social learning to make one or more layers of social resilience. Those layers might be emotional, physical, psychological or financial. Therefore, resilience and learning are examined as related contextual (i.e. situated and temporal) social processes that impact individual identity and well-being. Wenger's (2018) framework of social learning and Wenger-Trayner and Wenger-Trayner's (2020) broader definition of social learning spaces are used to analyse the layered relations within and between intersectionality, social resilience, and social learning.

A visual and a digital story version is included for each of the three narratives, the aim being to ensure that both the participants and the collaborative nature of the research are represented so that those core aspects of the work remain centred. Having presented the analysis of each narrative, the chapter concludes by discussing the similarities and differences in the mothers' experiences.

Sarah's Story

> We feared our husbands who were fighting us, and now you've got to fear a system. What's the point?

Sarah was a single mother when we met. She had spent years living as an asylum seeker with her children before being granted 'Discretionary Leave to Remain'[1] as her immigration status on compassionate grounds. Sarah's transitions with marital and immigration status destroyed her independence, self-esteem, and support networks. She had to rebuild them all. Sarah had lived independently financially and as a mother for years before arriving in the UK. She had arrived in Wales on a spousal visa, with the right to work, but intimate partner violence left her in a precarious position as her right to be in the UK had been dependent on her abusive (ex-)spouse. She then moved through a cycle of asylum claims and appeals, denied the right to work at the same time as getting divorced and becoming a single mother. Sarah was granted leave to remain before our first interview but was not granted refugee status and five years' leave to remain. Instead, she was given two and a half years of discretionary leave to remain. She and her children now live with a short cycle of repeated claims – and associated costs – for leave to remain.

Family detention
Sarah began her story by recounting her experiences of intimate partner violence (domestic abuse). Her husband had been violent during their time in their home country. The situation worsened when they arrived in the UK, and Sarah found, by and for herself, British resources that gave her the terminology and the knowledge to describe what was happening to her and leave. However, leaving did not lead her to freedom from abuse and fear, as the quotation above

shows so clearly. It led her from abuse from her husband to the 'slow violence' (Mayblin et al., 2020; Saunders and Al-Om, 2022) of the UK's asylum system. It is from that point that Sarah's story is shared and explored.

Sarah described Image 6.1 as representing a type of detention centre, a psychological and symbolic one rather than a physical one. She stated that her sons are trapped, and there is only one way out. The people who can open that exit or who are 'capable of snapping the wire' are on the outside, not inside with her. It is in this aspect of the image, her not having the tools required to get out, that one can most clearly see Sarah's intersectional oppression as an 'absence of choices' (hooks, 2000: 5). Those on the outside do not understand.

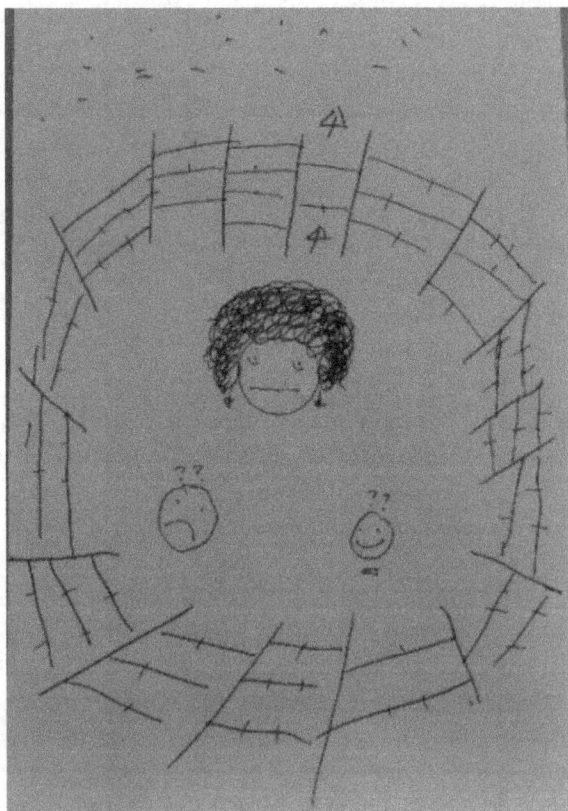

Image 6.1 – 'Family Detention'

Sarah said no one truly understood what she and her children were going through. Although she and her children have 'freedom' in their metaphorical enclosure, they are alone and want to leave, so it is a false freedom. She cannot leave the enclosure without getting 'cut' or hurt, but she wants to go out. She is also trapped, not truly knowing how her children feel or how they are coping because their outward expressions of emotion can change. Phillimore and Cheung (2021) discuss the 'violence of uncertainty', which goes beyond individual health and well-being for Sarah and her children. Those slow harms of uncertainty impact the family relationships and Sarah's understanding of her children's emotional needs (and her ability to meet those needs). Sarah even emphasised her coily hair to reflect her 'brain that is coily' as she's 'always thinking what to do'. She is trapped with the ongoing constant thoughts of her situation and her children but has no escape or relief from them as she has no control.

Sarah talked about the impacts of the situation in terms of learning, education, skills and self-esteem:

> What is happening to your experience? What is happening to your degree? It's getting older. What is happening to your confidence? It goes to the floor. And that is what happened to me. So, instead of being able to lift myself up, I went back to the floor, and I was just there.

Sarah had arrived in the UK as a highly educated, skilled and experienced professional. She had spent time working and caring for her eldest child alone while her husband worked or studied overseas. She was used to being 'quite an independent woman' and confident in caring for herself and her family. In Wales, she initially had some economic capital, with the right to work as a spouse to a migrant. She was forced to claim asylum when she fled from her husband, resulting in being stripped of her right to work and, therefore, her access to any economic capital.

Sarah's words in the extract above describe the impact of those dehumanising processes on her self-esteem. She has not unlearned anything. Her capabilities have not changed. Instead, she has been systematically denied the capacity to access or develop her capital and live a life rather than live in limbo. Sarah and her children spent years not just living in limbo and uncertainty but in a metaphorical cage, with her capacity to cope reduced by external factors (and not her skills and abilities).

Open prison

When meeting the researcher for the second time, Sarah had just been re-granted discretionary leave to remain, giving her family two and a half years of security. She had temporary relief from the slow violence and corrosion of uncertainty (Canning, 2020; Mayblin et al., 2020). She had also been in her job for a few months. Her second drawing represents those changes in her life.

Sarah's drawing (Image 6.2) shows a transition and a shift in her perspectives compared to communication through her first drawing. Sarah talked about the drawing, saying she had 'put on a bit of weight' and has folded her hands to show that she is more comfortable. Sarah explained that life has become 'quite a bit bearable'. It is significant that Sarah has not represented her children in this drawing, as it suggests that she can focus on herself, knowing her children are settled for a fixed period. Sarah's drawing shows the impacts of an increase in symbolic capital (Bourdieu, 1977, 2002) from her renewed leave to remain and economic capital from completing a probationary period in employment. One can also see the intertwined increased social and cultural capital (networks), with increased exits in the barbed wire to the outside world. Those exits are now bi-directional, and Sarah can see the grass and growth on the other side. She commented that 'maybe the job has contributed a lot', explaining that she has found work-based role models from whom she learns new skills and gets support as a colleague and a woman.

Sarah's life has reached this stage through her determination to resist the harm that the asylum system (and her ex-husband) inflicted on her. She talked through her learning experiences and directly linked them to her development of social resilience. Sarah had no choice but to pick herself off 'the floor' because, as she explained, she had two children depending on her. She started by going to community groups for mothers and children. It was in and through those spaces that Sarah learnt about short courses that were running and voluntary opportunities that might be available. These experiences were a lifeline for Sarah: 'All these little things, they start to lift your

Image 6.2 – 'Open Prison'

confidence over time. They start to build you up, lift your confidence'. In Sarah's narrative, one can see the communities that have enabled Sarah to participate and engage with others. She found a sense of belonging and, through that, could rebuild her sense of self (Wenger, 2018). Social learning has been vital for Sarah's well-being and resilience.

Eventually, through one of the community groups, Sarah was offered the opportunity to do a postgraduate qualification. The course required practitioner hours, and she carried out those hours as a volunteer in the same community groups she had once attended. She said: 'So you can see these things work. They don't; they need to give funding these little projects. They look little, but they are life savers for some people.' Those experiences preceded the researcher's relationship with Sarah but, during their second interview, she spoke a lot about them. Changes that had happened in Sarah's life could be seen through the combination of her words and her drawing. The value learning created was and is Sarah rebuilding herself, contributing to her community and going on to support others.

Resilient motherhood

Image 6.3 was taken during the Covid-19 pandemic and shows a snapshot of Sarah and her children's involvement in a digital community. The photograph shows Sarah and her children participating in a virtual church service. They were dressed in church clothes and focused on the service on the laptop screen. This photo also represents the duality of Sarah's narrative and the societal expectations she lives with. Sarah's journey in the asylum system is not over. She is now in a cycle of repeated claims for discretionary leave to remain every two and a half years. She needs resilience for herself and her children in the face of that ongoing stress, uncertainty, financial cost, and systemic harm. Sarah's narrative is 'about you as a woman and what you, the society, put you through' and her role as a mother. She told me, 'You have to make them responsible adults because it's my job to help these boys be what they can be.' Sarah carried the load of minimising

Image 6.3 – 'Lone and Digital Motherhood'

her children from harms caused by others, including the asylum system, plus the responsibility of ensuring her children grow up to be 'good refugees' or 'good citizens' (Gabriel and Harding, 2009). Yet, Sarah also explained that: 'My major motivation was the children. To encourage them to keep going. I didn't want them to see me sad and crying all the time, so I did all these other things.'

Motherhood was and is not simply a societal and biological duty for Sarah. When stripped of all other forms of identity, she retained her identity as a mother, which was her motivation. She took her children out to community groups, which helped her to rebuild herself and their lives and find some sanctuary in Wales. It was clear how important keeping busy was for the family. The present findings in this area reflect those from research with young people in Wales seeking asylum (Iqbal, 2016) and Morrice's (2007) earlier research with mothers in England. In an incremental, not always linear, process, she could start engaging in wider (albeit still limited) communities. Those communities included a church, a space where she gained support and a place of belonging for herself and her children.

That church community became so important to Sarah and her children's lives that they continued to join the community online during the Covid-19 pandemic. The importance of the family to Sarah is shown through her choice to send the researcher a photograph of them engaged in a virtual service. They joined from home, digitally, still presenting themselves in smart attire – showing the importance Sarah has placed on their cultural community and its role in helping her raise her boys to be 'what they can be' in Wales.

Irene's Story

Irene spoke very little English when she met the researcher, so she expressed herself fluently through her drawings. Her detailed pictures convey so much. This narrative will try to convey the overall message Irene was trying to communicate through each of them. She talked at length with the present writer but with the help of family members to translate (and some of the writer's limited knowledge of her 'first' language). Irene's perception of her lack of English linguistic skills was significant to her story – she spent more time with her drawing than with the interview dialogue, demonstrating the value of visual communication when language barriers exist. Irene's story is presented with an in-depth focus on her images, supported by her words, but not through equal representation. The aim is to represent best how she presented her narrative and generated data for the research.

One day at a time

Irene arrived in the UK with her family – husband and two children – and they were all quickly dispersed to Wales. Irene had had to leave behind a career she loved, and she spoke no English when she arrived. When she met with the researcher for the first time, Irene and her family had been living in Wales for a few months.

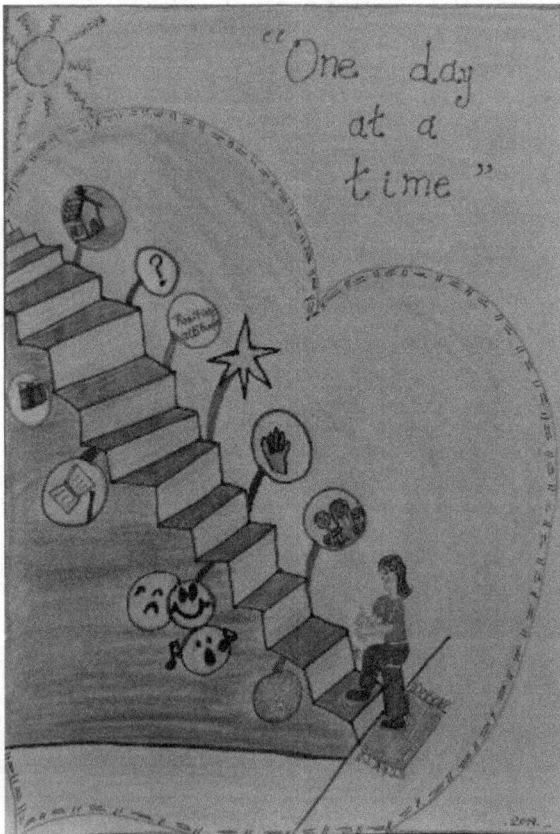

Image 6.4 – 'One Day at a Time'

Irene described Image 6.4 as representing the start of a new journey/chapter in her life. It is a drawing in which one can see the multiple layers of interactions that develop capital and build social resilience, as Obrist et al. (2010) defined. Fleeing to safety and arriving in Wales is not the end of her story; it is the beginning. Irene depicted a journey that is hers – not the same as her husband's and children's, even though they share critical parts. Irene's drawing reflects much positivity, but that is not how she initially felt in Wales. She said, 'when we arrived, I cried a lot'. At times, she found it hard to find the strength to cope with the situation of 'new customs, new rules, new speak, new all'. In those words, one can see how the forced transition to Wales has resulted in Irene's loss of cultural and social capital and her need to learn new norms and values (Lamba, 2003; Bourdieu, 2018).

Irene and her family had left behind everything they knew – their community, home, jobs/studies, everything. For Irene, the losses continued as she could not speak English when she arrived and could not offer her professional, educational skills in any context in Wales. In Irene's sense of loss, one sees her loss of identity, purpose, and belonging. Language was a key barrier for Irene.

Irene's family could participate more in life in Wales as they spoke more English. They had more quickly engaged in social learning and building new identities. Irene simultaneously felt both sad for herself and 'happy for family'. The latest lives she could see her husband and children experiencing helped her find a 'positive attitude' for herself, and she also had hope for a new start and future in their new country. Irene's drawing shows that while her journey is an individual one, she will also take each step with community support alongside her. That support is demonstrated by the image of her family (the four people), a hand (help), the globe (the international local community) and the yellow faces (activities in which she participates). Irene explained that her drawing includes support in social spaces and places where she could practise speaking English and finding information. She is alone on her journey, but there is support from people and learning (the book) along the way. In this way, one sees elements of a 'community of practice' (Wenger, 1998) in which Irene is an active participant and her new life and identity are being formed. The local community is alongside Irene on her journey, helping her with those steps. With her 'positive attitude' and belief, she will get to the top, taking 'one day at a time'.

Continue the process

When meeting for the second time, Irene had recently been granted Refugee Status, which was the conversation's key focus. She also went into detail about what she had been doing since the first interview. The effect of getting 'Leave to Remain' status is evident in Irene's second drawing. She explained that she is still on a journey with a long way to go, but she is no longer at the start of it. Irene depicted her journey's process in Image 6.5.

Again, Irene chose to depict her individual journey in Image 6.5; it is a journey on which she will need support, including ideas, from other people. Irene has now started along the journey, with some of it behind her, and the path is marked with concepts rather than social/community spaces this time. She also represented the growth in her life with the flowers to the bottom left of the image. This depiction of growth and life depicts a sense of sanctuary through new life in Wales. The details in her drawing show Irene's development in confidence and purpose; she is underway on her journey of citizenship, starting with the cultural aspects (O'Neill, 2018). The 'preparation' she does now and the people who support her will help bring new opportunities for her. One can also see that the nature of Irene's journey ahead and her reflections on the journey so far have changed; she is no longer facing an uphill journey with many steps and 'bumps'. Her life ahead and that journey will not be straightforward, as shown through the bends in the path. But, we can see that the path straightens towards the end, with arrows guiding the way.

Irene depicts herself as 'preparing' for her journey. She explained that the study and training described in her drawing refer to ESOL classes and perhaps re-skilling in a new profession or adapting her existing professional expertise. Irene is rebuilding her life and identity through social learning in a new community. Irene's drawing echoes much existing discourse on the value of paid work over unpaid labour (often carried out by women) and formal qualifications as a pathway to paid labour. Irene is already studying English and is a very active volunteer in her community. However, these activities are considered preparatory work, not end goals or achievements.

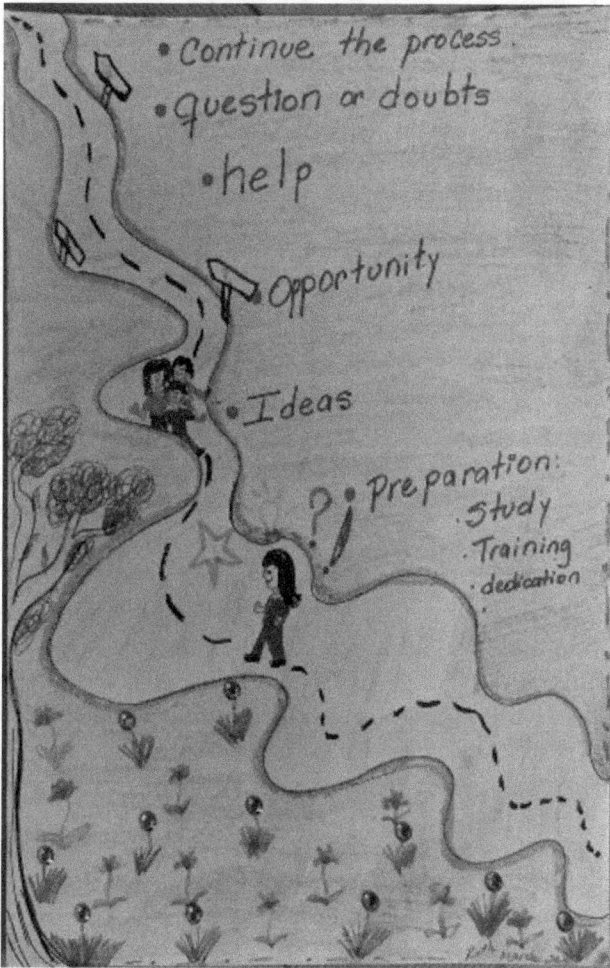

Image 6.5 – 'Continuing the Journey'

Through Irene, one sees a reflection in Wales of Morrice's (2007) argument that the importance of informal learning for building women refugees' social capital is undervalued, reflecting the continued lack of value given to much of women's unpaid labour in society. In Irene's second drawing, the viewer can see that she is walking towards something, but that final destination is not yet known – it is literally off the page. Irene's 'process' can be seen as the social learning process of community engagement and interaction through which

Irene is rebuilding her identity in a new home. She had stopped crying daily, and the whole family was 'showing, by fitting in, by helping and by continuing with life'. She had also found support 'to advance'. That process of social learning is one that should be recognised and valued more as a form of sanctuary provision in Wales.

Growing self-care

During the Covid-19 pandemic, in-person community activity stopped for prolonged periods. Irene sent her set of photographs during the first UK lockdown. In the explanations/descriptions accompanying her photographs, Irene explained that it had become vital to her to find other ways to keep busy and have a sense of purpose. So, she started gardening, growing plants such as strawberries, radishes and herbs; plants could be grown in window boxes indoors or in small garden pots. She also took the time to craft butterflies and other art objects. Irene sent several photographs of her engaging in these nurturing and creative activities, highlighting their significance as acts of self-care, including Image 6.6. The pandemic and the UK lockdowns plunged Irene's family into isolation (as it did for everyone). The Covid-19 pandemic lockdowns meant that Irene's direct engagement with the broader community ceased, so she had to focus on herself rather than social spaces and learning to maintain her mental and emotional well-being. Irene sent several photographs of her gardening and crafting activities with the words 'keeping busy during lockdown'. From the researcher's own earlier findings and research from scholars such as Iqbal (2016), it is known that keeping active and occupied is a core coping mechanism for asylum seekers and refugees. In community spaces, Irene had found ways to keep her mind busy, so she would not dwell on the past and the trauma of her losses. Irene's messages with her photographs explained that she had found new ways to cope during lockdowns by teaching herself new home-based gardening and crafting skills. It was significant that Irene chose to grow practical plants – food – and craft items associated with new life and beauty, such as butterflies, that could be used to decorate the home and garden. It seemed that she was keeping her hands and mind busy and creating a positive environment in a practical, nurturing and creative way, too.

Image 6.6 – 'Growing Self-Care'

Pam's story: 'I survive on people'

Pam had run a small business and lived with her husband and children until her husband was murdered for political reasons. Pam then needed to flee for her safety and arrived in Wales, both widowed and alone. She left her children with a relative, believing that to be both the safest and a temporary option for them all. She has spent over a decade living alone in Wales as an asylum seeker.

Surviving alone

When Pam met the researcher, she had lived in Wales for about a decade and was still in the asylum system without 'Leave to Remain' status. Pam had run her own small business in her country of origin, raising her children with her husband. She fled to the UK when her husband was murdered for political reasons. The Home Office took four years to process Pam's first claim and rejected it. Since then, she has been through legal processes for an appeal, exploring alternative options and a fresh claim. As Pam did not have 'Leave to Remain' status, she could not bring her children to join her, nor could she work in Wales to provide for them financially. One of her children has now been missing for several years. Pam talked to me about how she has coped with her traumas. Much of her focus was on the limbo and disconnections in her life and the impact on her emotionally and mentally. Her image of disembodied heads was a visual embodiment of life in Wales.

In Pam's first drawing (Image 6.7), shown overleaf, she represented three critical stages of her life in Wales. Those stages reflected her transition from arrival, being utterly alone and sad, to finding

Image 6.7 – 'Surviving Alone'

a means of survival through human interaction. She said, 'The first place I went to when I was new in this country was a church'. Pam's new religious community provided her with an initial social network. It taught her about options for everyday life as an asylum seeker with no capital in any form in Wales:

> Yes, yes, then I find those people in church. Then I talked to them; they will talk. Then they start telling me about, cos they ask do you have family here 'no'. 'Do you have this, do you have ...' They until we reached on that point. 'What do you do in the house on this month?' I said, 'Just sit, when it is Sunday, come'. Then they explained to me that there is a place where you can go and meet people and do this and this. I said, 'How do you do that?' They explained.

Pam explained that the church community was where she started learning about everyday life in Wales and places where she could meet other people. Pam had added: 'I started getting exposure with people. That's how I started.' The community church's role for Pam was supportive, providing her with the beginnings of some social networks and informal community and social learning. Pam's experiences support Morrice's (2007) and O'Neill and Hubbard's (2010) argument that informal learning in social spaces is significant. Pam's story shows how informal social learning moved her towards a sense of belonging, cultural and social citizenship or integration. Pam learned about volunteering opportunities and places where she could do short courses from that initial church community. Pam wants to work. Her interest in education and learning is a route to be seen as employable as soon as she gets (hopefully) the right to work. She talked about volunteering and courses in that context, saying:

> If I decided to do ... this course ... Then, volunteer, I want to ... I can't say ... is it skills, to improve skills ... I don't see which skills! But at least to get experience. And to interact with people. Because the more you interact with people, the more ideas and advices from different people. To meet friends because you don't know who gonna help you. Different...

that's why I told you I survive on people. [Ellipses are used in this extract to indicate a pause from Pam in her speech.]

Pam cannot always see which skills she might gain from short courses and volunteering, but she is clear about what she gains from human interaction. She makes friends in those spaces, learns from them and has developed a support network through them. In this way, one can see that Pam's participation in a community space and the engagement of others with her are social activities such as learning. This form of learning is also how Pam keeps herself mentally healthy by keeping her mind busy and demonstrating her contributions to Welsh society. There is a symbiotic role and mutual benefit for communities in informal learning. The community gains Pam's time and contributions as a volunteer, while Pam gains advice and vital support. Pam told me: 'I survive on people', something which has remained true for her beyond her early days – and years – in Wales. Her means of survival is also her means of community participation and contribution.

Persisting
In the second conversation, Pam talked more deeply about community support, particularly concerning her capacity to cope. She explained that while she may have no power or control over Home Office decisions, she can keep herself 'busy, busy, busy' and often 'busy from nine in the morning till ten at night'. Pam's busyness is through social interaction in community spaces of learning. In her second drawing, compared to the first, there is no longer an image of disembodiment but rather whole people in groups.

In her second drawing (Image 6.8), Pam represented the people surrounding her now – her support system that she had developed to survive. She represented her primary social communities – a support group, a church, and her friends from those places. She describes these communities as the people who 'make my life keep going'. That sense of survival through human support comes across strongly from this drawing, as it did with her first. Pam volunteers in several places, including at a local support/community group and her church. Those spaces are where Pam has built localised social capital and the strength to cope with the trauma and the challenges she continues to face. Pam's social networks provide her with spaces for learning and

Image 6.8 – 'Keep on Going'

practical and emotional support. She is trying to find sanctuary in a life of asylum limbo, separated from her children. Through her social networks, she has found a sense of solidarity and belonging that we see also discussed in Maggie O'Neill's work (2018a).

Pam's words show a shared experience with other participants, such as Irene. The communities that support Pam sometimes give financial support or help with clothes or food. But, for Pam, the support most vital for her comes in less tangible ways:

So sometime people from the church there is like, um, I think it's like an organisation … Sometime after, like two weeks, they give you £30. They help other people like that. So that's the life we are living in. But we have to socialise with people. You can't use the rate for yourself because of your status. But most people when they get such a refusals, they get really down. Some of them they go through the, I don't know, the depression or whatever. Because they put them to the wall, they don't know what to do. But I'm always telling them: I say, that is not the end of the world. Because if it was, maybe we should have been removed a long time ago. But there is a reason, because I'm always telling, we are not criminals, we are not doing anything so … we just go and socialise with people and do what you can do.

Pam had been talking about the ban on working for asylum seekers just before the above excerpt. So, she described that sometimes she can get small amounts of money from the church as a gesture of help and kindness but not as payment for work. However, she continued to talk about the impact of being refused asylum, and that 'most people when they get such a refusals, they get really down … the depression or whatever'. Pam explained that she has avoided severe depression through her interactions in community learning. Once again, Irene and Sarah shared an experience about the role that learning plays in mental health. Pam and other participants discussed the discourse of criminalisation of asylum seekers and how vital learning is for mental health in the context of the 'hostile environment' created and weaponised by the Home Office (Webber, 2019).

Continuing alone

The asylum system has, I argue, held Pam hostage for over a decade. She has been kept apart from her children by immigration rules, she has been excluded from full participation in society by asylum regulations, and she lives with the burden of having to prove her worth with limited agency to do so. Although Pam is not lonely anymore and shows she has people to help in her drawing 'Keep on Going' (Image 6.8), she is ultimately still alone with a life on hold or in limbo, as shown in 'Still Alone' (Image 6.9).

Pam sent several photographs during the first UK Covid-19 lockdown and Image 6.9 is arguably the one that best represented

Pam's situation. In the photograph, Pam sits alone outside the building of one of the first communities she joined. Pam was alone in all
the pictures she sent. She drew herself surrounded by others, but
the snapshots of her life on camera were of a woman alone. Pam has
built herself a support network, but in so many ways, she is still just
as alone as she was when she first arrived. Overall, Pam's drawings,
words and photographs reflect just how limited her development of
social capital has been beyond a source of survival.

Pam's narrative shows us that there might be much community and civil society support for sanctuary seekers in Wales, but that

Image 6.9 – 'Still Alone'

support has limitations. Pam has not built significant social networks beyond very localised community spaces. She does not have support from or in networks with direct political or legal power or influence. There is a Welsh Government Nation of Sanctuary plan (2019), and numerous civil society organisations are working towards that goal. Local community spaces available for Pam have been a lifeline for her. Yet, the development of social and cultural capital beyond the refugee support community is just as limited for Pam in Wales as it is for sanctuary seekers in England/at the UK level (Zetter et al., 2005; Cheung and Phillimore, 2017) and other Global North countries (Lamba, 2003; Kindler et al., 2015).

Pam's life has been on hold for a decade while life around her, she feels, continues. Pam's children have now grown up, and one is missing. They may never be reunited. Her motherhood is primarily invisible in Wales as few people around her know the extent of her circumstances – many do not even know she is a mother. Pam told me she feels too old to pursue a nursing career, which she considered when she first arrived. She now wonders how she will support herself as she grows old, deprived of the ability to prepare for that stage of life. Pam's life in isolated limbo is represented so well by photographs of her alone yet in her local spaces of social networks.

Her experiences support the findings of other researchers on the gendered harm isolation caused by the isolation and uncertainty of the asylum system (Canning, 2020; Phillimore and Cheung, 2021). A decade after Pam's arrival in the UK, her church community, refugee support group, and the places she volunteers remain Pam's primary sources of social support. Not much has changed since her early months in Wales. Furthermore, Pam is alone in many ways, as shown in the photograph. Yet, the backdrop of the picture, her church, reflects how much Pam relies on those communities for support – to keep alive that glimmer of hope that she will, 'maybe one day', start living, and not just surviving.

Discussion and Conclusion

This chapter has presented an interpretation of narratives from three women whose experiences are connected only by immigration status and motherhood. It has shown that social learning must be recognised for Wales to become a Nation of Sanctuary. Sarah, Irene and Pam all experienced exclusion from work or formal education, which added to their trauma. Yet, they all also rebuilt their lives and supported their mental health through social learning. Building a sense of personal identity through active participation that benefits one or more communities is a process of social learning and sanctuary building. That process came through formal education, Sarah's university course and Irene's ESOL classes, community learning, Sarah's social groups for mothers, Pam's church and community groups, and Irene and Pam's voluntary work. The presenting of Sarah, Irene and Pam's stories has highlighted some significant ways in which learning is a social phenomenon that can either hinder or help the development of individual social resilience and ensure communities in Wales become genuine places of sanctuary.

The analysis found that the women's learning experiences were wide and varied. Formal education through educational institutions or classes for qualifications had played a significant role for Sarah, with a lesser role for Irene and very little for Pam. Formal education, at different levels, was seen by the women as a route to a career and building a secure future. Still, entry criteria and class/course availability were the critical barriers for them, alongside childcare needs in Sarah's case.

Sarah, Irene and Pam's learning experiences differed, but their mental health and well-being and a sense of belonging were common themes throughout their narratives, along with the data generated with mothers in the writer's research. In Sarah, Irene and Pam's experiences of community spaces, it was found that supportive, perhaps empowering, social learning was taking place. For example, it was through community social learning that Sarah could build social resilience to enrol in a postgraduate course in a field that had been new to her. Through those spaces, she was able to build social resilience and find employment. Pam, for example, built a social network that was her source of survival. Social learning could most clearly be seen as a social process of community engagement and participation (Wenger, 2018).

The women valued their social networks as lifelines. The size of those networks was not as significant as those networks' role. It was found that the women were learning in social spaces – in communities of practice. Social learning supported and enabled transitions, and the women developed social resilience through the process. Sarah lifted her self-confidence back off the floor through her social learning spaces, which included short courses and the support and encouragement of others. Irene has been developing her English skills, a sense of purpose, and a new identity through her social learning spaces and volunteering. She turned to crafting and learning in the natural environment during the isolation of lockdown. Pam has found a support system for people to help her survive and keep herself well mentally, maintaining those connections through worship and volunteering during lockdowns. Through and in those social learning spaces, all three women have found, built and solidified social and well-being support.

All three women have faced challenges and hardships since they arrived in Wales, including the denial of fundamental human rights, intimate partner violence, long-term separation from children, a loss of identity and self, and the loss of a previous life. They have faced obstacles and barriers to building their forms of capital, including legal restrictions on fundamental rights, exclusionary eligibility criteria for courses, exclusionary educational spaces for mothers with infants/very young children, and lack of recognition of pre-existing skills and experience. Those obstacles come from socio-legal misrecognition as part of a hostile and coercive system that harms mothers and children (Shobiye and Parker, 2023).

Yet, through community (and education) social learning spaces, they have developed social resilience to the harms they face. Recognition of the importance of social learning spaces in Wales is still needed. The process of social learning and the spaces in which that happens creates a support system for asylum seekers and refugees, one that is arguably particularly important for women and mothers who are often more isolated than their male counterparts. That support is a form of sanctuary, as shown in Sarah, Irene and Pam's stories. We can see that sense of sanctuary in rebuilding identities, creating a sense of belonging and active socio-cultural contributions in communities. Social learning does not negate the coercive harms of the UK's immigration and asylum systems, but it does provide a means of support for coping with those harms. Given its significance and its role in providing sanctuary, social learning could help make Wales a Nation of Sanctuary.

Notes

1   'Leave to Remain' is the term used when permission to stay and reside in the UK is granted by the Home Office. The duration granted depended on the accompanying status/the reason given, but the maximum period was five years for refugee status at the time of writing.

Bibliography

Bhattacharyya, Gargi. 2018. *Rethinking Racial Capitalism: Questions of Reproduction and Survival*. London: Rowman and Littlefield International.

Bourdieu, P. 1977. 'Cultural Reproduction and Social Reproduction'. In D. Grusky and S. Szelényi (eds), *Power and ideology in education*. New York: Oxford University Press, pp. 487–511.

Bourdieu, P. 2002. 'The Forms of Capital'. In N. Woolsey Biggary (ed.), *Readings in economic sociology*. Chichester: John Wiley and Sons Ltd, pp. 280–91.

Canning, V. 2020. 'Corrosive Control: State-Corporate and Gendered Harm in Bordered Britain'. *Critical Criminology*, 28/2, 259–75.

Cheung, S. Y. and Phillimore, J. 2017. 'Gender and Refugee Integration: A Quantitative Analysis of Integration and Social Policy Outcomes'. *Journal of Social Policy*, 46/2, 211–30.

Chick, M. and Hannagan-Lewis, I. 2019. 'Language Education for Forced Migrants: Governance and Approach'. *Languages*, 4/3, 74.

Gobo, G. and Marciniak, L. T. 2016. 'What is Ethnography'. In D. Silverman (ed.), *Qualitative Research*, 4th edn. London, Thousand Oaks and New Delhi: Sage, pp. 103–20.

Hammersley, M. 2018. 'What is ethnography? Can it survive? Should it?'. *Ethnography and Education*, 13/1, 1–17.

Higham, G. 2014. 'Teaching Welsh to ESOL Students: issues of intercultural citizenship'. In D. Mallows (ed.), *British Council Innovation Series: Language and Integration*. London: British Council,, pp. 111–22.

Higham, Gwennan. 2020. *Creu Dinasyddiaeth i Gymru: Mewnfudo Rhyngwladol a'r Gymraeg*. Cardiff: University of Wales Press.

Higham, G. 2025. 'International Migration and the Welsh Language: Exploring an Interdisciplinary Framework for Linguistic Integration'. In C. W. Edwards, L. Shobiye and Rh. Dafydd Jones (eds), *A Welcoming Nation? Intersectional Approaches to Migration and Diversity in Wales*. Cardiff: University of Wales Press.

Holtom, Duncan and Iqbal, Hibah. 2020. *Refugee Employment and Skills Support Study*. Cardiff: Welsh Government.

hooks, bell. 2000. *Feminist Theory: From Margin to Center*, 2nd edn. London: Pluto Press.

Iqbal, H. 2016. 'Precarious Journeys: Exploring the Stories of Young People Seeking Asylum'. Unpublished PhD thesis, Cardiff University.

Kindler, M., with Ratcheva, V. and Piechowska, M. 2015. 'Social networks, social capital and migrant integration at local level European literature review'. IRiS Working Paper Series No. 6/2015. Birmingham: Institute for Research into Superdiversity, University of Birmingham.

Lamba, N. K. 2003. 'The Employment Experiences of Canadian Refugees: Measuring the Impact of Human and Social Capital on Quality of Employment'. *Canadian Review of Sociology/Revue canadienne de sociologie*, 40/1, 45–64.

Mayblin, L., Wake, M. and Kazemi, M. 2020. 'Necropolitics and the Slow Violence of the Everyday: Asylum Seeker Welfare in the Postcolonial Present'. *Sociology*, 54/1, 107–23.

Morrice, L. 2007. 'Lifelong learning and the social integration of refugees in the UK: The significance of social capital'. *International Journal of Lifelong Education*, 26/2, 155–72.

Mueller, R. A. 2019. 'Episodic Narrative Interview: Capturing Stories of Experience With a Methods Fusion'. *International Journal of Qualitative Methods*, 18, 160940691986604.

Neale, B. 2017. 'Generating Data in Qualitative Longitudinal Research: A methodological review'. Timescapes Working Paper Series, 8, University of Leeds.

Obrist, B., Pfeiffer, C. and Henley, R. 2010. 'Multi-layered social resilience: a new approach in mitigation research'. *Progress in Development Studies*, 10/4, 283–93.

O'Neill, M. 2018. 'Walking, well-being and community: racialized mothers building cultural citizenship using participatory arts and participatory action research'. *Ethnic and Racial Studies*, 41/1, 73–97.

O'Neill, M. and Hubbard, P. 2010. 'Walking, sensing, belonging: Ethno-mimesis as performative praxis'. *Visual Studies*, 25/1, 46–58.

Phillimore, J. and Cheung, S. Y. 2021. 'The violence of uncertainty: Empirical evidence on how asylum waiting time undermines refugee health'. *Social Science & Medicine*, 282/June, 114–54.

Saunders, N. and Al-Om, T. 2022. 'Slow Resistance: Resisting the Slow Violence of Asylum'. *Millennium: Journal of International Studies*, 50/2, 1–23.

Shobiye, L. 2023. '"I survive on people": (Mis)recognising the value of social learning for mothers seeking sanctuary in Wales'. Unpublished PhD thesis, Cardiff University.

Shobiye, L. and Parker, S. 2023. 'Narratives of coercive precarity experienced by mothers seeking asylum in the UK (Wales)'. *Ethnic and Racial Studies*, 46/2, 358–77.

Webber, F. 2019. 'On the creation of the UK's "hostile environment"'. *Race and Class*, 60/4, 76–87.

Wenger, E. 2018. 'A social theory of learning'. In K. Illeris (ed.), *Contemporary theories of learning: learning theorists in their own words*, 2nd edn. London: Routledge, pp. 219–28.

Wenger-Trayner, Etienne and Wenger-Trayner, Beverly. 2020. *Learning to make a difference: Value creation in social learning spaces*. Cambridge: Cambridge University Press.

Zetter, R., Griffiths, D. and Sigona, N. 2005. 'Social capital or social exclusion? The impact of asylum-seeker dispersal on UK refugee community organizations'. *Community Development Journal*, 40/2, 169–81.

CHAPTER 7

EU Migrants in Wales: Still Welcome?

Stephen Drinkwater, Taulant Guma,
Bryonny Goodwin-Hawkins and Rhys Dafydd Jones

Introduction

The summer of 2016 evokes two photographs. The first is the well-known UKIP campaign poster during the European Union (EU) membership referendum. Entitled 'Breaking Point', it showed 'mostly non-white migrants and refugees' (Stewart and Mason, 2016) crossing into the EU at the Croatia–Slovenia border. The imagery drew on and reproduced threats associated with race, religion and hypermasculinity, ignoring the reasons that people fleeing conflict in Syria and Iraq were seeking sanctuary in the summer of 2015 (and overlooking the fact that the UK was not party to the Common Asylum Policy). The second photograph is of a young woman in a Wales football shirt holding the EU flag at the Northern Ireland versus Wales match in the 'Last 16' round of the 2016 UEFA Men's European Championships. This was the first time since 1958 that Wales had qualified for a major football tournament, and, in addition to the on-field excitement of reaching the semi-finals, was also seen as part nation-building project; the Welsh team would be exposed to millions of viewers as representing a nation in its own right, and praise given to the Football Association of Wales's bilingual practices. These ends followed a long geopolitical history of positioning Wales within Europe as a small, modern European nation. The match took place on Saturday, 25 June, two days after a small majority of the Welsh electorate (similar to the UK as a whole) voted to leave the EU.

The juxtaposition of the Welsh team's success in Europe with the referendum result in Wales creates discomfort for proponents of Wales as an inclusive European nation. While it is not suggested that all those who supported leaving the EU did so for xenophobic or racist reasons, it is noted that the referendum campaign, exemplified by the UKIP poster, drew on and reproduced xenophobia and racism (Stewart and Mason, 2016). The sharp growth in reported hate crime during and after the campaign period, peaking the week after the referendum, is well documented. As has been discussed elsewhere (Guma and Dafydd Jones, 2019), many EU citizens in Wales felt that they were no longer welcomed or wanted, often challenging a previously fostered sense of belonging. In some instances, these feelings were very personal, affecting a sense of self. Others experienced uncertainty around what rights they would have after the UK's eventual withdrawal from the EU, and considered whether they should move elsewhere.

This chapter draws on Engbersen and Snel's (2013) notion of 'liquid migration' to understand empirical examinations of the nature of EU citizens' migration to Wales. Quantitative (mainly Census) data is used to undertake a statistical analysis and document how the number and origin of international migrants living in Wales has evolved over recent decades. Migration following the EU enlargements between 2004 and 2011 has been a key factor in the changing picture of Wales's non-UK born population. This mainly involved migration from the eight central and eastern European states that joined the EU in May 2004 (collectively known as the A8 or EU8 group of countries). Relatively high levels of immigration occurred partly because there were few restrictions on migration from the EU8 to the UK immediately following the accession, whereas most other existing EU member states had imposed transitional arrangements to limit EU8 migration flows. It was estimated that more than 1 million EU8 migrant workers moved to the UK between May 2004 and June 2010 (McCollum and Findlay, 2011), marking the first substantial peak in migration from the EU, with the second peak being triggered between 2013 and 2015 by migration once restrictions on Romanian and Bulgarian citizens' right to work were lifted (Cuibus, 2023).

This study also focuses on certain social aspects of migration, especially those relating to migrants who arrived in Wales from the

EU8 following the 2004 enlargement. Political issues and changes that have helped shape patterns of migration to and from Wales, as well as public attitudes towards migrants who have settled in Wales, are central to the discussions. Most notably, the decision that the Welsh/UK electorate took to leave the EU in June 2016 is emphasised. The legal and social changes affecting EU migrants who had been resident in Wales during the referendum led many migrants to question whether they were (still) welcomed and if they wanted to remain in Wales or to return to their home countries or move elsewhere in the EU. To recount the ways in which EU citizens in Wales have experienced the 2016 referendum campaign, its aftermath, and the run-up to the UK's withdrawal from the EU in January 2020, discussion draws on qualitative datasets from two projects: a work package of the ESRC WISERD Civil Society research centre,[1] and parts of the Welsh case study of a work package for the Horizon2020 IMAJINE project.[2]

The WISERD data involved twenty-five interviews from eighteen organisations, as part of a broader project exploring EU citizens' engagement with civil society in Wales. Interviews were conducted between February 2016 and October 2018, and across Wales. Most respondents were from Poland, Czechia, Slovakia, Hungary and Latvia; due to similarities encountered during fieldwork, including shared respondents, Portuguese respondents (including some born in former Portuguese colonies) were also included. The IMAJINE interviews were conducted between February and September 2019 as part of a study on migration to economically peripheral regions. The case study used here focused on the experiences of German nationals in Ceredigion and Romanian nationals in Swansea (including one Hungarian-speaking Romanian-born respondent who had taken Hungarian citizenship), but other parts of the study also included Danish, Estonian and Irish citizens (as long-term residents or in-migrants). 'European citizen' is taken as a broad definition, as some may have arrived in the UK before the state of their citizenship (e.g., Poland and Romania) joined the EU; some had also acquired British citizenship alongside their initial citizenship; some also had been raised outside the EU, such as Portuguese citizens from former Portuguese colonies in Africa. These attest to the diversity of lived experiences and citizenship.

Liquid Migration and European Citizenship

Bauman (2000) characterised late capitalism as having a liquid condition: a free-flowing, dynamic form that can be difficult to contain and predict. Engbersen and Snell (2013) developed this ontology to understand contemporary migration that is beyond the linear 'A–B (and staying)' movement that has characterised traditional accounts of migration. Liquid migration accounts for return and circular migration, as well as a hypermobility enabled by low-cost air travel, underpinned by international agreements. Liquidity is an appropriate analogy for migration: it can flow at different rates, and different filters in the form of state migration regimes will allow some (deemed 'desirable' or 'legitimate') through, while attempting to block others. Liquidity is also a suitable concept to understand international migration within EU member states, from one member state to another.

Against this fluid backdrop, migration scholars have developed the notion of 'anchoring': a suitable metaphor for establishing some stability among turbulence and the potential for rapid flows (Grzymala-Kazlowska, 2018). Meeting a partner, raising children, getting to know neighbours, developing a career in a collegial workplace, joining sports clubs, as well as volunteering are all examples of anchoring activities that can contribute to a sense of attachment or belonging to place, although the latter notion may also depend on external validation and recognition.

The 1992 Maastricht Treaty, which saw the European Community (EC) evolve into the EU, not only facilitated liquid migration through freedom of movement (alongside other developments, such as the Open Skies agreement, the ending of many state monopolies on public services and major industries, and the end of the Cold War), but also ideas of citizenship. At the same time, increasing numbers of resident non-citizens led to new approaches to citizenship in the late 1980s and 1990s. Brubaker (1989, 1990), drawing on Turkish Gastarbeiter living in (West) Germany, advanced the notion of 'denizenship' to describe an additional rights tier, whereby non-citizen residents have some rights but not the full entitlement of citizenship; for EU citizens, this may include the right to vote in some elections. Soysal (1994) goes further, arguing that global bodies and international agreements had moved to provide rights based on human subjectivity rather than membership of national (state) communities, which she termed 'post-national citizenship'. Soysal argued that EU citizenship falls in this category. As a transnational form of governance, EU citizenship works by placing a 'thin layer of additional rights on top of a thicker national citizenship' (Bauböck, 2000: 310). As demonstrated in the present chapter, the vulnerability of this 'thin layer' of EU citizenship has been particularly exposed in the context of ongoing political changes exacerbated by the Brexit vote.[3]

In the UK context, EU membership afforded member states' citizens particular privileges. They were allowed to move to another state to find a job within three months, the 'free movement of labour', a central reciprocal EU treaty right. They were also granted many of the same rights as citizens ordinarily resident in another state, such as access to benefits and higher education fees at rates for local residents. EU citizens have thus often been characterised as 'privileged' or 'invisible' migrants, who were not typically subject to the same state controls of migrants from outside the EU.[4] There is now a well-established literature which has shown how these rights and privileges are questioned in practice (Guma, 2020) and how EU migrants are also subject to hostility, stigmatisation and racialisation by British media and political discourses (Burrell, 2010; Fox et al., 2012; Rzepnikowska, 2019). Much of this hostility has been directed mainly to 'East Europeans' and has pre-dated Brexit, although, as shown below, these negative experiences are now affecting a wider range of EU citizens, including groups such as those from northern and western Europe who had not been targeted previously.

Migration from EU Countries to Wales

Migration to (what is now) Wales from within Europe of course pre-dates (and is not restricted to) the EU. Historically, prehistoric people, the Celts, Romans, Vikings and Normans all came from mainland Europe, as well as migration from Ireland (settling the kingdom of Brycheiniog) and within the British Isles. More recently, migration to the industrial areas of Wales from Ireland, Italy and Spain are well documented (Evans, 2003). During the First World War, refugees from Belgium took sanctuary in Wales, and *Y Gadair*

Ddu ('The Black Chair'), the bardic chair won posthumously by Hedd Wyn in 1917, was crafted by a Belgian refugee. Some 1,800 Irish republicans involved in the Easter Rising, including Michael Collins, were imprisoned in Frongoch, Meirionydd in 1916. Forced migration also continued in the run-up to and during the Second World War, with numerous accounts of people seeking sanctuary from Nazism arriving in Wales (Hammel, 2022), while Italian and German prisoners of war were incarcerated in camps in Llandysul and Bridgend.

European migration after the war was characterised by those from eastern Europe who decided to stay in the UK as the region fell to communism. This included Polish immigrants who settled in localities such as Lampeter, Rhosllanerchrugog and Penrhos (Gwynedd). The UK's accession to the EC in 1973 saw some further migration from the EC to UK but the numbers were low, 'averaging 7,000 per year across the UK' (WJEC, 2023: 4). Generally, in the post-war period it is immigration from outside Europe and especially Commonwealth countries which has been a significant development both in statistical terms as well as with regard to policy changes, rather than migration from Europe.

The 2004 expansion of the EU brought a significant change to the European immigration landscape. Much of this recent migration has been driven by migration from post-socialist countries in central and eastern Europe (Czechia, Estonia, Hungary, Latvia, Lithuania, Poland, Slovakia and Slovenia). Only the UK, Ireland and Sweden essentially allowed these countries' citizens to enjoy the same freedom of movement as other EU citizens.

The following analysis is based on examining different years of Census of Population data, especially information taken from the most recent 2021 Census.[5] These data have been supplemented with information from other sources such as the Annual Population Survey (APS), European Union Settlement Scheme (EUSS), and applications collected by the Home Office and the Department of Work and Pensions' database on new National Insurance numbers (NINo) issued to overseas nationals.

Table 7.1 reports the population of Wales according to country of birth for the 2001, 2011 and 2021 Censuses. It splits UK-born residents according to their nation of birth as well as identifying non

Table 7.1: Population in Wales by Country of Birth: 2001–21.

	2001		2011		2021	
	Number	%	Number	%	Number	%
Wales	2,188,754	75.39	2,226,005	72.66	2,202,820	70.89
England	589,828	20.32	636,266	20.77	659,084	21.21
Scotland	24,389	0.84	24,346	0.79	21,975	0.71
Northern Ireland	7,851	0.27	8,253	0.27	7,803	0.25
UK (Not Specified)	772	0.03	715	0.02	383	0.01
EU14	34,355	1.18	38,518	1.26	41,588	1.34
Other Europe	7,324	0.25	34,934	1.14	58,554	1.88
Africa	10,722	0.37	22,006	0.72	28,760	0.93
Asia	27,304	0.94	57,929	1.89	69,328	2.23
The Americas	7,656	0.26	10,310	0.34	12,631	0.41
Oceania and Antarctica	4,130	0.14	4,174	0.14	4,573	0.15
Total residents	2,903,085	100.00	3,063,456	100.00	3,107,499	100.00

Source: Census of the Population.

UK-born residents by their continent of birth. People born in Europe have been split into those born in countries that were EU members before 2004 (the EU14) and an 'Other Europe' category. The first thing to note from the table is that the percentage of non UK-born residents in Wales rose from 3.2 per cent in 2001 to 5.5 per cent in 2011 and 6.9 per cent in 2021. The increase was evenly split between people born in European and non-European countries: the percentage born in the former rose from 1.4 per cent in 2001 to 3.2 per cent in 2021, whilst the equivalent change for the latter group was from 1.7 per cent to 3.7 per cent. The biggest increases in the non UK-born population were observed for Other European (1.63 percentage points) and Asian countries (1.29 percentage points). In terms of residents born in the UK, there was a small increase in the English-born from 20.2 per cent in 2001 to 20.8 per cent in 2011 and 21.2 per cent in 2021, whilst the percentage of Welsh-born residents fell from by 4.5 percentage points between 2001 and 2021.

Table 7.2 presents information on the twenty countries from outside the UK with the highest populations in Wales in 2021. For each country, a country grouping is also reported: that is, whether the country belongs to the EU2 (Bulgaria and Romania), EU8, EU14 or non-EU. The are no countries from the Other EU grouping reported in the table. The greatest number of migrants were born in Poland, with almost 25,000 Welsh residents in March 2021 indicating that they were Polish-born. This was over 10 per cent of Wales's non-UK born population in this year. The other countries

Table 7.2: Countries of Birth with Highest Number of Residents in Wales: 2021.

	Country Grouping	Number of Residents	% of All Non-UK Born
Poland	EU8	24,832	11.53
India	Non-EU	13,399	6.22
Germany	EU14	11,114	5.16
Ireland	EU14	9,998	4.64
Romania	EU2	8,520	3.95
Pakistan	Non-EU	7,103	3.30
Bangladesh	Non-EU	6,752	3.13
China	Non-EU	6,304	2.93
South Africa	Non-EU	5,733	2.66
Philippines	Non-EU	5,542	2.57
Italy	EU14	4,650	2.16
United States	Non-EU	4,625	2.15
Nigeria	Non-EU	3,891	1.81
Hong Kong	Non-EU	3,715	1.72
Portugal	EU14	3,664	1.70
Iraq	Non-EU	3,164	1.47
Spain	EU14	3,068	1.42
Australia	Non-EU	3,008	1.40
Turkey	Non-EU	2,886	1.34
Zimbabwe	Non-EU	2,801	1.30

Source: Census of the Population.

making up the top five in terms of birthplaces were India, Germany,[6] Ireland and Romania. The Census figures for some countries such as Romania and Poland are relatively low compared to the number of registrants on the EUSS. For example, according to Home Office statistics there were 27,130 and 12,660 respective EUSS registrations from Polish and Romanian nationals from the scheme opening in August 2018 to the end of March 2021. This compared to 24,832 and 8,532 people born in these countries recorded in the 2021 Census respectively.[7] This suggests substantial amounts of short-term and return migration from these countries to the UK, including to Wales (Drinkwater and Garapich, 2015; Knight et al., 2017; Andrén and Roman, 2016), supporting the liquid migration thesis.[8]

Statistics on the distribution of the migrant population across the twenty-two Welsh Unitary Authorities (UAs) in 2021 can be found in Table 7.3. It shows that the UAs with the highest percentage of non UK-born residents are the three city-based regions in southern Wales: Cardiff (16.5 per cent), Newport (12.2 per cent) and Swansea (9.4 per cent). This percentage was lowest in Caerphilly (2.9 per cent) and Blaenau Gwent (3.2 per cent) in the southern valleys, followed by the Isle of Anglesey (3.3 per cent). Similarly, the percentage of residents born in non-EU countries was relatively high in Cardiff (11.7 per cent), Newport (7.2 per cent) and Swansea (6.0 per cent). This is to some extent due to the presence of overseas students: according to the 2021 Census there were around 6,700 non-European born full-time students aged 16 and over in Cardiff, and over 2,000 in Swansea, compared to just over 600 in Newport. In contrast, migration from EU countries was relatively more important in other UAs. For example, in Flintshire, EU-born migrants accounted for 4.5 per cent of the population compared to 2 per cent from non-EU countries. Similar patterns were also observed in Merthyr Tydfil (3.6 per cent from EU and 2 per cent from non-EU countries) and Wrexham (5.0 per cent from EU and 2.2 per cent from non-EU countries). The percentage of residents born in EU14 countries was highest in Cardiff (2.6 per cent), for EU8 countries in Wrexham (2.8 per cent) and for EU2 countries in Flintshire (1.1 per cent).

Table 7.3: Distribution of Residents Across Welsh Unitary Authorities by Countries of Birth: 2021.

	% UK Born	% EU14 Born	% EU8 Born	% EU2 Born	% Other EU Born	% Non-EU Born	Total Residents
Blaenau Gwent	96.79	0.55	1.07	0.19	0.04	1.36	66,906
Bridgend	95.70	0.92	0.83	0.26	0.09	2.21	145,488
Caerphilly	97.06	0.76	0.52	0.14	0.06	1.45	175,950
Cardiff	83.48	2.61	1.52	0.55	0.15	11.68	362,309
Carmarthenshire	94.94	1.02	1.44	0.26	0.06	2.28	187,900
Ceredigion	92.94	1.55	1.61	0.30	0.09	3.50	71,476
Conwy	94.82	1.53	0.68	0.23	0.07	2.66	114,741
Denbighshire	95.29	1.09	0.58	0.20	0.06	2.79	95,820
Flintshire	93.54	1.23	2.08	1.10	0.09	1.96	154,963
Gwynedd	94.58	1.21	0.70	0.33	0.06	3.12	117,393
Isle of Anglesey	96.67	1.21	0.24	0.11	0.08	1.68	68,878
Merthyr Tydfil	94.42	0.95	2.18	0.43	0.04	1.97	58,839
Monmouthshire	94.50	1.42	0.58	0.22	0.09	3.18	92,954

	% UK Born	% EU14 Born	% EU8 Born	% EU2 Born	% Other EU Born	% Non-EU Born	Total Residents
Neath Port Talbot	96.36	0.82	0.44	0.24	0.06	2.08	142,292
Newport	87.84	1.50	2.53	0.82	0.10	7.20	159,583
Pembrokeshire	95.18	1.57	0.54	0.22	0.12	2.36	123,356
Powys	95.15	1.17	0.83	0.30	0.07	2.48	133,171
Rhondda Cynon Taff	96.26	0.80	0.53	0.16	0.09	2.17	237,649
Swansea	90.58	1.48	1.29	0.54	0.08	6.03	238,487
Torfaen	96.43	0.84	0.52	0.12	0.05	2.04	92,284
Vale of Glamorgan	94.22	1.58	0.43	0.15	0.15	3.47	131,940
Wrexham	92.13	1.39	2.82	0.75	0.08	2.83	135,113
Wales	93.07	1.34	1.13	0.38	0.09	3.99	3,107,492

Source: Census of the Population.

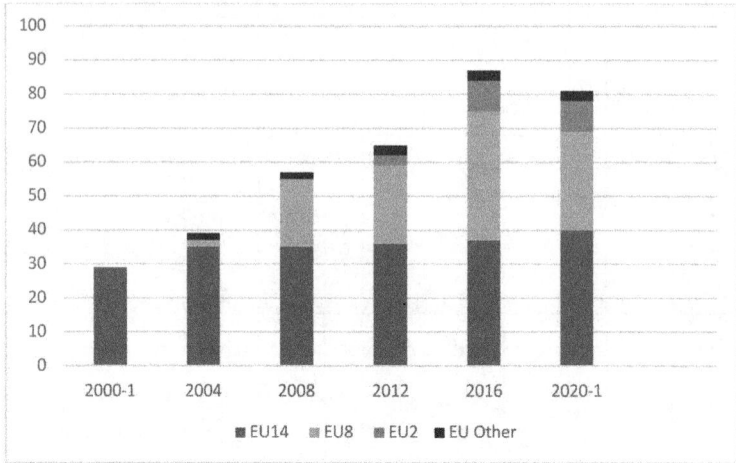

Figure 7.1: Estimated Population of Wales Born in EU Countries: 2000–1 to 2020–1. Source: Annual Population Survey.

Figure 7.1 shows the estimated EU-born population in Wales from 2000/1 to 2020/1. These data have been taken from the APS. This is a regular survey that provides frequent estimates of demographic and labour market trends across the UK. However, given that the survey is based on a sample of the population, estimates for some sub-groups may be imprecise.[9] This is because of issues such as sample non-response and attrition, although relevant weights are attached to the data so that they reflect the size and composition of the general population (ONS, 2012). Nevertheless, the general patterns indicated by APS and Census data are similar. For example, Figure 7.1 shows the large increase between 2004 and 2016 in Welsh residents who were born in the EU8, as well as the growth in the EU2-born population after 2012. NINo statistics further emphasise the significance of Polish and Romanian migrants for these two groups in slightly different periods. Almost half of the Polish nationals registering for a NINo between March 2002 and March 2021 did so in the five years between 2004–5 and 2008–9. whilst over 80 per cent of the registrations by Romanian nationals occurred between 2014–15 and 2018–19. In addition, Figure 7.1 provides some interesting information on inter-Census periods. Notably, a post-referendum decline in migrants from EU8 countries can be seen with the EU8-born population in Wales falling from a peak of around 38,000 in 2016 to 29,000 in 2020. This 23.4 per cent reduction in the estimated EU8 population living in Wales was slightly higher than the equivalent decline (20.9 per cent) recorded across the UK over the same period. Moreover, the ONS's long-term international migration estimates indicate that there was a net in-migration of 184,000 people from the EU to the UK in 2019 but that this had become a small net outflow in 2021 and risen to a net outflow of 51,000 in 2022.

Labour Market Integration of EU Migrants in Wales

Considering the integration of EU migrants in Wales, existing evidence for the labour market indicates that recent migrants, especially from the EU2 and EU8, have relatively high levels of employment but tend to be in low-skilled occupations, and as a result relatively low levels of claims for work-related benefits. This has been particularly noticeable amongst post-enlargement Polish migrants to Wales (Drinkwater and Garapich, 2015; Knight et al., 2017). However, some Polish migrants have been able to progress in the Welsh labour markets by moving to higher status jobs, especially in the cities of southern Wales (Knight et al., 2014).

To provide a more detailed and contemporary comparison of labour market outcomes for migrants in Wales, including in relation to those living in other parts of the UK, Table 7.4 reports information from the APS for 2022–3. The table shows that there are relatively high employment rates of EU migrants in both Wales and the rest of the UK. For example, in Wales the employment rate of EU migrants aged 22-64 years old is 6.8 percentage points higher than the equivalent group of UK-born individuals. Rates are particularly high for migrants from the EU14 and Rest of the EU (which includes the EU2) but relatively low for the EU8. This appears to be driven by low rates of employment among women born in these countries (around 66 per cent, compared to around 86 per cent for men). In terms of occupational attainment, the table also shows that EU8 workers are more likely to be employed in routine or semi-routine jobs. Almost 40 per cent of EU8 migrant workers in Wales were employed in such occupations compared to under 22 per cent of UK-born workers. A

Table 7.4: Labour Market Outcomes in Wales and Other Parts of UK by Countries of Birth: April 2022–March 2023.[1]

	Employment Rate		% Professional/ Managerial		% Routine/ Semi-Routine		Gross Average Hourly Earnings		% with Degrees	
	Wales	Other UK	Wales	Other UK	Wales	Other UK	Wales	Other UK	Wales	Other UK
UK Born	76.1	79.5	48.2	53.7	21.5	18.0	16.39	18.70	39.8	43.4
EU Born	82.9	86.5	45.3	45.8	26.9	24.9	14.78	18.13	48.3	48.4
EU14	85.7	85.7	58.4	63.9	14.7	14.1	16.94	21.97	60.1	63.6
EU8	76.0	87.3	26.3	31.0	38.5	35.1	12.22	14.26	35.3	37.9
Rest of the EU	92.1	86.8	46.9	32.4	38.5	30.6	12.97	15.88	42.4	34.2
Non-EU Born	74.1	75.0	51.6	54.7	22.7	20.2	15.97	19.72	41.0	46.0
Unweighted N	8,439	79,759	6,253	61,369	6,253	61,369	3,980	38,616	6,159	60,558

Source: Annual Population Survey.

[1]Statistics in the table relate to a sample of the population aged between 22 and 64 and are based on weighted data. Self-employed workers are included in those in employment, as well as in the occupational categories but they are not asked any questions on their earnings. The earnings questions also tend to have fairly high levels of non-response. % with degrees just relates to those in employment.

similar percentage of migrant workers from the Rest of the EU living in Wales could also be found in routine or semi-routine occupations. However, in Wales, a relatively high percentage of this group (around 47 per cent) were in professional or managerial occupations. This was much higher than the equivalent percentage for EU8 migrants (26 per cent) but below that of the UK born (48 per cent) and especially EU14 migrant workers (58 per cent). These occupational variations are, unsurprisingly, reflected in earnings differentials. Employees born in EU8 countries have the lowest average earnings, followed by employees born in the Rest of the EU. In contrast, workers born in the EU14 had higher average earnings than those born in the UK. The same patterns occur in the rest of the UK, but for each of the groups average earnings in Wales are typically around 20–5 per cent lower, which is consistent with lower overall earnings in Wales.

Additionally, although the average earnings of workers from the EU8 and the rest of EU are relatively low, these groups do not have low average levels of education. In fact, Table 7.4 indicates that over 42 per cent of workers from the rest of the EU living in Wales had a degree or equivalent qualification. This is higher than the comparable percentages for the same group in other parts of the UK (34.2 per cent) and the UK-born living in Wales (39.8 per cent). Moreover, over a third (35.3 per cent) of EU8 workers in Wales have a degree or equivalent qualification. This picture is consistent with Dustmann et al.'s (2013) argument that many immigrants experience significant occupational downgrading in the UK labour market, either because employers may not recognise the type or value of overseas qualifications or due to discrimination. This aspect is likely to have been exacerbated by restrictive public attitudes, language barriers and ethnic stereotyping. In addition, there is often a link between the labour market and social integration (Dickey et al., 2018), with both types influenced by the future migration intentions. The latter is particularly relevant given increased uncertainties following Brexit.

Still Welcome?

Most EU citizens interviewed initially had a little awareness of Wales prior to migration (see also Guma and Dafydd Jones, 2019). One

German migrant noted that she was initially drawn to an educational exchange in Wales (before returning and staying) out of curiosity:

> When I did the British Studies Programme in [city] there was always stuff about Scotland and always about Ireland on the syllabus and English by default. I just thought well they're pushing these four nations, what's going on with the fourth nation. I'm sure it can't be that boring. (Lisa, German, Ceredigion)

Others described being unaware of Wales's distinct national consciousness and language (as well as climate):

> I had no idea it was a different country. I remember crossing the bridge and I was in a National Express bus and looking at the sign and it said 'Welcome to Wales' and then something in another language. I thought 'Oh my God, they have a different language'. I was so shocked because I knew nothing about Wales. Then all of a sudden to realise this is nothing like England. Nothing at all like England. Even the people were different. The way that they're speaking was different and I remember feeling shocked, like they made the English language sound very different. It was a strong da, da, da. A different inflection and you make it like a song almost. It was such a shock the first time and it was November, and it was raining like crazy. We went to visit Gower and I was thinking, 'Oh my God this country is full of sheep'. (Cristina, Romanian, Swansea)

Nonetheless, many respondents alluded to the friendliness encountered in Wales. While this notion – part of the discourse of a 'tolerant nation' (Williams et al., 2003) – has been critiqued (Evans, 2003; Jackson and Dafydd Jones, 2014; Guma and Dafydd Jones, 2019), there was, nonetheless, some sense of welcome. This is not to say that such accounts should be reified, nor that they should be dismissed: rather, they attest to the complexities of attachment and belonging. For example, some felt that a bilingual societal culture with a minority language brought openness to other languages being spoken:

We do events here in this Welsh pub. We do our meetings up here. So, we're already using a Welsh place where at main points there's the Portuguese and the Welsh crowds because it's the way it is. (Luciana, Portuguese, northern Wales)

[I]n Wales, being bilingual, there's a great openness to other people who speak another language. But in England, it was not possible to speak German [at work] … It wasn't appreciated at all to speak German. (Peter, German, Ceredigion)

As argued elsewhere (Drinkwater et al., 2022), participation in civil society is a form of anchoring. So, too, are developing friend, work and family networks, raising children, and operating businesses. The 2016 referendum, however, challenged this sense of belonging. Guma and Dafydd Jones (2019) provide evidence for experiences of hostility and anxiety among migrants from particular EU countries, and the extent to which these migrants felt they belonged in Wales. They report that some migrants were subjected to hostility during the Brexit referendum campaign and following the result. As a result, they argue that the uncertainty and insecurity that accompanied this period affected migrants' sense of identity and belonging. Furthermore, Drinkwater et al. (2022) report that there was a sharp increase in reported hate crimes across police force areas in Wales, as well as in other parts of the UK, in the immediate aftermath of the Brexit referendum.

It would be reductive and overly simplistic to argue that the referendum campaign and result provoked a sea-change in attitudes towards immigration in Wales in particular and the UK in general: it did not. Evans (2003) recounts several xenophobic and racist incidents in the late nineteenth and early twentieth century, at times and places associated with the sense of solidarity that supposedly gave Wales its tolerant outlook. More recently, Mann and Tommis (2012) show very polarised attitudes towards immigrants in Wales, while Anglophobia and anti-English sentiments are mainstreamed. Moreover, the genealogy of the UK's citizenship legislation (Tyler, 2010) reveals long-standing racist underpinnings and attempts to exclude. While the Commonwealth Immigrants Act 1962 and Immigration Act 1971 restricted access to British citizenship for British subjects in former colonies under Conservative governments, notable recent restrictions came from New Labour, including the Immigration and Asylum Act 1999, which paved the way for the rise of a hostile asylum system and removed asylum seekers' rights to work. In the 2010s, Conservative-led UK governments sought to reduce net immigration to 'tens of thousands', leading to Theresa May's 'hostile environment'. The Immigration Acts of 2014 and 2016 further expanded immigration controls into all aspects of life in Britain, giving immigration-related powers to actors including landlords, doctors, teachers and employers, and effectively turning them into border-guards (Hall, 2015; Yuval-Davis et al., 2018). The net effect of the 'hostile environment' 'has been to sensitise people to who carries a British passport and who does not' (Yuval-Davis et al., 2018: 238), creating tensions in targeted communities, which are often hyper-diverse localities. The Brexit referendum campaign did, however, mainstream and validate xenoracist sentiments, and disrupted senses of belonging within some communities.

There also tend to be geographical variations in public attitudes towards migrants. For example, it is often argued that urban residents display more tolerant views in comparison to rural inhabitants because the former generally have more contact with migrants and therefore feel more comfortable when new people arrive in their areas (Allport, 1954). Crawley et al. (2019) examine views towards asylum seekers in rural compared to urban parts of Britain and find evidence that supports this idea. More generally, there is evidence to indicate that racism may be more acute in rural parts of Wales because individuals tend to have less exposure to more diverse populations (Robinson and Gardner, 2006).

Respondents also noted that markers of difference which emphasised their Europeanness were targeted: a Polish grocery in mid-Wales was graffitied and their planters upturned, and a Portuguese café in northern Wales was vandalised. Lisa (German, Ceredigion) mentioned anxieties around speaking in a public setting shortly after the referendum, where her accent may be used to identify her, but noting how her 'whiteness' and German accent could provide her with relative privilege:

It also happened that we're white and we don't have accents that are not [sic.] likely to be heard on the street, like Polish

or ... any Slavic accent ... In that case, we would probably get
a lot more [hostility].

These accounts attest to Rzepnikowska's (2019) finding that other
'markers of difference', such as dress and appearance, as well as linguistic markers (Botterill and Hancock, 2019), signified a European 'otherness', and attempts were sometimes made for dissimulation (Scott,
1985) to hide these for self-preservation. As Lisa acknowledges here,
this 'marking out' has been already in place for those with the 'wrong'
European (i.e., 'Slavic') accents, thus highlighting the ongoing hostility towards 'Eastern Europeans' (Fox et al., 2012; Guma and Dafydd
Jones, 2019; Rzepnikowska, 2019). Her quotations also show that,
following the EU referendum, other EU citizens like her from EU14
states who were perhaps less visible became also 'targeted' and suddenly seen as 'immigrants', although Wales's bilingual and thus more
tolerant linguistic context may have shielded them from some of this
'marking out', as Peter, another German participant, noted above.

Many of these accounts personalised a sense of non-belonging.
These included children being bullied at schools and suffering verbal
abuse on the street. These led people to question whether they, and
the contributions they had made to their communities, were appreciated. Some spoke of disappointment when people previously considered friends or allies made xenophobic or racist comments; these
were sometimes followed by the clichéd excuse 'But we don't mean
you'. These experiences disrupted established senses of identity and
belonging, as one respondent noted: 'I haven't felt like an immigrant
for a while – the whole EU referendum hit back and made me feel a
bit like one again' (Emilia, Polish, 38).

However, respondents equally encountered solidarity from
non-migrant residents. These included individuals apologising on
behalf of the national vote pattern: '[M]y closest neighbours ... they
apologised the day after, 'what on earth was Wales thinking?' (Mar-
got, German, Ceredigion). In Aberystwyth, a rally was held to voice
solidarity with European citizens a week after the referendum, coin-
ciding with a pre-scheduled 'Global Village' festival in Merthyr Tydfil.

The referendum was followed by three and a half years of uncertainty around the UK's future relationship with the EU. The referendum had produced a negative result on the UK's status quo,

rather than endorsing any alternative vision, and internal divisions in the Conservative party meant a lack of support for the different post-Brexit plans. This uncertainty translated into a lack of clarity for respondents around their future intentions for remaining in Wales. Some spoke of moving to Scotland, which was seen as more tolerant and welcoming (although see Botterill and Hancock, 2019), while others considered 'seeing how things go', return or onward migration. Some voiced concern about whether their British spouses would have residency rights in their states of origin, and how children with limited proficiency in other languages would cope.

Against this turbulent backdrop, some respondents spoke about acquiring UK citizenship. This was often a tactical decision. In some instances, the decision had been taken before the EUSS was launched nationally in March 2019. The scheme initially could only be completed via an Android app, or at a local authority venue (potentially necessitating a long and costly round-trip) and had an initial application fee of £65 for adults and £32.50 for individuals aged under 16, which was quickly removed following a public backlash. There were accounts of partners with the same migratory history being given different statuses (pre-settled for one, settled for the other), and complications in being able to produce documentation to prove they met residency requirements. The 'Windrush Scandal', emerging in 2018, had revealed how many people who came to the UK from the Caribbean in the mid-twentieth century could not definitively prove their residency, some subsequently being deported, which did not fill people with confidence in negotiating a hostile state bureaucracy. For some German migrants, the timing was crucial, as Germany only allowed dual citizenship with other EU states (which could be retained once the UK left the EU). However, obtaining citizenship is a costly and lengthy process, often requiring travelling some distance to test centres and venues for the compulsory citizenship ceremony. Others did not consider taking citizenship, as they felt this would assert a formal attachment to the UK while potentially limiting future return or onward migration or was incompatible with their sense of identity.

While obtaining British citizenship creates a (pragmatic) attachment to the UK state, a small but significant number of respondents sought to create attachments with the Welsh nation. These included learning Welsh and sending children to Welsh-language schools, and membership of *YesCymru*, the pro-independence campaign group. While the discourse of a welcoming and tolerant Welsh nation needs to be problematised, and the co-option of migrant and minoritised groups into national secession politics is viewed with caution (Bassel and Emejulu, 2017), there is nonetheless a clear attraction to try and fashion an alternative, inclusive national politics. This aligns, to some extent, with recent initiatives from the Welsh Government and Welsh Parliament, such as the Senedd and Elections (Wales) Act 2020, which extended the franchise to all those aged 16 and over 'legally resident' in Wales (and ending the hierarchy where EU and Commonwealth Citizens could vote in elections in Wales other than those to the UK parliament, but other nationals could not), and the Nation of Sanctuary (see Chapter Four). While there is scope for further developments in these and other areas, there is ground for optimism that the Welsh Government has refrained from reproducing a similar anti-immigration climate to that of the UK government. However, there is also a real need to understand the way the 'hostile environment' is enacted in Wales, including the anti-immigrant sentiments (including anti in-migrant and Anglophobic discourses) held by Welsh people and people in Wales.

Conclusions

International migration to Wales from the EU has increased substantially in recent decades, both in terms of the number of foreign-born people and in the diversity of migrants' regions/countries of origin. Engbersen and Snel's notion of 'liquid migration' (2013) is a helpful conceptualisation, as it allows understanding of dynamic, non-linear forms of migration that can appear and change quickly, as well flows which are facilitated or restricted by filters such as state immigration policies. However, the extent to which migrants (continue to) feel welcome has now been brought into question, especially given the higher levels of hostility directed towards migrants in the wake of the Brexit referendum. Evidence presented in this chapter suggests that migrants' concerns have risen since the UK electorate voted to leave the EU and they have become more uncertain about how long they wish to stay in Wales. Despite attachments developed and affinities with Wales expressed, the operation of the 'hostile environment' in Wales, both by UK governments but also the everyday xenoracist abuse suffered, illustrates the clear limitations of Wales being viewed as a welcoming nation. An intersectional approach highlights the different experiences of these everyday hostilities and allows understanding of how specific groups are othered. This can include national origin informed by geopolitical imaginations ('EU14' versus 'EU8' and 'EU2' or 'western'/'northern' versus 'eastern'/'southern'), race and ethnicity, and gender can bring different experiences of encountering hostility targeted in different ways.

The reduction of migrants from certain parts of the EU, most notably EU8 countries such as Poland, has been another aspect of Brexit and its aftermath, which has included the requirement for EU migrants living in Wales/the UK to apply to the EUSS. The fall in migrants from the more recent EU member states is likely to have exacerbated problematic (economic) issues that have emerged following the Covid pandemic, such as hiring difficulties experienced by employers and spiralling inflation (Portes and Springford, 2023). Moreover, Wales's ageing population implies that migration should play an increasing role in sustaining public services. Therefore, policy-makers will need to consider the impact of everyday hostility on the vitality of many Welsh localities, particularly in areas where population decline was identified in the 2021 Census. Future research could thus focus on how the changing migration patterns following Brexit may have had differential effects across Wales in terms of both the provision of services and in addressing sectoral skill shortages.

Notes

1   Project reference ES/L009099/1.
2   Grant Agreement ID 726950.
3   As the UK government has stripped some of its citizens (who held dual citizenship) of their UK citizenship, it would also be naïve to assume that the 'thick layer' of state citizenship is a guarantor of security and human rights.
4   EU citizens – particularly those from central and eastern Europe – have also been othered (see Rzepnikowska, 2019).
5   The Census is administered in England and Wales by the Office for National Statistics (ONS).

6   A high percentage of the German-born residents in Wales are British citizens, and likely to reflect birth to military families stationed in Germany.
7   Just under 85,000 EUSS applications were submitted by EU27 Nationals in Wales up until 31 March 2021. The total number of EU-born people living in Wales in the 2021 Census, excluding those born in Ireland, was similar at around 81,500. However, EU nationals have continued to make applications to the EUSS. Around 24,000 additional applications from EU nationals in Wales were made between the end of March 2021 and March 2023 even though the scheme was initially supposed to close at the end of June 2021.
8   According to the NINo database, over 45,000 new national insurance numbers were issued to Polish nationals in Wales between January 2002 and March 2021, while for Romanian nationals the equivalent figure was 15,400.
9   The ONS has suspended the publication of country of birth statistics using the APS after releasing information for the July 2020–June 2021 period because the APS needs to be compared with more comprehensive Census 2021 data to create weights that produce more accurate population estimates.

Bibliography

Allport, G. W. 1954. *The Nature of Prejudice*. Cambridge, MA: Addison-Wesley.
Andrén, D. and Roman, M. 2016. 'Should I stay or should I go? Romanian migrants during transition and enlargements'. In M. Kahanec and K. Zimmermann (eds), *Labor Migration, EU Enlargement and the Great Recession*. Berlin: Springer.
Bassel, Leah and Emejulu, Akwugo. 2017. *Minority Women and Austerity: Survival and Resistance in France and Britain*. Bristol: Policy Press.
Bauböck, R. 2000. 'Introduction: Dual and supranational citizenship. Limits to transnationalism'. In T. A. Aleinikoff and D. Klusmeyer (eds), *From Migrants to Citizens: Membership in a Changing World*. Washington, DC: Brookings Institution Press.
Bauman, Zygmunt. 2000. *Liquid Modernity*. Cambridge: Polity Press.
Botterill, K. and Hancock, J. 2019. 'Rescaling belonging in "Brexit Britain": Spatial identities and practices of Polish nationals in Scotland after the UK Referendum on European Union membership'. *Population, Space & Place*, 25/1, e2217.
Brubaker, W. R. 1989. 'Membership without citizenship: The economic and social rights of noncitizens'. In W. R. Brubaker (ed.), *Immigration and the Politics of Citizenship in Europe and North America*. Lanham, MD: University Press of America.
Brubaker, W. R. 1990. 'Immigration, citizenship and the nation-state in France and Germany: A comparative historical analysis'. *International Sociology*, 5/4, 379–407.

Crawley, H., Drinkwater, S. and Kausar, R. 2019. 'Attitudes towards asylum seekers: Understanding differences between rural and urban areas'. *Journal of Rural Studies*, 71, 104–13.

Cuibus, M. 2023. *Briefing: EU migration to and from the UK*. Oxford: Oxford University Migration Observatory. Available from *https://migrationobservatory.ox.ac.uk/wp-content/uploads/2020/10/MigObs-Briefing-EU-migration-to-and-from-the-UK.pdf* (accessed 21 December 2023).

Dawney, L. 2008. 'Racialisation of Central and East European migrants in Herefordshire'. Working Paper, 53, Sussex Centre for Migration Research.

Dickey, H., Drinkwater, S. and Shubin, S. 2018. 'Labour market and social integration of Eastern European migrants in Scotland and Portugal'. *Environment and Planning A: Economy and Space*, 50/6, 1250–68.

Drinkwater, S. and Garapich, M. 2015. 'Migration strategies of recent Polish migrants to England and Wales: Do they have any at all?'. *Journal of Ethnic and Migration Studies*, 41/12, 1909–31.

Drinkwater, S., Guma, T. and Dafydd Jones, Rh. 2022. 'Xenophobia, hostility, and austerity: European migrants and civil society in Wales'. In P. Chaney and I. R. Jones (eds), *Age of Uncertainty – Civil Society: Institutions, Governance and Existential Challenges*. Bristol: Policy Press, pp. 163–85.

Dustmann, C., Frattini, T. and Preston, I. P. 2013. 'The effect of immigration along the distribution of wages'. *Review of Economic Studies*, 80/1, 145–73.

Engbersen, G. and Snel, E. 2013. 'Liquid Migration: Dynamic and Fluid Patterns of Post-accession Migration'. In B. Glorius, I. Grabowska-Lusinska and A. Rindoks (eds), *Mobility in Transition: Migration Patterns After EU Enlargement*. Amsterdam: Amsterdam University Press, pp. 21–40.

Evans, N. 2003. 'Through the prism of ethnic violence: Riots and racial attacks in Wales, 1826–2002'. In C. Williams, N. Evans, and P. O'Leary (eds), *A Tolerant Nation? Exploring ethnic diversity in Wales*. Cardiff: University of Wales Press, pp. 93–108.

Fox, J. E., Moroşanu, L. and Szilassy, E. 2012. 'The racialization of the new European migration to the UK'. *Sociology*, 46/4, 680–95.

Grzymala-Kazlowska, A. 2018. 'From connecting to social anchoring: Adaptation and "settlement" of Polish migrants in the UK'. *Journal of Ethnic and Migration Studies*, 44/2, 252–69.

Guma, T. 2020. 'Turning citizens into immigrants: State practices of welfare "cancellations" and document retention among EU nationals living in Glasgow'. *Journal of Ethnic and Migration Studies*, 46/13, 2647–63.

Guma, T. and Dafydd Jones, Rh. 2019. '"Where are we going to go now?" European Union migrants' experiences of hostility, anxiety, and (non-) belonging during Brexit'. *Population, Space and Place*, 25/1, e2198.

Hall, S. M. 2015. 'Migrant urbanisms: Ordinary cities and everyday resistance'. *Sociology*, 49/5, 853–69.

Hammel, Andrea. 2022. *Finding Refuge: Stories of the Men, Women and Children Who Fled to Wales to Escape the Nazis*. Aberystwyth: Honno.

Jackson, L. and Dafydd Jones, Rh. 2014. '"We'll keep a welcome"? Proximity, distance, and hospitality towards migrants in Wales'. *Contemporary Wales*, 27/1, 82–104.

Knight, J., Lever, J. and Thompson, A. 2014. 'The labour market mobility of Polish migrants: A comparative study of three regions in South Wales, UK'. *Central and Eastern European Migration Review*, 3/2, 61–78.

Knight, Julie, Lever, John and Thompson, Andrew. 2017. *Labour, Mobility and Temporary Migration: A Comparative Study of Polish Migration to Wales*. Cardiff: University of Wales Press.

Mann, R. and Tommis, Y. 2012. *Public Sentiments Towards Immigrants Living in Wales*, WISERD Research Report 009. Bangor: Bangor University.

McCollum, D. and Findlay, A. 2011. 'Trends in A8 migration to the UK during the recession'. *Population Trends*, 145, 77–89.

Office for National Statistics. 2012. *Annual Population Survey (APS) QMI*. Available at: *https://www.ons.gov.uk/employmentandlabourmarket/peopleinwork/ employmentandemployeetypes/methodologies/annualpopulationsurveyapsqmi*

Portes, J. and Springford, J. 2023. 'The impact of the post-Brexit migration system on the UK labour market'. *Contemporary Social Science*, 18/2, 132–49.

Robinson, V. and Gardner, H. 2006. 'Place matters: Exploring the distinctiveness of racism in rural Wales'. In S. Neal and J. Agyeman (eds), *The New Countryside? Ethnicity, Nation and Exclusion in Contemporary Rural Britain*. Bristol: Policy Press, pp. 47–72.

Rzepnikowska, A. 2019. 'Racism and xenophobia experienced by Polish migrants in the UK before and after Brexit vote'. *Journal of Ethnic and Migration Studies*, 45/1, 61–77.

Scott, James C. 1985. *Weapons of the Weak: Everyday Forms of Peasant Resistance*. London: Yale University Press.

Stewart, H. and Mason, R. 2016. 'Nigel Farage's anti-migrant poster reported to police'. *The Guardian* (16 June). Available at *https://www.theguardian.com/ politics/2016/jun/16/nigel-farage-defends-ukip-breaking-point-poster-queue-of-migrants*

Soysal, Yasemin Nuhoglu. 1994. *Limits of Citizenship: Migrants and Postnational Membership in Europe*. Chicago: University of Chicago Press.

Tyler, I. 2010. 'Designed to fail: A biopolitics of British citizenship'. *Citizenship Studies*, 14/1, 61–74.

Williams, Charlotte, Evans, Neil, and O'Leary, Paul (eds). 2003. *A Tolerant Nation? Exploring Ethnic Diversity in Wales*. Cardiff, University of Wales Press.

WJEC. 2023. *Patterns of Migration: The Welsh Context*. Available at: *https://www. gwegogledd.cymru/wp-content/uploads/2019/02/patterns-of-migration-welsh-context.pdf* (accessed 22 December 2023).

Yuval-Davis, N., Wemyss, G. and Cassidy, K. 2018. 'Everyday bordering, belonging and the reorientation of British immigration legislation'. *Sociology*, 52/2, 228–44.

CHAPTER 8

Ageing and Migration into Rural Wales: A Counter-Narrative to the Rhetoric of Burden and Dependency

Jesse Heley and Rachel Rahman

Introduction

This chapter pulls together findings and reflections on studies which variously explore the interactions between migration, ageing, and health. More specifically, it considers long-standing policy narratives on rural mid-Wales which tend to characterise this space as problematic in terms of demographic trends. In turn, a complementary account is put forward which rather underscores some of those more encouraging aspects of older age in-migration as relayed in a qualitative study in one community in mid-Wales, as well as within a wider suite of research in this field nationally and internationally. The latter part of the discussion sets out further grounds for positivity with reference to a series of opportunities that might address challenges to successful ageing in rural places. Inclusive of long-standing residents and in-migrants, these include the important voluntary contributions of older adults to the Welsh health and social care sector. Coupled with a parallel consideration of how technological interventions are supporting healthy and independent living, it is argued that those bleak accounts of rural ageing in place have a critical counterweight. The discussion draws upon a range of research undertaken within the Wales Institute of Social and Economic Research and Data

(WISERD) and as part of the Centre for Excellence in Rural Health Research (CERHR) at Aberystwyth University, which involves a wide-ranging research focus on Wales, and rural Wales in particular.

A historical trend of out-migration among younger age-groups coupled with mid-Wales's attractiveness as a destination for retirement in-migration has precipitated concerns regarding the social, cultural and economic vitality (and potentially viability) of its constituent communities in the mid-to-long term. Here, trepidation has emerged around the issue of service provision and healthcare delivery, in particular. An issue which is of national concern given the current cost-of-living crisis, 'real-terms' cuts in service delivery, and the growing number of people living longer (often with complex conditions), the motif of the 'ticking time bomb' has been widely used in this context – including by the Welsh Government in their recent Age Wales report (2021). The health-centric account of 'grey in-migration' into rural Wales overlaps and interacts to a lesser extent with those long-standing cultural-political anxieties regarding 'Anglicisation' and the potentially deleterious impact of English settlement in the Welsh 'heartland' (Day et al., 2010). As such, the apparent attractiveness of rural Wales as a retirement destination for those 'over the border' since at least the 1960s has been seen by some as further undermining the well-being of the Welsh language and culture. A perspective which has been challenged using Census data, and on the grounds of costs to the devolved state and potential prejudice (Lloyd, 2019), it is one that has nevertheless gained currency through the Covid crisis and in terms of pressures on the housing market in rural Wales. With rising house prices and rents being allied to a growing demand from migrants from beyond mid-Wales and England, this picture typically includes second-home owners, empty nesters, and retirees. This has sparked considerable public dialogue and understandable concerns for those on lower incomes, first-time buyers and renters, as well as for the cohesion of certain communities as a result of a lack of stable neighbourhoods due to holiday letting, or who face significant isolation when second-home owners return to their city dwellings. This is a complex scenario which belies easy description and bedevils a sweeping policy response (Goodwin-Hawkins et al., 2023).

The purpose of this contribution is to provide an alternative account of older in-migration into rural Wales which is intended not to discredit or undermine those very real concerns regarding the social, economic and cultural implications of this process, but rather to emphasise a heterogeneity of experiences between communities and individuals, inclusive of a range of potentially positive outcomes. In so doing, we echo calls made elsewhere and by ourselves to reject a-priori constructions of older people which operate along two main axes. First, the discussion adds critical weight to calls to move beyond the narrow and often unhelpful perspective of older people as service users as opposed to service providers. This construction is especially powerful in portraying 'deep rural' locations in Wales where accessibility is (by definition) much lower than in other, predominately urban, localities. Coupled with the growing costs of service delivery and increasingly difficult decisions pertaining to priorities and cuts in public service budgets, this has precipitated a rather unhelpful view that older residents constitute a relative 'burden' to wider society. While not advocating skating over a 'rural health deficit' (Bourke et al., 2012) as a real and imminent political challenge, the discussion is mindful of Best and Myer's (2019: 198) directive to not uncritically replicate the view of rural health and social care delivery as an inherently problematic and potentially unsolvable environment (also Malatzky and Bourke, 2016). In accordance with this, the chapter's second aim is to challenge and discredit these broad-brush stereotypes from both an economic and a social standpoint, as well as provide a critical counterpoint to the characterisation of (older) in-migrants as being culturally deleterious in Wales.

Methods and Data

This chapter takes the form of a comparative analysis of existing data on the contributions older residents make in rural contexts, the dynamics of older in-migration in the countryside, and that limited body of research which connects these two (largely distinct) fields of enquiry. Setting the Welsh experience within international case-studies, the scale is shifted with reflection on the findings from a place-based study of older volunteering undertaken in two neighbouring villages in Ceredigion, mid-Wales (Jones and Heley, 2016). This project involved interviews with approximately forty residents over the age of sixty who were implicated in the delivery support of services or were coordinating activities that impact the welfare and well-being of the wider community. Undertaken during 2014 and early 2015, it should be noted that this project was not predominately concerned with processes of in-migration. Nevertheless, a significant proportion of interviewees identified themselves as in-migrants while other respondents talked to the capacity of 'in-migrants' to maintain and contribute to community sustainability through their activities. Obviously, how the 'local/incomer' was defined and reproduced by interviewees varied (as might be expected), but it is not in the scope of this paper to address those long-standing debates on the cultural construction of the countryside (e.g., Heley and Jones, 2012; Woods, 2010).

Subsequent to this place-based case study, attention is shifted to the regional scale of mid-Wales and focuses on the contributions of older people to health and social care provision. Drawing on a cross-section of research identified and undertaken by the Centre for Excellence in Rural Health Research (CERHR), based in Aberystwyth University, the discussion highlights a lack of extant research on the role of older in-migrants as part of landscape of care, and makes the case for the potential role of technological innovations in securing improved quality-of-life outcomes for individuals with more restricted social and familial networks.

Older In-Migration to Rural Wales: Historical Trends and Academic Perspectives

With a population of just over 3.1 million at the time of the 2021 Census, there were more people in older age groups than at any time previously. With 21.3 per cent of the population aged over 65 (662,000), as a share of the overall population this represents a significant increase on the 2011 figure of 18.4 per cent (ONS, 2021). Moreover, the proportion of the population aged 90+ (29,700) has also increased over this period from 0.8 to around 1.0 per cent. At a regional and local level, the demographic picture is much more complex. In spatial terms, the most densely populated areas are in the south and southeast, centred on Cardiff, Swansea and Rhondda

Cynon Taf, as well as in the northeast around Wrexham. Those local authorities in the lowest population densities include Powys, Ceredigion, Carmarthenshire and Gwynedd, which cover mid-Wales. Between 2011 and 2021 these authorities also experienced population decline (Ceredigion, Gwynedd) or comparatively low levels of population growth (Carmarthenshire). Furthermore, the age structure of these predominately rural counties is such that they have a comparatively high proportion of residents aged 65 years and over, with Powys having the largest percentage of people in this cohort for Wales as a whole (27.8 per cent). This has potential implications in terms of those services required, desired and used by residents in these counties.

Figures and patterns for net migration in mid-Wales over this period are more complex and do not allow for neat description or clear-cut claims to causality. Referring to the Office for National Statistics' (ONS) most recent statistical bulletin for internal migration in England and Wales (ONS, 2016), the picture at the local authority level is varied. Authorities in rural mid-Wales, for example, largely experienced a positive net migration rate (i.e., influx) between July 2014 and June 2015, including Carmarthenshire (2.97 per cent), Gwynedd (1.15 per cent) and Powys (2.9 per cent). Over the same period, however, Ceredigion experienced a net movement of people out of the county to other parts of the UK (–11.72 per cent). In comparison, figures for the previous year (ONS, 2014) demonstrate a similar net loss for Ceredigion (–9.1 per cent), but also a net loss for Gwynedd (–2.8 per cent). It should be noted that these figures are for periods prior to the Covid-19 pandemic and exclude international moves in or out of the UK, as well as moves within a single local authority. They are, however, useful in demonstrating variation in migration rates across mid-Wales over time, although robust comparisons with more recent periods are not possible following the discontinuation of local area migration indicator publications by the ONS after 2020. For migration data at a more granular level, including age, it is necessary to refer to the 2011 Census. Over the 12 months prior to the survey, of those 2,993 in-migrants to Carmarthenshire from the UK and internationally, 7.3 per cent were over the age of 65. Figures for Ceredigion were 4,594 (4.7 per cent of which were over 65), 5,306 (9.6 per cent) for Gwynedd, and 3,841 (13.1 per cent) for Powys.

With in-migrants to local authorities in mid-Wales over the age 65 constituting a comparatively small proportion of total arrivals to these areas, the cumulative impact of these migration flows over multiple years can, nevertheless, be substantial. Moreover, these figures do not account for second-home ownership and reoccurring seasonal residency in mid-Wales among older people. For example, data from the 2021 Census shows that over 1,100 people over the age of 65 have registered second homes in Ceredigion. These individuals have not permanently relocated to the county but are likely spend a significant proportion of time in the area, during which periods they might access (and contribute to) a range of services, including health and social care (West Wales Regional Partnership Board, 2022).

In statistical terms, older age in-migration into Wales is a complex picture with considerable variation temporally and spatially. Just as there are significant variations between city and country, there are differing trends within these contexts. While it is the case that in-migration is an established feature of rural society across the UK more generally, the literature also demonstrates a growing array of characteristics and motivations undergirding this process (Phillips et al., 2022; Stockdale, 2006; Willett, 2023). Different localities attract different cohorts of in-migrants for diverse reasons, although there remains an ongoing tendency across the broader geographical and sociological literature to effectively pigeonhole motivations into the category of lifestyle factors (Benson and O'Reilly, 2009; Cawley, 2020; Fielding, 2012). This is a point well made by Stockdale (2014): she deftly argued that the decision-making processes attendant to rural in-migration have been over-generalised and, in many cases, reduced to the status of 'sound-bites' allied to the of the rural idyll. Such formulaic motivations, it is argued, effectively reduce 'what is likely to be a complex interplay of individual and personal factors and influences, to a one dimensional and highly simplistic understanding of the actual decision-making process associated with a move to rural areas' (Stockdale, 2014: 171).

Looking to unravel the complexities of individual migrant rationales for moving into rural areas, Stockdale's research (2006; 2010; 2014; with MacLeod, 2013) has employed a life-course approach which recognises that prompts to migration are subjective, multifaceted, and positioned within the innate 'messiness' of everyday life. Life-events are seldom uniform and predictable across multiple households and often involve compromise between parties involved. Moreover, Stockdale's work is positioned among those few studies that have directly addressed older-age migration into contemporary rural Wales. In this vein, we include: investigations by Day and colleagues (2010) and Milbourne (2011), which also tackle the theme of English in-migration; explorations of in-migration and support networks among older people living in Welsh rural communities by Burholt and Sardani (2018); and the interplays between in-migration, volunteering and community engagement by Heley (with Jones, 2013; 2016; with Jones and Yarker, 2020).

Using survey and interview data collected from mid-life (aged 50–64 years) English (defined by prior residence) in-migrants to Powys, Stockdale's study identifies a significant variation in the decision-making process underpinning respondents' motivations to move and their choice of destination. These were not collectively reducible to retirement and aspirations for the 'good life'. Driving factors included exiting the job market, but relative to combinations of health, bereavement (primarily of parents), inheritance, and children leaving home, which in some cases, but not all, were working in tandem with anti-urban or pro-rural sentiment. On their own, however, Stockdale noted that 'such sentiments present only a partial and simplistic explanation of the decision to move and rarely represent[ed] the dominant influence within the decision-making process' (Stockdale, 2014: 168). In respect to the destination of migrants, a tendency towards compromise and negotiation was also identified. In many cases, the choice of rural mid-Wales was premised on affordability (particularly in contrast to areas of the English countryside), alongside accessibility considerations, notably proximity to friends and relations in Manchester, Birmingham and the English midlands. Representing a material choice more so than a social or environmental rationale, these 'value for money' sentiments also seemingly trumped the selection of retirement destination according to the prospect of ageing and the potential need for services and amenities. Where respondents did take specific locational factors into account, such as 'proximity to a local pub or whether or not it was close to medical facilities ... this was the exception and not the norm' (Stockdale, 2014: 171). Feeding into those debates on the relationship between the housing market in rural Wales, migration and property prices, Stockdale's study adds credence to those noted concerns regarding a limited interest or willingness on the part of some English in-migrants to engage with their new communities on practical and cultural terms.

Older In-Migrants and Assimilation:
Stereotypes and Challenges

The interaction between an endogenous Welsh population and incomers has been a major topic of public debate and academic scrutiny since at least the 1960s, with different aspects of this incursion being the focus of attention at different times. Here, Day and colleagues (2010) highlight the impact of rural redevelopment initiatives and small-scale industrialisation during the 1960s and 1970s which brought in key workers and skilled labour (particularly from the English midlands and southeast), as well as the well-documented emergence of the 'second/holiday-home problem' over the same period. Through the 1980s and 1990s, critical attention shifted to the out-migration of younger people from Wales and counterflow of English settlers attracted by environmental factors and relatively cheap house prices. As discussed above, this rhetoric rather oversimplifies the process of relocation, but the power of prevailing stereotypes cannot be dismissed. Among the most powerful of these is the archetype of the English incomer as an 'arrogant, assertive individual, often from economically privileged background, who takes control of organised social life, monopolises the better jobs, and attempts to impose lifestyles that are "alien" to Wales' (Day et al., 2010: 1408; see also Robinson and Gardner, 2006). What is more, this widely portrayed image overlaps and interacts with other common tropes, including the 'social misfit' foisted on Wales by English local authorities and that of the 'ageing, economically inactive person who drains local resources' (Day et al., 2010: 1408). None of these constructs is flattering, and their reproduction belies the limited effort undertaken to rigorously explore the experiences of those English in-migrants who have settled in Wales, older or otherwise.

For their part, Day et al. (2010) have addressed this critical lacuna through undertaking research in northern Wales with English in-migrants in communities across Gwynedd and Conwy. Involving interviews with respondents with ages ranging from thirty to seventy, the greater proportion of participants were aged over fifty. Findings provided a 'degree of confirmation for retirement or downsizing tendencies among migrants' (Day et al., 2010: 1411), a significant proportion had relocated to Wales prior to retirement. In keeping with those participants in Stockdale's (2014) project in Powys, a significant proportion of respondents in Day et al.'s northern Wales research noted proximity to family in England and quality of life as major motivations underpinning their choice of destination. However, there are also marked contrasts between the two studies. Notably cheaper housing did not feature as a major theme in northern Wales, and a 'very high proportion' of those questioned specified prior familiarity with the area to which they had moved (Day et al., 2010: 1412). In this regard they reported a strong connection with tourism and revealed a history of family holidays. A sizeable number also indicated that they had owned a second home in Wales prior to permanent relocation.

Turning to the attitudes and lived experiences of in-migration in rural Wales, the preponderance of English incomers who took part in Day et al.'s study felt that they had successfully embedded themselves in community life. Nevertheless, these sentiments were set against a degree of self-policing; there being a tendency to 'defer to local opinions and expectations, so as to maintain harmonious relations with their neighbours' (Day et al., 2010: 1420). In this way English inmigrants are acutely aware of those discursive constructions which position them as fundamentally lacking in those cultural competencies required of rural life in Wales (Cloke et al., 1995). Referential to and reinforcing what Cloke et al. (1997) referred to as the 'dominant axis of debate' over Welsh rural change over twenty-five years ago, accounts gathered over the intervening period would suggest that this narrative persists (including Bowie, 2020).

In their more recent overview of migration, conflict and rural community life, Day (2011) reminds us of the significant gaps which can and do exist between aggregate trends and the diversity of experiences revealed through closer inspection. On this point they note that it is 'all too easy to impute inappropriate attitudes and behaviours to an entire set of people on the basis of particular, even anecdotal, pieces of evidence' (Day, 2011: 39). This point is also made by Milbourne (2011), who has also taken aim at popular constructions of English in-migration to Wales in terms of class, income, occupation and age. Referring to their own research, they cite a high proportion of middle-age households with children within incomer flows in some localities; a trend that would rather tend to counteract the so-called 'ageing' of rural communities in Wales. Milbourne also emphasises the level of complexity and contingency associated with integration, with perceptions and experiences of this process varying considerably between localities, and between incomers and established residents. The latter, they note, are much more likely to 'provide less recognition of the contribution of incomers to local society' (Milbourne, 2011: 62). In contrast, incomers tended to construct community integration 'as a more positive and straightforward process than local groups, seeing themselves becoming integrated in a much shorter time and underestimating the role of the Welsh language within this process (Milbourne, 2011: 62).

Quantifying and Qualifying Contributions to Economic, Social and Cultural Life

When considering contributions to community life, it is important to recognise that there are many types of involvements. They may be more, or less, 'formal', qualified, recognised or requiring of consistent engagement over time, but just as critical in sustaining communities and underpinning their outlook and vitality. Such activities might include playing on the rugby team, cleaning the church or chapel, or organising informal childcare, whilst others might be less ambiguous. Here, for instance, Edwards and Woods (2004: 188) note that being a member of the Women's Institute or running a youth rugby team might embed individuals within wider networks or governance, tap into new resources and shape the future for others. Similarly, there are those whose activities focus on specific needs or interest groups within communities or across wider territories. In this category Edwards and Woods include volunteers in meals-on-wheels services and youth group leaders (2004).

The extent to which older people play a part in rural life was not directly addressed in Edwards and Woods' (2004) study, being more directly concerned with institutional governance. However, a significant body of relevant research has emerged in the ensuing period. This includes work on older volunteers and caregivers undertaken in North America (see Colibaba et al., 2022; Glasgow et al., 2012) and Europe (Mettenberger and Küpper, 2019), including the UK (see Munoz et al., 2014; Yarker et al., 2020). A comparatively large body of research of this type has also been undertaken in Australia, with Winterton and Warburton contributing a great deal in this area (Warburton, 2010; Winterton and Warburton, 2014; 2017). Taken together, these analyses tend to draw on the conceptual framework of social capital, being attentive to networks of engagement, cooperation and reciprocity (after Putnam, 1993). Moreover, this research also shares common ground insofar as it uniformly highlights the crucial role that 'informal volunteering' can and does play as a social glue, defined as the multitude ways through which people sustain families, friends and community through 'unofficial' and often (but not always) unstructured ways (Wilson and Musick, 1997).

Work which pulls together a concern with older in-migrants, civic participation and volunteering remains somewhat under-researched. Outside rural contexts and in more general terms, notable contributions have been made been by Haas (2013), and Torres and Serrat (2019). In respect to rural change and resilience, contributions are sparser still, but a series of papers published over the past decade or so suggest we have turned a corner. Here we include Winterton and Warburton's (2015) exploration of the civic activities of retirement migrants across six rural communities in Victoria, Australia. Focus group data gathered in this project indicates that many in-migrants to these localities have had little problem integrating in their new communities, and that many have taken on a range of roles and responsibilities within social clubs, service organisations and sporting associations. Moreover, they are identified as being particularly active in helping disadvantaged groups and individuals through, for example, work at food banks, fundraisers and doing 'odd' jobs for senior citizens (Winterton and Warburton, 2015: 169). Stakeholders also suggested that retirement migrants were more likely to volunteer within areas relating to the arts, culture and tourism. More specifically, they were also identified as fostering an entrepreneurial spirit in several localities, and of bringing vital skillsets, enthusiasm and energy to public facing institutions, including visitor information centres and recreation sites. This resonates with Glasgow and colleagues' (2012) overview of social entrepreneurship and volunteering tendencies among older in-migrants to rural communities in the United States. Drawing on the Cornell Retirement Migration Study (see Brown and Glasgow, 2008) and findings from four case study 'amenity' destinations in rural Arizona, Maine, Michigan and North Carolina, their analysis of survey data and interviews indicate that in-migrants to these communities have contributed greatly to socio-economic resilience. More than this, the energy and creative drive of some of these incomers has purportedly 'promoted economic development in rural retirement destinations' (Glasgow et al., 2012: 247).

While these accounts of social participation among older immigrants in Australia and the US are widely optimistic in terms of the broader benefits to rural communities, the extent and patterns of engagements described is inevitably variable, nor uniformly positive and well received within the wider social milieu. For example, the relative buoyancy in recruitment for civil society institutions in the main in Winterton and Warburton's (2015) Australian case study communities was allied to older in-migration, but engagement was apparently selective. This was identified by some respondents as running contrary to – and as having implications for – the ongoing viability of other, 'more traditional' groups. Here, for example, it is reported that one 'agricultural community' was subject to substantial decline in membership in some long-standing, service-orientated institutions due to high levels of attrition among ageing cohorts coupled with a 'lack of interest among newcomers' (Winterton and Warburton, 2015: 169). Moreover, across those communities examined, the positive impact of older immigrants was reportedly tempered by: a tendency for some newcomers to expect higher levels of monetary and technical input than feasible in some situations; of being more sporadic and less committed in their contributions to more mundane elements of local civil society; and of occasionally failing to consider alternative points of view of other (often financially disadvantaged) residents (Winterton and Warburton, 2015: 172). The same caveats are also made by Glasgow et al. in respect to their US case studies, noting that – irrespective of their intentions – 'older in-migrants sometimes displace longer-term residents, older and younger, from cultural, political and economic roles, and sometimes in-migrants have different social and political agendas than their new neighbours' (Glasgow et al., 2012: 248). On this point, one can certainly see parallels with narratives of English in-migration and the rhetoric of an incomer/local dichotomy in parts of rural Wales as discussed earlier (Day et al., 2010; Day, 2011; Milbourne, 2011).

Older Incomers and Community Contributions in Wales: Emerging Evidence and Themes

Turning to that work which directly addresses older incomers and civic contributions in rural Wales, the range of available data is – expectedly – thin on the ground. Nonetheless, some indicative studies have surfaced in recent years. Included within this research is Burholt and Saradani's (2017) overview of mobility, population turnover and support networks among older people living in the Welsh countryside. Through examining evidence from the Cognitive Functions and Ageing Study (CFAS) in northern Wales, they argue that 'stayers' (defined as those who were born in an area and lived in this locality for 25+ years prior to taking part in the survey) were more likely to have 'family dependent' networks. These typically involved shared households and proximity between accommodation (often allied to widowhood and poor health) but were also characterised by limited interaction with friends and neighbours, and by reduced levels of community involvement. Another cohort of older stayers were attributed with 'locally integrated' associations, defined by close relationships with family, friends and neighbours, and strong and varied links with community organisations.

Considering non-stayers (those born outside the local authority), a substantial cohort were identified as tending to inhabit 'private restricted networks', categorised by an absence of kin, little contact with neighbours, low involvement in community groups, and with smaller than average networks. Another significant group of older incomers, however, surveyed had cultivated 'wider community focused (WCF) networks' in their retirement destinations, referring to a proliferation of local friends and establishing meaningful relationships with neighbours (Burholt and Sardini, 2017: 8). This group, Burholt

and Sardini note, tended to inhabit areas characterised by outmigra-
tion of young working/university age populations, an influx of pre-
retirement migrants and significant churning of the population aged
65+ years. Elaborating on this point they note that 'those with WCF
networks are more likely to be migrants than stayers themselves, and
to be involved in community activities, while not having any proxi-
mal kin' (Burholt and Sardini, 2017: 8). Burholt and Sardini identify several limitations of their study, including the influence of 'the
type of rural area' in their analyses and connections to migration, the
types of networks involving older residents, as well as the need for
further research which takes 'into account differences in norms and
expectations between types of rural communities rather than turnover' (Burholt and Sardini, 2017: 9). What this research does, however,
do is pointedly destabilise the notion that those older incomers into
rural Wales are necessarily less willing and able to play an active part
in community life. Indeed, the CFAS indicates that they can and do
play a significant role in voluntary groups.

Other studies which also underscore the importance of older
(predominately English) in-migrants to sustaining rural communities in Wales include projects undertaken by the authors (see Heley
and Jones, 2013; Jones and Heley, 2016; Jones et al., 2020; Yarker et
al., 2020). Undertaken as part of the ESRC WISERD research centre,
this research focuses on older volunteers in rural communities and/
or with rural organisations, inclusive of motivations, experiences
and outcomes (for both individuals and wider society). Drawing on
a wide body of literature on volunteering practices among the over
fifties, these studies do not directly address the figure of the older
incomer to rural communities as part of their original aims. However, this cohort did emerge through the research process, with the
analysis demonstrating the important function that retirement migrants were playing in servicing many of those formal and informal
institutions that contribute to community life in mid-Wales. Common themes emerging in the researchers' interviews with later-life
arrivals included an importance attached to remaining physically
active and mentally occupied and making the most of increased free
time to pursue hobbies. This was often tied to the landscape and
rural pastimes (including walking and fishing), resonating with established trends in other countries including England (Gilbert et al.,

2006), Ireland (Walsh and O'Shea, 2008) and Scotland (Flynn and Kay, 2017).

Taking part in local life was also prompted among some respondents by the desire to 'give something back' to society more broadly, and not just within those communities where this cohort have previously lived and worked. For example, one participant in their late sixties who had moved to the study site fifteen years prior discussed the importance they attached to working in the village shop, which he described as a 'lifeline' to some locals in both material and social terms. This, they noted, included the elderly, but also younger mothers and members of the farming community. This respondent also detailed the role they had played in establishing a heritage walking tour of the area, tailored to tourists, groups of children for local schools and other members of the community who 'have lived here for years and who might not be aware of the local history'. Another respondent, who had lived and worked in the English midlands before moving to rural Wales, talked about the importance of social interactions and a willingness to get involved as a basis for well-being amongst older incomers. This ethos of 'taking part' was deemed to be more important than local family ties, being raised in the locality or in being Welsh:

> There are so many newcomers come to villages like this ... because they want to live in the countryside. When it comes down to it, they really do need to have some sort of social intercourse rather than being right out in nowhere. But I don't think having lived in Wales as such is important, it's about living in a community and being part of it. (Jill, 63)

For Jill, being 'part of the community' involved becoming a member of the Women's Institute and also the Royal Voluntary Service, which in turn prompted her to regularly take part in a local meals-on-wheels service (primarily delivering to elderly residents in Ceredigion). Moreover, Jill also volunteered for the National Trust and spent a significant proportion of her spare time involved in the upkeep of a local historical property and tourist destination. Jill was one of a number of respondents who highlighted the value of volunteering and 'stepping up' as a means of demonstrating commitment and value to other, long-standing residents. This was also noted by Bob, originally from urban southern Wales, who strongly identified with his role as a community councillor:

> People in rural communities support each other. I strongly agree with that, and it's important to have good family and friends nearby ... Volunteering is important as a way of getting that social contact. (Bob, 72)

The importance of getting involved in community activities for older in-migrants was also noted by Audrey (76), who highlighted proactivity as a means of replacing social networks lost or depleted by distance:

> That [loss of friends] is one of the problems with older people moving to a completely new place ... I mean some people get very involved with the communities but some don't. It might get lonely unless you're prepared to go out and mix with people. But I think that it's quite a difficult thing to do. (Audrey, 76)

In terms of contributing to community life and local organisations, Jill, Bob and Audrey were seemingly more involved and industrious than many older incomers. However, they were not an outlier in these terms, with several other respondents demonstrating a clear desire to protect and preserve their host communities and exercise a 'stewardship of place' in later life (Yarker et al., 2020: 190). For some respondents, this came with a recognition that those in retirement had more resources in the form of time and money in comparison to younger people in work. This was noted, for example, by Victoria, a recent in-migrant and retiree from England:

> We would love some younger people in the WI [Women's Institute]. I feel young ... But young people can't because you've got to have two people earning in a family now and when you come home in the evening you're tired, you've got to get the kids to bed, you've got to get the food, you know, the woman's not free. (Victoria, 75)

Other participants in the study emphasised the importance of informal and contingent practices in maintaining neighbourly relations and attending to their own needs and those of others in terms of social interaction and practical needs. This included Mary, who had moved to the area from England eleven years prior to interview. Although she evaluated her involvements in village life as 'fairly limited', Mary nevertheless took time to organise and run a Tai Chi class in the village once a week. Unable to drive, she highlighted the important role their neighbours played in making her life easier in terms of picking up groceries and taking them to appointments. She also took time to outline the contributions she made to their lives:

> They are very neighbourly. I make a frock for one of his grandkids at times. I also make cakes for [him] sometimes and he takes me about and that, in the snow and brings me stuff if I can't get out. (Mary, 75)

Mary was unusual in that, while professing limited interest in rural community life and social infrastructure per se, she thought it was important to take part in our study and support research that looks to understand the lives and needs of people more generally.

As with many studies, however, those who were less willing and able to participate in local life were likewise less willing to take part in the research process, but – as with Glasgow and colleagues – the present research would tend to indicate that these included those 'older-old individuals with substantial health problems' (2012: 240). Somewhat perversely, this also included stakeholders who were too busy to take part in the study (on two occasions the researchers were unable to schedule an interview with potential participants due in part to their other commitments), and those who were more introverted in nature.

In parallel to a series of studies pointing to the positive contributions older in-migrants to rural Wales can make to community life, advances in research and service delivery suggest that interrelated challenges of a healthcare 'timebomb' allied to demographic ageing is also a problematic discourse. In this regard, research indicates that older incomers can and do play a part in delivering both formal and informal services allied to health and social care (both themselves and other residents), whilst continuous improvement in rural health-care processes are also bringing an increased quality of life for (older) residents, in-migrant or otherwise.

Older Adults and Their Contribution to Health and Social Care

The demands on the global health workforce, alongside a significant recruitment and retention challenge, have been well documented, with the WHO identifying a likely shortfall of 10 million staff health workers globally by 2030 (WHO, 2016). The NHS in Wales faces its share of these demands with the added pressure of recruiting professionals to work in its largely rural areas, known to be an additional recruitment challenge (Welsh Government, 2023). In-migrants to Wales, from other regions of the UK and perhaps more significantly from beyond, are an important source of workforce; although the UK workforce numbers do not delineate between the Welsh and wider UK population. Over the past five years, Wales's health workforce has also increased in age, with 20 per cent of the workforce aged 56–65; an increase of almost 3 per cent, with some individuals continuing to work in the health service into their 70s (Welsh Government, 2023). However, there is limited research that specifically identifies the numbers of in-migrant workers who remain living and contributing to Welsh society in retirement.

Volunteers and unpaid carers without a training in healthcare also provide a vital source of health and social care support in rural Wales (and the UK) whether through formal volunteering or unpaid care. Wales has the highest proportion of older carers in the UK, with carers in Wales providing more than fifty hours of care a week (Welsh Government, 2021). The positive trend of adults living longer means that a large proportion of this unpaid care is provided by older adults caring for family members who represent the 'oldest old'. While the potential health implications that providing unpaid care can cause should not be understated, the contribution that unpaid carers make has been and continues to be critical for supporting stretched health and social care services.

While a wide range of society contribute in different ways to volunteering activities, older adults make up a significant proportion of volunteers, with example motives for engagement being reported as a desire to give back to society, revival in religiosity, or seeking support and friendship post-retirement or following bereavement (Russell et al., 2022). Voluntary contributions to the health and social care related third sector are wide ranging, including acting as community first responders, expert patients, offering sitting services to enable unpaid carers respite, and befriending services that offer lonely or isolated members of the community access to forms of social and practical support, to name but a few. Local delivery of social care support such as lunch clubs, or transport schemes to facilitate access to medical or social engagements, have also been vital for enabling less mobile or vulnerable residents to maintain independence and be actively involved in society (Cameron et al., 2021). The act of volunteering in older age has been shown consistently to offer health and well-being benefits for the volunteer in addition to recipients of the support offered (Russell et al., 2021). The opportunity to socialise, integrate into communities and feel valued are all positive attributes reported by older adults who volunteer in their communities. The contribution of older adults volunteering in the health and social care sphere therefore appears to offer multiple benefits: from supporting stretched rural health and social care services to forming closer community connections and involvement while supporting their own healthy ageing.

While the understanding of whether the older people supporting health and social care services in rural Wales are indigenous to Wales or in-migrants remains unclear, what is clear is that older adults make an essential contribution to the Welsh society, economy and landscape. Edwards et al. (2018) found that the economic value of the contribution made by older people in Wales was estimated to be £2.19 billion per annum, with £483 million of that being through the benefit of their volunteering contribution. Moves to ensure older adults are valued and supported to remain living well are therefore vital for future prosperity. Support can come in a variety of ways; however, technology has been one such area of interest, particularly in rural areas where the challenges of geography and lack of effective public transport infrastructure have been identified as barriers to engagement or access to services. Health service innovation using technology and telehealth has been identified as an acceptable way to improve access to services for older adults in receipt of palliative care, preventing unnecessary travel and stress, and enabling patients to receive support closer to home (Rahman et al., 2020; Keenan et al., 2021); and the rapid development of technological solutions means that remote monitoring of vulnerable older adults is enabling them to live independently and safely for longer in a number of Welsh rural county councils (Powys County Council and Aberystwyth University, 2023). However, while older adults are becoming more adept and confident with technology, there remains a proportion who lack the necessary skills, confidence or infrastructure to engage, running the risk of increasing health inequality and isolating members of the community. Strategies therefore emphasise the importance of up-skilling the digital skills of older adults as innovation continues to develop (Welsh Government, 2021).

Conclusions

As Brown and Schaft (2011: 228) point out, the recognition that strong communities are characterised by a higher quality of life and are more resilient is not particularly helpful 'unless one understands why some places are better able to develop stronger social structures, and more effective social relations than others'. Without this understanding and the underlying research that supports this, the task of formulating and modifying policy interventions is precarious at best. Meeting this challenge, we are reminded by Gardner (2011: 103), is contingent on recognising increased diversity and cultural shifts in the countryside and abandoning the 'apparent assumption that geographical communities represent arenas of broad consensus'. It is, however, also dependent on not overplaying stereotypical divisions and tensions within rural Wales, including those interlaced tropes of the ageing countryside, in-migration, non-engagement and dependency.

In the case of Wales, as with Australia, it is appropriate to paraphrase Warburton and McLaughlin (2015: 715) and emphasise the integral role older people (inclusive of incomers) can and do play in rural civil society and, therefore, that social policy must embrace the positive contributions of this cohort rather than emphasising the costs of demographic change in the countryside in a blunt and formulaic manner. As Edwards et al. (2018) note, the economic contribution made by older people in Wales is significant, and this is before social processes are taken into account. In rural Wales, evidence indicates that older incomers can and do sustain community infrastructure through their involvements. Coupled with a range of interventions focused on physical and mental health, the parallel challenges of living and ageing well in rural place as experienced by long-term residents and in-migrants alike can be variously addressed. However, it is important to be mindful of the positive role that many older people and older in-migrants play in sustaining their communities, and those technological interventions in healthcare discussed cannot be seen as a panacea or an easy-fix for rural resilience. Real-terms cuts in services (notably transport) and growing financial constraints as detailed in the Age Wales report (2021) are likely to reduce the capacity of many rural residents to maintain existing engagements and activities, much less allow for extending them. This will inevitably have a knock-on effect in terms of individual well-being and community health.

Bibliography

Benson, M. and O'Reilly, K. 2009. 'Migration and the search for a better way of life: a critical exploration of lifestyle migration'. *The sociological review*, 57/4, 608–25.

Best, S. and Myers, J. 2019. 'Prudence or speed: Health and social care innovation in rural Wales'. *Journal of Rural Studies*, 70/1, 198–206.

Bourke, L., Humphreys, L., Wakerman, J. and Taylor, A. 2012. 'Understanding drivers of rural and remote health outcomes: a conceptual framework in action'. *Australian Journal of Rural Health*, 20/6, 318–23.

Bowie, F. 2020. 'Wales from within: Conflicting interpretations of Welsh identity'. In S. Macdonald (ed.), *Inside European Identities*. London: Routledge, pp. 167–93.

Brown, David L. and Glasgow, Nina. 2008. *Rural retirement migration: Past, present and future*. Dordrecht: Springer.

Brown, David L. and Schaft, Kai, A. 2011. *Rural People and Communities in the 21st Century: Resilience and Transformation*. Cambridge: Polity.

Burholt, V. and Sardani, A. 2018. 'The impact of residential immobility and population turnover on the support networks of older people living in rural areas: Evidence from CFAS Wales'. *Population, Space and Place*, 24/4, 2132–46.

Cameron, A., Johnson, E., Lloyd, L., Willis, P. and Smith, R. 2021. 'The contribution of volunteers in social care services for older people'. *Voluntary Sector Review*, 13/2, 260–77.

Cawley, M. 2020. 'Rural out-migration and return: perspectives on the role of the everyday reality and the idyll in Ireland'. *Documents d'anàlisi geogràfica*, 66/2, 289–305.

Cloke, P., Goodwin, M. and Milbourne, P. 1995. 'There's so many strangers in the village now'. Marginalisation and change in 1990s Welsh rural lifestyles'. *Contemporary Wales*, 8/1, 47–74.

Cloke, Paul., Goodwin, Mark and Milbourne. 1997. Paul, *Rural Wales: community and marginalization*. Cardiff: University of Wales Press.

Colibaba, A., Skinner, M. and Russell, E. 2020. 'Supporting Older Volunteers & Sustaining Volunteer-Based Programs in Rural Communities', https:// vitalptbo.ca/wp-content/uploads/sites/65/2023/06/BBD-older-volunteers. May24.22b. pdf

Day, G. 2011. 'The Englishing of rural Wales? Migration, conflict and integration in community life'. In P. Milbourne (ed.), *Rural Wales in the Twenty-first Century: Society, Economy and Environment*. Cardiff: University of Wales Press, pp. 23–45.

Day, G., Davis, H. and Drakakis-Smith, A. 2010. 'There's One Shop You Don't Go Into If You Are English: The Social and Political Integration of English Migrants into Wales'. *Journal of Ethnic and Migration Studies*, 36/9, 1405–23.

Edwards, B. and Woods, M. 2017. 'Mobilising the local: community, participation and governance'. In M. Kneafsey and L. Holloway (eds), *Geographies of rural cultures and societies*. London: Routledge, pp. 173–96.

Edwards, Rhiannon, Spencer, Llinos, Bryning, Lucy and Anthony, Bethany. 2017. *Living well for longer: The economic argument for investing in the health and wellbeing of older people in Wales*. Bangor University: Centre for Health Economics and Medicines Evaluation.

Fielding, Tony. 2012. *Migration in Britain: Paradoxes of the present, prospects for the future*. London: Edward Elgar Publishing.

Flynn, M. and Kay, R. 2017. 'Migrants' experiences of material and emotional security in rural Scotland: Implications for longer-term settlement'. *Journal of Rural Studies*, 52/1, 56–65.

Gardner, G. 2011. 'Community action in rural Wales'. In P. Milbourne (ed.), *Rural Wales in the Twenty-first Century: Society, Economy and Environment*. Cardiff: University of Wales Press, pp. 81–112.

Gilbert, A., Philip, L. and Shucksmith, M. 2006. 'Rich and poor in the countryside'. In P. Lowe and L. Speakman (eds), *The ageing countryside: The growing older population of rural England*. London: Age Concern, pp. 69–93.

Glasgow, N., Min, H. and Brown, D. 2012. 'Volunteerism and social entrepreneurship among older in-migrants to rural areas'. In D. Brown and N. Glasgow (eds), *Rural aging in 21st century America*. Dordrecht: Springer, pp. 231–50.

Goodwin-Hawkins, B., Mahon, M., Farrell, M. and Dafydd Jones, Rh. 2023. 'Situating spatial justice in counter-urban lifestyle mobilities: relational rural theory in a time of crisis'. *Geografiska Annaler: Series B, Human Geography*, 105/4, 379–94.

Haas, H. 2013. 'Volunteering in retirement migration: meanings and functions of charitable activities for older British residents in Spain'. *Ageing & Society*, 33/8, 1374–1400.

Heley, J. and Jones, L. 2012. 'Relational rurals: Some thoughts on relating things and theory in rural studies'. *Journal of Rural Studies*, 28/3, 208–17.

Heley, J. and Jones, L. 2013. 'Growing older and social sustainability: considering the "serious leisure" practices of the over 60s in rural communities'. *Social & Cultural Geography*, 14/3, 276–99.

Jones, L. and Heley, J. 2016. 'Practices of Participation and Voluntarism among Older People in Rural Wales: Choice, Obligation and Constraints to Active Ageing'. *Sociologia Ruralis*, 56/2, 176–96.

Jones, L., Heley, J. and Yarker, S. 2020. 'Retiring into civil society'. In S. Power (ed.), *Civil Society through the Lifecourse*. Bristol: Bristol University Press, pp. 161–84.

Keenan, J., Rahman, R. and Hudson, J. 2021. 'Exploring the acceptance of tele-health within palliative care: a self-determination theory perspective'. *Health and Technology*, 11/2, 575–84.

Lloyd, A. 2019. Nation Cymru (4 August). Available at: *https://nation.cymru/opinion/why-its-young-people-moving-out-not-retirees-moving-in-thats-a-burden-on-wales/*

Malatzky, C. and Bourke, L. 2016. 'Re-producing rural health: challenging dominant dis-courses and the manifestation of power'. *Journal of Rural Studies*, 45/1, 157–64.

Mettenberger, T. and Küpper, P. 2019. 'Potential and impediments to senior citizens' volunteering to maintain basic services in shrinking regions'. *Sociologia Ruralis*, 59/4, 739–62.

Milbourne, P. 2011. 'The social and cultural impacts of English migration to rural Wales'. In P. Milbourne (ed.), *Rural Wales in the Twenty-first Century: Society, Economy and Environment*. Cardiff: University of Wales Press, pp. 46–64.

Munoz, S., Farmer, J., Warburton, J. and Hall, J. 2014. 'Involving rural older people in service co-production: Is there an untapped pool of potential participants?'. *Journal of Rural Studies*, 34/1, 212–22.

NHS Wales. 2022. NHS Wales Workforce Trends (as at 31 March 2022), *https://heiw.nhs.wales/files/nhs-wales-workforce-trends-as-at-31-march-2022/*

Office for National Statistics. 2022. 'Population and household estimates, Wales: Census 2021' (June 2022), *https://www.ons.gov.uk/peoplepopulationandcommunity/populationandmigration/populationestimates/bulletins/populationandhouseholdestimateswales/census2021#main-points*

Office for National Statistics. 2016. 'Internal Migration, England and Wales: Year Ending June 2015' (June 2016), *https://www.ons.gov.uk/peoplepopulationandcommunity/populationandmigration/migrationwithintheuk/bulletins/internalmigrationbylocalauthoritiesinenglandandwales/yearendingjune2015*

Office for National Statistics. 2015. 'Internal Migration, England and Wales: Year Ending June 2014' (June 2015), *https://www.ons.gov.uk/peoplepopulationand*

community/populationandmigration/migration withintheuk/bulletins/internalmigrationbylocalauthoritiesinenglandan dwales/2015-06-25

Phillips, M., Smith, D., Brooking, H. and Duer, M. 2022. 'The gentrification of a post-industrial English rural village: Querying urban planetary perspectives', *Journal of Rural Studies*, 91, 108–25.

Powys County Council and Aberystwyth University. 2023. 'Technology Care Programme Success', *https://en.powys.gov.uk/article/14843/ Technology-Care-Programme-Success*

Putnam, R. 1993. 'The prosperous community: Social capital and public life', *The American*, 4, *https://prospect.org/infrastructure/prosperous-community-social-capital-public-life/*

Rahman, R., Keenan, J. and Hudson, J. 2020. 'Exploring rural palliative care patients' experiences of accessing psychosocial support through telehealth: A longitudinal approach', *Qualitative Research in Medicine and Healthcare*, 4/1, pp. 31–42.

Robinson, V. and Gardner, H. 2006. 'Place matters: exploring the distinctiveness of racism in rural Wales'. In Neal, S. and Agyeman, J. (eds), *The New Countryside? Ethnicity, Nation and Exclusion in Contemporary Rural Britain*. Bristol: Policy Press, pp. 73–98.

Russell, A., Storti, M. and Handy, F. 2022. 'Volunteer Retirement and Well-being: Evidence from Older Adult Volunteers'. *International Journal of Community Well-Being*, 5/2, 475–95.

Stockdale, A. 2006. 'The role of a "retirement transition" in the repopulation of rural areas'. *Population, Space and Place*, 12/1, 1–13.

Stockdale, A. 2010. 'The diverse geographies of rural gentrification in Scotland'. *Journal of Rural Studies*, 26/1, 31–40.

Stockdale, A. 2014. 'Unravelling the migration decision-making process: English early retirees moving to rural mid-Wales'. *Journal of Rural Studies*, 34/2, 161–71.

Stockdale, A. and MacLeod, M. 2013. 'Pre-retirement age migration to remote rural areas'. *Journal of Rural Studies*, 32/1, 80–92.

Torres, S. and Serrat, R. 2019. 'Older migrants' civic participation: A topic in need of attention'. *Journal of Aging Studies*, 50/1, 100790.

Walsh, K. and O'Shea, E. 2008. 'Responding to rural social care needs: older people empowering themselves, others and their community'. *Health & Place*, 14/4, 795–805.

Warburton, J. 2010. 'Volunteering as a productive ageing activity: Evidence from Australia'. *China Journal of Social Work*, 3/2, 301–12.

Warburton, J. and McLaughlin, D. 2005. 'Lots of little kindnesses: valuing the role of older Australians as informal volunteers in the community'. *Ageing & Society*, 25/5, 715–30.

Warburton, J. and Winterton, R. 2017. 'A far greater sense of community: The impact of volunteer behaviour on the wellness of rural older Australians'. *Health & Place*, 48/1, 132–8.

Welsh Government. 2021a. *Digital strategy for Wales: How we will use digital, data and technology to improve the lives of people in Wales.* Cardiff: Welsh Government.

Welsh Government. 2021b. *Age friendly Wales: our strategy for an ageing society.* Cardiff: Welsh Government.

Welsh Government. 2023. *National Workforce Implementation Plan: Addressing NHS Wales Workforce Challenges.* Cardiff: Welsh Government.

West Wales Regional Partnership Board. 2022. *Older People: Overview and key messages, https://www.wwcp-data.org.uk/older-people*

Willett, J. 2023. 'Counter-urbanisation and a politics of place: A coastal community in Cornwall and rural gentrification'. *Habitat International,* 141/1, 102935.

Wilson, J. and Musick, M. 1997. 'Who cares? Toward an integrated theory of volunteer Work'. *American Sociological Review,* 62/5, 694–713.

Winterton, R. and Warburton, J. 2014. 'Healthy ageing in Australia's rural places: the contribution of older volunteers'. *Voluntary Sector Review,* 5/2, 181–98.

Winterton, R. and Warburton, J. 2015. 'Civic and voluntary contributions of retirement migrants and their impact on rural community sustainability'. In M. Skinner and N. Hanlon (eds), *Ageing resource communities: New frontiers of rural population change, community development and voluntarism.* London: Routledge, pp. 164–78.

Woods, Michael. 2010. *Rural.* London: Routledge.

World Health Organization. 2020. *Global strategy on human resources for health*: *Workforce 2030, https://www.who.int/publications/i/item/9789241511131*

Yarker, S., Heley, J. and Jones, L. 2020. 'Stewardship of the rural: Conceptualising the experiences of rural volunteering in later life'. *Journal of Rural Studies,* 76, 184–92.

Index

A

Abergavenny 69

Aberystwyth 10, 13, 82, 183

Aberystwyth University 192, 194

Afghanistan 77, 107, 115

Afghan resettlement scheme 35, 40

   see also refugees, Afghan

Aliens Restriction Act (1905) 103

Aljumma, Zaina 57, 70–1

Amendment Act (1919) 103

Amnesty International 2

Anglesey *see* Isle of Anglesey

Anglophobia 181, 185

   see also anti-English sentiment

Annual Population Survey (APS) 170, 176, 178

anti-Catholicism 3

anti-English sentiment 7, 181

   see also Anglophobia

Anti-Racist Wales Action Plan (2022) 7, 34

Antoniw, Mick 6, 94

Arabic language 63

Arizona 202

assimilation 37, 198

Asylum and Immigration Act (1993) 104

asylum seekers 3, 6, 9, 10, 21, 35, 38, 42, 43, 48, 53n2, 53n3, 68, 78–82, 84–93, 95, 96, 97n2, 103–4, 107, 110, 112–17, 121, 127–9, 130n4, 135, 139, 150, 151, 153, 156, 160, 182

Atlantic Ocean 8

Australia 5, 172, 201–2, 210

B

Bannau Brycheiniog National Park 69

Banwen 11

Barti Ddu 8

Bhogal, Inderjit 80

bilingualism 19, 32, 33, 49, 50, 51, 52, 165, 180–1, 183

bisexuality 117–18

Blaenau Gwent 173–4

Blair, Tony 2

Bosse-Griffiths, Kate ix, 77

Brexit 17, 22, 179, 184, 186

   2016 EU membership referendum 35, 165, 169, 181–2, 185

Bridgend 12, 170, 174

Bristol 8

British citizenship 2, 3, 4–5, 34, 103, 167, 181, 184, 187n6

   British Dependent Territory Citizen 4

   British Overseas Citizen 4

British Commonwealth *see* Commonwealth of Nations

British Empire 4, 5

British Nationality Act (1948) 4, 103

Brittany 11
Brown, Gordon 2
Bulgaria 17
    Bulgarian citizens 166

C
Caernarfon 11
Caerphilly 173–4
Calderón, Luisa 8
Cameron, David 82
Canada 38, 71,
Canton 14
Cardiff 6, 8, 13, 14, 24, 59, 71, 78–9,
    81, 94, 110, 122, 130, 173–4, 194
    Bay Barrage 69
    City Hall 8
    Race Riots 12
Cardiff University 13, 73
Caribbean, the 3, 4, 5, 13, 184
Carmarthen 8
Carmarthenshire 8, 195
    County Council 8
Catalan language 51
Catalonia 32, 37, 51
Centre for Excellence in Rural Health
    Research 192, 194
Cenedl Noddfa 43
    see also Nation of Sanctuary
Ceredigion 42, 167, 174, 193, 195–6,
    205
Chetty, Darren 18
China 64, 172
churches 144
civil society 6, 157, 167, 181, 202, 210
    migrant 6, 87, 158
    rural 210
class 14, 16, 18, 200
'clear water' 6, 15
Collins, Michael 12, 170
colonialism 5, 7–9
    logic 49
    settler 8
Colston, Edward 8
Commonwealth Immigrants Act
    (1962) 3, 181

Commonwealth of Nations 4, 5, 103,
    130, 170
Conservative party 1, 2, 184
Conwy 174, 199
Covid-19 pandemic 7, 10, 15, 65–8,
    137, 144–5, 150
    lockdowns 65–8
    regulations 15
creative methods 137
Crenshaw, Kimberlé 15, 126
Cricieth 12
Critical Participatory Action Research
    39
cultural capital 138, 142, 158
Cymdeithas yr Iaith Gymraeg 32
Cymraeg 2050 33
Czechia 64, 167, 170

D
Danish people 167
devolution 6, 9, 14, 17, 33, 43
    2011 referendum 9
disability 16
Displaced People in Action 80–1, 97
dispersal 3, 9, 17, 82, 96
    accommodation 110–11, 112, 127
    areas 110
    no-choice 110
    policy 3, 10, 110
domestic abuse 139
Drakeford, Mark 7, 35

E
Eames, Marion 11
Easter Rising 12, 170
Edwards, Aled 80
Elis, Rowland 11
emigration (from Wales) 8, 9, 13, 24
Empire Windrush 4
England 3, 11, 14, 16, 89, 136, 171,
    186n5, 195, 199, 204, 207
English Channel 1
English language 19
    English for Speakers of Other
        Languages (ESOL) 19, 34, 36,

40, 44–9, 57, 59, 61, 62, 65, 74,
    136, 148, 159
Teaching English to Speakers of
    Other Languages 59
enslavement 7, 8, 12, 25n6
    chattel slavery 8
Estonia 170
    Estonian people 167
ethnicity 4, 5, 22, 104, 107, 122, 186
ethnography 21, 78, 137
European Union 9
    2004 expansion 9, 13, 22, 166
    citizens 9, 10, 22, 165–90
    citizenship 168
    Settlement Scheme 170
evacuees 10, 12
Evans, Ellis Humphrey *see* Hedd Wyn
Evans, Neil 9
exclusion 8, 18–19, 22, 33, 88, 92,
    105, 118, 120, 122, 136, 159, 160
    exclusionary politics 83–4, 86–7

F
First Minister of Wales 79
    see also Drakeford, Mark; Jones,
        Carwyn
First World War 10, 13, 77
Flintshire 173–4
Floyd, George 7
Football Association of Wales 165
forced migration 3, 20–1, 58, 60, 62,
    63, 103–34, 170
free movement of labour 9, 169
free movement of people 169
French language 37, 51
Frongoch 12, 170

G
gender 16, 18, 21, 22, 104–7, 119,
    123–4, 127–8, 130n3, 186
    gendered harm 158
Geneva Convention (1951) 2
Gerald of Wales 11
Germany 168, 172–3, 184, 187n6
    Nazi Germany 95

Glasgow 16
Glitter Cymru LGBTQ+ Action Plan
    110
Gnagbo, Joseff 77
Great Depression, the 13
Government of Wales Act (2006) 9
Grangetown 14
Gwynedd 170, 174, 195, 199

H
Hamilton, Neil 94
Hedd Wyn 170
Henry VII *see* Harri Tudur
Herman, Josef 77
Home Office 34, 42, 48, 61, 70,
    104–5, 114–15
homophobia 111–12, 113, 116, 121,
    123, 129
homosexuality 116
Hong Kong 4, 130n1, 172
Hope not Hate 95
hospitality 18–19, 20, 43, 78, 83–4,
    86–8, 93, 95–7
    host/guest relationship 38, 44,
        83–5, 98n5
    linguistic 32, 38, 41, 43, 49, 52
hostile environment 2, 5, 7, 15, 22,
    35, 43, 48, 61–2, 69, 78–9, 84–8,
    91–3, 96–7, 97n3, 103–34, 156,
    182, 185–6
hostility 10, 12–13, 22, 52, 86, 97,
    116, 129, 169, 181, 183, 185–6
Hungary 64, 167, 170
    Hungarian language 167
Hutt, Jane 6, 90–1

I
*Iaith Pawb: A National Action Plan for
    a Bilingual Wales* 33
Illegal Migration Act (2023) 2, 18
Illegal Migration and Borders Bill 6
Immigration Act (1971) 3, 181
Immigration Act (1981) 4, 103
Immigration Act (2014) 2, 182
Immigration Act (2016) 2, 182

Immigration and Asylum Act (1999)
   2, 10, 17, 182
Immigration Bill: an End to Free
   Movement 103
inclusion 7, 18, 37, 49, 57–76, 92,
   120, 122
   social 136
   see also integration
India 5, 16, 64, 71, 172–3
indigenous people 5, 36
in-migration
   English in-migration to Wales 23,
      198–200, 203
interculturalism 37–8, 43, 51
integration 61, 65, 72, 79, 83, 90, 92,
   104, 107, 118–19, 121–2, 127–9,
   136, 153, 200–1, 209
   community integration 49, 104,
      129, 200
   economic 121
   linguistic 18–19, 31–56
   social 36, 130, 179
Iran 64, 77, 124
Iraq 10, 64, 71, 79, 165, 172
Ireland 3, 9, 11, 169, 170–3, 180, 187,
   205
Isle of Anglesey 173–4
Issa, Hanan 18
isolation 15, 18, 65–6, 71, 98 n6,
   104–5, 110, 113, 118, 121, 127,
   129, 150, 158, 160, 192, 209–10
Italy 64, 169, 172

J
Jamaica 8
James, Julie 90
Jones, Carwyn 79, 80
jus soli 4, 103

K
Karkoubi, Mohamad 43
Kindertransport 77
   see also refugees from National
      Socialism
King's College, London 73

L
labour 12
   market 13, 89, 120, 176–9
   requirements/shortages 3, 9, 103
   skilled 198
   unpaid/paid 148–9
Labour party 34
   New Labour 2, 24, 182
   Welsh 79
Lampeter 10, 13, 24n6
   see also St David's College
Latvia 167, 170
leave to remain 89, 91, 139, 142, 144,
   148, 151, 161n1
   discretionary 139
Lek, Karel 77
LGBTQ+ 20–1, 103–34
Libya 77
Liberal Democrats 2
liquid migration 166, 168, 173, 185
Lithuania 170
Llandysul 12, 170
Llanelli 10, 95
Llantwit Major 94–5
Llanybydder 9, 13
Local Government and Elections
   (Wales) Act (2021) 89
London 3, 11, 16, 68–9, 111, 136
loneliness 68, 156, 206, 209

M
Maine 202
Manchester 16, 73, 197
Mauritania 107, 110
May, Theresa 2, 61, 182
Merthyr Tydfil 173–4, 183
Michigan 202
Minneapolis 7
Minnesota 8
monolingualism 35, 44, 49
Morgan, Eluned 91
Morgan, Harri 8
Morocco 124
motherhood 137, 144–5, 158–9
Muse, Grug 18

multiculturalism 9, 37, 51, 103
   Anglophone 51
   liberal 36
   Welsh 34, 51

N

National Asylum Support Service
   (NASS) 104, 110, 128
National Centre for Learning Welsh
   (NCLW) 32, 36, 47
National Health Service (NHS) 2, 89,
   91, 208
National Museum of Wales 8
National Trust 8, 205
nationalism
   civic 19, 33, 87
   moral 84, 86, 96, 97
   nation-building 19, 20, 33, 165
Nationality and Borders Act (2022)
   2, 18
Nationality, Immigration and Asylum
   Act (2002) 34
Nation of Sanctuary (NoS) 6, 15, 18,
   20–3, 31, 35, 38, 40, 41, 43–4, 47,
   50, 53n3, 58, 61, 74, 77–9, 80–5,
   87, 89, 90, 92–7, 97fn1, fn3, 136,
   158, 159, 161, 185
Nazism 10, 12, 170
   see also Kindertransport; refugees
     from National Socialism
Neath 11, 175
   New Asylum Model (NAM)
     113–14
Newport 71, 81, 173, 175
Ngalle Charles, Eric 77
non-binary people 21, 117–18, 129,
   130n3
North Carolina 202
Northern Ireland 3, 165, 171

O

Oasis 6, 73
Offa's Dyke 11
Ohio 11
othering 2, 5, 8, 22, 24n2, 86, 118, 130

O'Leary, Paul 9
Oxford 11

P

Pakistan 124, 172
Patagonia 8
Pembrokeshire 11, 92, 175
Penally 53 fn3, 92, 94–5
Pennant family 8
   see also Penrhyn Castle
Penrhyn Castle 8
Phillips, Thomas 24n6
photo elicitation 137
Phule, Savitrabi 16
Picton, Thomas 8
Poland 3, 13, 64, 167, 170, 172–3, 186
Pontypridd 59
Portugal 172
   Portuguese colonies 167
positionality 39, 40, 97, 106–7
post-war migration 12, 170
post-national citizenship 169
Powell, Enoch 5
Powys 175, 195, 197, 199
prisoners of war 12, 170

Q

Québec 32–3, 37–8, 51
queer people 21, 108, 117, 123
   asylum policy 105

R

race 3–5, 7–9, 16, 18, 22, 24n3,
   103–4, 107, 122, 165, 186
Race Council Cymru 13
Race Relations Act (1968) 5
racialisation 16, 22, 169
racism 2, 5–6, 7, 9, 12–13, 16, 18, 22,
   24n3, 49, 92, 112, 119, 122, 166
   cultural 5
   institutional 7, 9
   rural 10, 182
Ramadan 71
refugees
   2015 'refugee crisis' 17, 81, 103

Afghan 35, 39, 40–1, 43, 77, 107, 115
Basque 10, 77
Belgian 10, 77, 170
from Communism 10
from National Socialism 12; *see also Kindertransport*
'genuine' 83
status 148
Syrian 42, 81–2
Ukrainian 6, 41, 72, 95
relationality 86, 97
religion 5, 104, 165
religious community 153
religious beliefs 111
religious diversity/disparities 9, 112
religious persecution 11
return migration 14, 24, 173
Rhondda Cynon Taf 175, 194–5
Rhosllanerchrugog 10, 170
Rhyl 77
Riverside 14
Roberts, Bartholemew *see* Barti Ddu
Roma 24
Romania 13, 64, 167, 172–3
Romanian people 166–7, 173, 176, 187n8
Royal Voluntary Service 205
Russia 71
Rwanda 1, 43, 53
Safety of Rwanda (Asylum and Immigration Act) (2024) 1
Rwanda Migration and Economic Development Partnership 1, 43, 53n2

S
St David's College 24n6
St Kitts 12
St Patrick 11
St Vincent 13, 24n6
sanctuary 18
City of Sanctuary 73–4, 79, 80, 82, 97

people seeking 1–2, 6, 10, 15, 19–20, 58, 59, 60–1, 62, 66, 68, 70, 74, 79, 91, 92, 95, 170
university of 73
see also Nation of Sanctuary
scale 15, 20, 78, 82–4, 86–7, 92, 96–7, 193–4, 198
Scotland 3, 17, 32, 38, 171, 180, 184, 205
Scottish Government 97, 97n3
second homes 192, 196, 198
owners 15, 34, 199
Second World War, the 3, 4, 77, 103, 170
semi-structured interviews 78–9
Senedd Cymru
Member of the Senedd (MS) 89, 90–1, 93–4
see also Welsh Parliament
Senedd and Elections (Wales) Act (2020) 88, 185
Seren Network 13
sexuality 16, 18, 107, 114, 116–18, 120, 123–4, 128
Sewell convention 6
Seymour, John 14
Show Racism the Red Card 95
Sianel Pedwar Cymru (S4C) 32
Slovakia 167, 170
Slovenia 170
social capital 135–6, 147, 149, 154, 157, 201
social care 191, 193–4, 207–9
social cohesion 35, 37, 49, 121, 123–4, 129
Somalia 77
Spain 12, 169, 172
Splott 6
Spanish Civil War 10, 12, 77
Stewart, Maria 16
Sudan 64
Swansea 12, 75, 78–9, 81, 112, 130, 167, 173, 175, 194
Swansea University 73

Sweden 9, 170
Symbolic capital 142
Syria 10, 59, 64, 70–1, 77, 79, 165
Syrian Vulnerable Persons Relocation
    Programme (SVPRP) 79, 81, 84,
    96–7

T
'Team Wales' 35, 40, 50
Tenby 69
Thailand 64
Tillich, Paul 95
transgender people 117, 130n3
trauma 12, 19, 48, 57, 60–1, 63,
    108–9, 110, 112, 116, 129, 150,
    152, 154, 159
    post-traumatic stress disorder
        (PTSD) 114, 127
Travellers 24
Trawsfynydd 12
Trinidad 8
Trinity Centre 70, 73
Truth, Sojourner 16
Tudur, Harri 11
Tunisia 107, 116, 121, 125
Tyne, Iestyn 18

U
Uganda 77
Ukraine 71
United Kingdom Independence Party
    (UKIP) 94, 165
UK government 1, 2, 18, 20–1, 33–5,
    51–2, 53n2, 61, 73, 79, 84–6, 88,
    92–3, 96–7, 97n2, 97n3, 103, 182,
    185, 186, 186n3
UK parliament 1, 5, 6, 89, 185
UK Supreme Court 1, 53n2
United States of America 16, 87, 172,
    202
University of South Wales (USW) 59,
    68, 70–1, 72, 73–4
Urdd Gobaith Cymru 19, 32, 35–6,
    39, 40, 41–2, 44, 48–9, 50–2

V
Victoria (Australian state) 201
Vietnam 77
volunteering 153–4, 160, 168, 193,
    197, 201–2, 204–6, 208–9
    schemes 81, 90

W
Wales Institute of Social and Econom-
    ic Research Data (WISERD) 23,
    74, 167, 192, 204
Wales Strategic Migration Partner-
    ship 6
Watson, Joyce 92–3
Wells, Nathaniel 12
Welsh Government 7, 13, 15, 18–19,
    20–1, 33, 35–6, 38, 40–2, 48, 53
    fn3, 58, 60, 61, 79, 80–1, 83–9,
    90–4, 96–7, 110, 120, 128, 158,
    185, 192
    Refugee and Asylum Seeker Plan
        35
Welsh language 15, 18–19, 31–56, 77,
    192, 200
    Society see Cymdeithas yr Iaith
        Gymraeg
    Welsh for Speakers of Other Lan-
        guages (WSOL) 19, 32, 36, 39,
        40–1, 44–9, 50–2, 136
    Welsh Language Act (1993) 32
    Welsh Language (Wales) Measure
        (2011) 33
Welsh Parliament 6, 20, 78–9, 80, 87,
    89, 90, 94, 185
    Equality, Local Government and
        Communities Committee
        (ELGCC) 78–81, 84, 88, 90, 96
    Member of the Senedd (MS) 89,
        90–1, 93–4
Welsh Refugee Coalition (WRC) 6,
    80
Welsh Refugee Council 59
West Virginia 11
white supremacy 5, 7, 8

Williams, Charlotte 7, 9
Windrush *see also* Empire Windrush
  generation 4, 13
  scandal 4, 184
  Windrush Cymru @ 75 (film) 13
Wladfa, y *see* Patagonia
Women's Institute 200, 205–6
Wood, Leanne 89, 93
Wrexham 10, 71, 81, 173, 175, 195

X
xenophobia 9, 129, 166
xenoracism 7, 22, 182, 186

Y
Yemen 77
YesCymru 185
Ystumllyn, John 12